To my informants and their families:

I came to you in search of klezmer.

I came home with the meaning of Torah in my heart.

OTHER BOOKS BY YALE STROM

World Music: Klezmer

The Book of Klezmer: The History, the Music, the Folklore, from the
Fourteenth Century to the Twenty-First

Quilted Landscape: Conversations with Young Immigrants

Uncertain Roads: Searching for the Gypsies

The Hasidim of Brooklyn: A Photo Essay

The Expulsion of the Jews: Five Hundred Years of Exodus

A Tree Still Stands: Jewish Youth in Eastern Europe Today

The Last Jews of Eastern Europe

A Journey Through

the Jewish Culture

of Eastern Europe

YALE STROM

with ELIZABETH SCHWARTZ

An Arthur Kurzweil Book

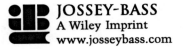

JOSSEY-BASS
A Wiley Imprint
www.josseybass.com

Published by Jossey-Bass
A Wiley Imprint
989 Market Street, San Francisco, CA 94103-1741   www.josseybass.com

Jossey-Bass books and products are available through most bookstores. To contact Jossey-Bass directly call our Customer Care Department within the U.S. at 800-956-7739, outside the U.S. at 317-572-3986, or fax 317-572-4002.

Jossey-Bass also publishes its books in a variety of electronic formats. Some content that appears in print may not be available in electronic books.

Library of Congress Cataloging-in-Publication Data

Strom, Yale.
    A wandering feast : a journey through the Jewish culture of Eastern Europe /
Yale Strom with Elizabeth Schwartz.
        p.   cm.
"A Wiley Imprint."
"An Arthur Kurzweil Book."
Includes bibliographical references.
ISBN 0-7879-7188-X (alk. paper)
        1. Jews—Europe, Eastern—Social life and customs—20th century.
2. Strom, Yale—Travel—Europe, Eastern.   3. Europe, Eastern—Description and travel.   4. Cookery, Jewish.   I. Schwartz, Elizabeth.   II. Title.
DS135.E83S76   2004
305.892'40497'09048—dc22   2004010051

FIRST EDITION
PB Printing 10 9 8 7 6 5 4 3 2 1

Contents

Acknowledgments   xi
Introduction   xiii
Glossary   xxiii

Chapter One

YUGOSLAVIA   1

RECIPES

Burek Sasirom Spinat (Yugoslavian Spinach and Cheese Pies)   12
Leek, Garlic, and Red Pepper Soup   23
Prebanac (Baked Beans)   35
Yugoslavian Chopped Salad   36
Hurmasice (Pound Cake in Syrup)   37

MUSIC

"Maestral Hora and Bulgar"   3
"Waltz from Senta"   9
"Khosn's March" (Groom's March)   32

Chapter Two

HUNGARY 39

RECIPES

Galuska (Hungarian Dumplings) 47
Letcho (Vegetable Stew) 48
Potato Paprikash 49
Lecso (Peppers and Eggs) 50
Flodni 56
Hungarian Mushroom Soup 72
Hungarian Cucumber Salad 73

MUSIC

"Katarina Maladitse" (Young Katrina) 58
"Yismakh Moyshe" (Moses Rejoiced) 70
"Tibi's Hora" 76

Chapter Three

CZECHOSLOVAKIA 84

RECIPES

Sweet Noodle Kugel with Raisins and Almonds 99
Bramborove Knedliky (Potato Dumplings) 100
Kuba (Barley Dish) 102
Latkes (Potato Pancakes) 122

MUSIC

"Malke Zhote" 95
"Oberek Palota" 103
"Bulbes / Beblekh" (Potatoes / Beans) 118

Chapter Four

POLAND 125

RECIPES

Kasha with Mushrooms and Onions 130
Kapusta z Jablkamy (Polish Cabbage with Apples) 131
Polish Poppy Seed Cookies 132
Pierogi 134
Zuppa Ogorkowa (Polish Sour Cucumber Soup) 156
Kutia (Poppy Seed and Walnut Spread) 160
Krupnik (Mushroom and Barley Soup) 165

MUSIC

"Ropshitser Nign" 145
"Doyne / Freylekhs" 154
"Drohobitsh" 162

Chapter Five

SOVIET UNION: UKRAINE 176

RECIPES

Galushke (Stuffed Cabbage) 188
Russian-Style Baked Mushrooms in Sour Cream 195
Ukrainian Honey Cake 196
Pokhlyobka (Vegetable Soup) 199

MUSIC

"On the Road to Salang" 192

Chapter Six

ROMANIA 201

RECIPES

Mamaliga 207
Sweet Noodle Kugel with Apples and Walnuts 208
Palave (Pilaf) 219
Mincare de Vinete cu Usturoi (Eggplant with Garlic) 224
Potato-Cheese Kreplach 225
Gogl-Mogl 227
Romanian Vegetable Latkes 233
Passover Macaroons 237

MUSIC

"Baveynen Di Kale" (The Lamenting of the Bride) 221
"Bosnian Waltz" 226

Resources 239
The Authors 241

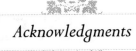

Acknowledgments

THANKS TO Archie Barkan, Bogdan Kaczerowski, Abraham and Ruth Taigman, and Isidor Strom for their excellent translation and to Brian Blue for the photography lessons and the loan of his camera. Thanks to Ron Robboy for not needing another fiddler and to Dr. Ita Sheres and Dr. Carrie Wall, who honed my intellectual curiosity. Thanks go to all my high school and college cross-country teammates, who taught me the true meaning of "no strain, no pain, no gain"—that, and not to ever be a choker. Thanks to Jeff Pekarek for his sensitive arrangements and to Jeff and Fred Benedetti for their musical virtuosity, which is eclipsed only by the quality of their friendship. Profound thanks to my siblings Shoshana, Avivah, Carmi, Lilah, Ari, Stephanie, and Tamar for their support and understanding of my wanderlust.

Most especially and lovingly, I must thank my parents: first, for steeping me in the love of Judaism and Yidishkayt and the spiritual and moral compass that guides me to this day. For that, and for not freaking out when I canceled law school. To my wife, Elizabeth, whose encouragement, support, and love give me the strength to let me be who I am . . . and who, as my first set of eyes, is the tsarina of grammar. And finally, to my *shmukler,* Tallulah-Nan-Hari-Naomi, whose effervescent spirit and Yiddish give me such pleasure and hope for the future of Yiddish culture.

—*Yale Strom*

xi

Thanks first to all my very game eaters, the friends and teachers who, during the development of these recipes, were my tasters (whether they knew it or wanted to be). Many of the recipes in this book were handed down to me by my mother, Sheila Schwartz, and my grandmother, Sylvia Frackman (who, while she was alive, was the best cook on the planet), and I am deeply grateful to them, as well as to the many friends, like Melna Katzman (the latke maven), who so generously shared their recipes with me. Thanks to my stepmother, Pearl Schwartz, for the Yiddish lessons and great cooking, and my father, Laskar Schwartz, for his loving memories about Romanian food (and thanks, Dad, for the Romanian *yikhes*). Special thanks to my brother, Jonathan Schwartz, for his advice and passion for cooking—beneath that Genius of Finance exterior, he is truly the best cook in the family. Thank you, Yale, for inspiring everything I do. And my biggest thank you goes to Tallulah, for inspiring every bit of joy in the doing.

—*Elizabeth Schwartz*

Together, we extend our most heartfelt thanks to our agent, Mary Jack Wald, and to our editors, Alan Rinzler and Catherine Craddock. Without their encouragement and advice, this book would not exist.

T-Bone, we miss you.

Introduction

Y OU COME BACK with the goods and we'll form a band that will blow away all the others."

My friend and klezmer collaborator Jeff Pekarek told me this just before I left on my year-long trek to Central and Eastern Europe in 1981, in search of undiscovered klezmer music—gems that had never before been recorded—for our newly formed band.

From before that trip to the present day, I have been deeply engrossed in klezmer music—playing it, studying it, teaching it, and using it in my other creative pursuits. The word klezmer comes from two Hebrew words: *kley,* meaning vessels or tools, and *zmer,* meaning melody. Klezmer was originally Ashkenazic folk dance music. Today the definition has broadened to include Ashkenazic vocal and melismatic instrumental music. The word *Ashkenaz* is Hebrew for German. The term specifically denotes the Jewish culture and Yiddish language that was born in the Rhine River valley, as opposed to the Sephardic culture, the Jewish cultural complex originating in Spain (the Hebrew word *Sepharad* means Spain).

When I hear klezmer, I hear the expression of both the ecstatic joy and profound despair of my people—the Jewish nation. When I draw my bow across the strings of my violin, I am not just making tonal vibrations; I am thinking and feeling out loud. Klezmer for me is the window into the soul of Yiddish culture, the culture of my *yikhes* (Yiddish, lineage, pedigree).

But I have never been content with playing what is already well known and recorded. In 1981, I was starting my own klezmer band, and I wanted to find the roots of klezmer music, its last songs and melodies, and the stories of its creators, so I decided to visit the birthplace of klezmer. I needed to see what was left of this beautiful and rich tradition.

I was confident I would find what I was looking for, despite the skepticism of many of the scholars I'd contacted—and even of some of my friends. They were under the impression that since the Holocaust, those few remaining Jews who'd returned to their former homes in Central and Eastern Europe had all but succumbed to their Stalinist-style governments; they'd assimilated or just disappeared into the fabric of the secular societies surrounding them. These communist regimes were not conducive to fostering or even maintaining any semblance of Yiddish culture, especially klezmer music. But I was not convinced by their lectures or by the articles they'd written to support their assumptions. I was determined to find out for myself not only what klezmer music remained, but what remained of Jewish life four decades after the end of the Holocaust.

I relished being an iconoclast; I learned early on that my last name, Strom, means stream in Yiddish, and that *"Er geyt kegn der shtrom"* (He goes against the stream) would become my mantra.

I found more than I could have ever imagined. I hope to convey to you, as you read this book, my sense of wonderment and surprise in the rich Jewish life I discovered. In fact, I found many pockets where the Jewish communities and individual Jews were not just satisfied with the status quo but wanted to create and promote new Jewish culture in the very places where it was nearly obliterated. Considering the bleak circumstances that surrounded Central and Eastern Europe, it seemed ironic at first that some of the best and most interesting klezmer music I heard was not in the United States but in the Eastern bloc, being sung and played by Jews and Rom (Gypsies).

During my travels, I saw many Jewish cemeteries, took part in several funerals, visited many abandoned synagogues, met several retired Jewish klezmorim, and played klezmer with Rom musicians. But this is only a small part of my story.

I want to share with you the amazing stories I heard from many Holocaust survivors and their children, stories of survival and perseverance. Through my descriptions, I want you to hear some of the Jewish songs I heard; through the recipes, smell and taste some of the Jewish dishes I enjoyed; and through my photography, meet some of the people I met. All five of my senses were constantly bombarded and astounded, which proved to me that Jewish life in Central and Eastern Europe not only survived the Holocaust but was sprouting tiny roots throughout the scarred landscape. The tree of life for the Jewish people in the Eastern bloc had been severed but not completely uprooted.

I have since made many trips to Eastern Europe, both before and after the wall came down, but it was that first trip in 1981 that made the most distinctive mark on me.

Many of those survivors I met during my trip were old enough to have memories that date from before World War I. A few even remembered their childhoods in the 1890s. These Jews were a vital link for me from the time when Yiddish culture was at its zenith to its nascent revival in 1981. Though most of the *kehiles* (Yiddish, Jewish communities) were small, they were still amazingly vibrant.

As we near the sixtieth anniversary of the end of World War II, I feel compelled to tell the story of a people who created a rich thousand-year-old Yiddish culture. Those eyewitnesses to the Holocaust who are still alive can teach us that if we do not learn from history, we are doomed to repeat it. Sadly, however, their numbers are fewer and fewer. And while the survivors' voices and memories fade to a flicker, the voices of those who deny that the Holocaust ever happened or the extent to which it happened have grown bolder and louder.

KLEZMER BEGINNINGS

One man I met in eastern Czechoslovakia, a klezmer musician named Yiska Eisikowicz, told me a story that set the tenor of my travels and echoed my own reasons for becoming a klezmer musician.

"I remember Yoel Simkhe the klezmer in my hometown of Velki Kapusany, Czechoslovakia. He played alto in his uncle's band, but lost his right hand in an accident at the lumber mill. Now he couldn't work at the mill or play alto. After several years, during which I hadn't seen Yoel, he appeared one day in our courtyard on Ulica Zydowski [Jew Street]. He was pushing a dilapidated carriage, and in it was a big gramophone with a big copper tube coming out of it. He had a few records he would play. After he played a couple of records, the people who were listening from their windows would throw Yoel a few kroner [coins], which he would stuff into a little purse that hung from his belt. He would come to our courtyard once a week. I looked forward to his visits even if he played the same tunes over and over again. I never thought of Yoel Simkhe as a beggar. When he appeared my mother used to say: 'God respects all Jews, especially those who bring joy to others.' That is when I decided I wanted to become a klezmer when I grew up."

Hearing Yoel Simkhe play klezmer in front of his home in 1931 left such an indelible impression on the young Yiska that he, too, became a klezmer musician. Half a century later, in 1981, I too was so moved by the haunting, mellifluous sounds of klezmer that I made the same choice.

At this time I was living in San Diego, on my way to law school and to what I thought would be the direction of my life. That all changed on March 1, the night I went to hear the Big Jewish Band, a klezmer group that had been playing concerts in San Diego for about a year. There were no chairs; everyone danced. My endorphins began raging during the first set. I was thoroughly enthused with the spirit and the sound of the music. The second set was just as good, and I was the last off the dance floor. Later that night, I was unable to sleep. By 4 A.M. I had an epiphany: forget law school. I would create my own klezmer band.

By this time, the bal-kulturnik movement was five years old (*bal-kulturnik* is a Yiddish word, meaning master of the culture and returnee to the culture, that I coined for those Jews who began the revival of klezmer in the mid-1970s). Klezmer bands like the Klezmorim, Kapelye, and the Klezmer Conservatory Band and klezmer musicians like Andy Statman and Zev Feldman were performing klezmer concerts throughout the United States. The Big Jewish Band was one of these groups. I had heard of it and even knew some of the musicians, but I had never been to one of their concerts until that fateful night in March.

Well, San Diego was big enough for two klezmer bands, I thought, and I was going to make mine unique. Most bale-kulturniks were learning their repertoire by transcribing tunes from 78 LPs and from the very few available Jewish music books. I decided that my band's repertoire should be based on tunes that had never been recorded, tunes that might be forgotten in archives and in the recesses of the memories of older Jews and Rom.

I called my San Diego band Zmiros (melodies). Jeff Pekarek and I were soon joined by guitarist extraordinaire Fred Benedetti (both of them remain in the band to this day). Within a year after my return from my trek to Eastern Europe we were the most popular klezmer band in Southern California. When I moved to New York City in 1987 I established my other band, Hot Pstromi. Both bands have collaborated on many recordings together. Several years ago I renamed the San Diego band Klazzj, to reflect the growing influence of jazz on the band's style of klezmer.

It is not a coincidence that various bale-kulturniks across the country, many quite separate from each other, also returned to the music of their grandparents at the same time in the 1970s and '80s. All had come from a positive Jewish upbringing, whether religious, secular, or a combination of both. Some of these musicians' parents were part of the American folk music movement that began in the late '50s. The liberal wing of this movement helped galvanize many people, including progressive Jews, to take control of their lives and fight for economic, social, and political justice after the searing McCarthy years. The growing diversity of the country and the rise of the African American and Chicano movements shattered assimilationist theories and encouraged other ethnic groups to slowly begin to research and extol their own unique cultures.

Consequently, many young Ashkenazic Jews (who were second- and third-generation Americans) began to examine and rediscover their Eastern European roots. Some felt disillusioned about the political situation in Israel, and they turned to these roots as an alternative. Others, tired of the focus of Eastern European Jewish history and culture on migration, pogroms, and the Holocaust, sought more positive aspects. Still others were completely assimilated; for them, returning to Judaism down the prescribed religious paths was not an option. Finally, many Jews who were brought up in homes that were devoid of any Jewish spirituality, or whose Hebrew school/ synagogue experience (particularly Reform) left them apathetic, found religious consolation in returning to their roots. Although many of these same disillusioned Jews wandered off searching for some kind of spiritual fulfillment in other religions and cults, others returned to Judaism through klezmer. Learning to play klezmer was often less intimidating than learning

Hebrew or studying Torah, and going to klezmer concerts was often easier than going to synagogue.

By the mid-1980s, after almost ten years of existence in America, klezmer had planted strong roots in American Jewish culture, having helped create a setting of "nostalgic diasporism." This phrase was coined by Mark Slobin in his book *Fiddler on the Move: Exploring the Klezmer World*. Since the klezmer bal-kulturnik movement began in the mid-1970s, it has created a yearning nostalgia for the Yiddish world that existed before the Holocaust. Many of the baby boomers of the 1950s and '60s had been reared in either assimilated or acculturated homes where Judaism was expressed solely by going to the synagogue on the High Holidays, going to Jewish Sunday school, having a bar or bas mitzvah, eating matzah during Passover, buying a tree for Israel, or contributing money to their local United Jewish Federation. But in the last thirty years, nostalgic diasporism has often taken the place of these activities. Signs of this include the creation of Jewish film festivals that have screened, among others, films about shtetl life before its destruction; the airing of klezmer music on Jewish radio programs; the screening of Yiddish-language films made between 1910 and the eve of World War II; the publication of new Jewish magazines like *Der Pakn Treyger* (The Package Porter) that focused on Yiddish culture; the proliferation of Eastern European Jewish studies courses and Yiddish graduate programs offered at Bar Ilan University, Columbia, McGill, Oxford, UCLA, Jagellonian, and other schools; the celebration of Eastern European Jewish culture and Yiddish art festivals throughout the United States, Canada, and Europe; the multitude of klezmer recordings; the increase in students taking Yiddish language courses; and the huge interest in Jewish genealogy and the subsequent growth of travel to former and current Jewish communities in Central and Eastern Europe.

A DISTINCTIVE CHILDHOOD

Although the night of March 18 triggered an epiphany to devote much of my life to klezmer music, my distinctive Jewish upbringing had just as much to do with this enduring passion for klezmer and my decision to go to Europe in search of its roots.

My father's maternal grandmother and grandfather were Hasidim from Stolin, Belarus, and followers of the Stoliner *rebe,* Rabbi Israel. My great-grandparents continued to follow the *rebe* and *davened* (prayed) at the Stoliner shul (synagogue; it became a Baptist church and then burned down) even after they'd immigrated to the United States and moved to Detroit. Rabbi Israel had six sons, four of whom remained in Eastern Europe. Two came to America, Rabbi Yaakov and eventually, Rabbi Yochanan (1948). Rabbi Yaakov lived in the Williamsburg section of Brooklyn, New York. Once a year he would travel to Detroit to visit his followers, providing them with spiritual sustenance and halakhic (Talmudic) advice. Whenever he was in Detroit, Rabbi Yaakov stayed only at my father's grandmother's. To have a *rebe* stay at your home was something special, and gave my father's family a higher level of *yikhes.* In 1946, just after Passover, the *rebe* actually died in my great-grandmother's home. In 1948, Rabbi Yochanan became the Stoliner *rebe* for his followers.

My family's relationship with the Stoliner *rebe* in Eastern Europe as well as in America provided fodder for many stories about the Stoliner *rebes.* The Stoliner Hasidim were known for composing some of the most beautiful *nigunim* (wordless melodies). Almost from infancy, I was infused with love and appreciation for these melodies.

My parents' home was by no means Hasidic. Rather, it was imbued with many of the traditions from Orthodox (keeping kosher, wearing a yarmulke while eating, and so on) as well as Conservative Judaism (such as going to Hebrew school). At the same time, the family politics were left-wing. When I tell people that my father was both descended from Hasidim *and* a socialist Zionist, they can appreciate how lively my home life was.

My parents sprinkled their English with many colorful Yiddish words, particularly adjectives and nouns that described certain people and situations. I still recall expressions such as "She is so *oysgeputst* but dresses still *vi a zhlob*" (She's so dressed up but still dresses like a yokel) and "What a *mumzer* he is, *oysgevarfn mit gelt*" (What a bastard, he has too much money).

Like many Jewish children, my early exposure to Yiddish came from when my *bobe* (grandmother) would come over to visit us and speak to me in her Yinglish. But when I would go to shul with my father, I learned Yiddish in an unexpected way: while my father was inside *davening,* I would be outside playing with the other boys, many of whom were the sons of the rabbi, *gabe* (trustee of the synagogue), or *shames* (sexton), or just came from *frume* (devout) homes. These boys spoke both Yiddish and English, and to be accepted, I learned their *gas Yidish* (street Yiddish). I remember catching *shpringers* (grasshoppers), seeing whose would jump the farthest. We would look for *fosiln* (fossils) of plants and seashells in the shul's *hoyf* (yard) and trade them with each other. And of course, we played *hilke-pilke* (baseball).

The Jewish holidays, especially Passover, trained me to never be afraid to take an unpopular stand on an issue. During Passover, the relatives all got together to celebrate, sing, eat, and argue. We were twenty-five to thirty people of all ages sitting around long tables set with all the traditional Passover foods and a lot of spilled wine on the tablecloths. My Uncle Harold was the family bard. At all holidays and *simkhes* (celebrations) he led the singing and reading in Hebrew of the Haggadah—the collection of tales, hymns, psalms, and songs recited during the Passover *seders,* the holiday meals for the first two nights. The Four Questions were sung in both Hebrew and Yiddish. The reading of the Haggadah was also sporadically interrupted by religious and social questions, which usually led to a political debate about socialism versus communism, Lenin versus Trotsky, or capitalism versus kibbutz life in Israel. The seders were clamorous, spirited, and fun.

I was fascinated with the stories about shtetl life I had heard from my Hebrew School teacher, Mrs. Pike. Mrs. Pike seemed to be at least ninety (she had taught my dad as well) and to have just stepped out of a Sholom Aleichem story as an emissary from the distant past. I was captivated whenever she read to us about the vanished Jewish world of my grandparents.

When I was eleven, our family moved from Detroit to San Diego. The Jewish life, the Jewish community, was not as vital as it had been in Detroit. Though there was a shul nearby, my father couldn't shake his lifetime habit of *davening* in a *shtibl* (small synagogue), so he and some other likeminded folk created a "storefront *shtibl*." These were places that during the day were homes or businesses but were transformed on Shabes into places of worship. I remember best the *shtibl* in a doctor's office. The Torah was brought out and laid on the examining table to be read. This was so strange, weird, and cool all at the same time that it made going to shul much more interesting. This core group of wandering worshippers would eventually form the base for the first Lubavitcher (Chabad) synagogue in San Diego.

Throughout high school my interest in Eastern European Jewish history continued, but it was rivaled by my love of long-distance running. The training and competition of those years helped to shape the person that I am today, and the endurance that I developed as an athlete certainly would come in handy more than once during my adult travels. This love of running continued into college and my first trek to Europe, where I traveled on my own during my junior year in college, living and studying in Uppsala, Sweden. When I wasn't in class I was traveling throughout Sweden; during the winter, spring, and summer breaks I ventured across the European continent. My experiences ranged from sleeping outside Rovaniemi, Finland (at the Arctic Circle) with some Laplanders, surrounded by their reindeer for warmth, to dancing and singing in the snow in a park with Soviet Jews on Purim (the KGB wouldn't let us into the synagogue). There was something about Europe that intrigued me and fed my curiosity. Living for a year in Europe and experiencing so many different cultures just whetted my appetite for more. Whatever reverse culture shock I felt when I returned to San Diego, I reassured myself that I would be back to Europe sometime soon.

And sure enough, after that memorable klezmer concert on March 18, I returned to Europe. The adventure I am about to share with you shaped me spiritually and artistically. Klezmer became my aesthetic palette for mining the riches of Yiddish culture. My role as a researcher, educator, artist, and entertainer has been not only to play klezmer music but to use it as a creative vehicle to explore other social aspects of Yiddish culture.

Klezmer and the life of the klezmer prior to World War II are common themes in all of the media in which I work: films, photography, books, and plays. The umbilical cord to my grandparents' continent had been severed by the Holocaust—my trek nourished and reconnected me. I rediscovered their history and what my Yiddish heritage means to me, and made many surprising discoveries and lifelong friends along the way.

Glossary

As with any foreign language with its own alphabet, Yiddish has often been spelled in other alphabets in the way the user deems closest to its sound. For example, Poles might write *mermelsztajn* (marble), while Americans, relying on the German spelling, would write *mermelshtein,* and those spelling it according to the YIVO (Yiddish Scientific Organization) standard would spell it *mirmelshtayn.* There are many spelling land mines in Yiddish because it is a language derived from several others (German, Hebrew, Polish, Russian, and French), all of which are in use today.

Because this is a book about Eastern European Jewish culture, in which the lingua franca for the vast majority of Jews was Yiddish, most Yiddish and Hebrew words herein are spelled according to the YIVO standard, which is recognized by academicians throughout the world. Those words that have crossed over into everyday English usage—such as Hanukkah, challah, Torah, and Haggadah—are spelled in their more common way and they are not set in italics. In this glossary the YIVO spelling follows the definition in parentheses, if it differs from the common spelling.

VOCABULARY

aliye . . . . To go up (Hebrew); to immigrate
ameyn . . . . "It is true"; amen
aveyre . . . . Sin (Hebrew)

bal-kulturnik . . . . . Master of the culture; one who returns to the culture (plural, *bale-kulturniks*)

bal-tfile . . . . One who leads prayers in the synagogue

bekeshe . . . . Long waistcoat

beshert . . . . Predestined; inevitable

besmedresh . . . . Small Orthodox house of worship

bimah . . . . Elevated platform in a synagogue (YIVO: *bime*)

bobe . . . . Grandmother

Borkhashem . . . . . . Thank God

brekhekhs tans . . . . . Vomit dance

bris . . . . Circumcision

bulgar . . . . An 8/8 tune, similar to a *freylekhs* in 2/4 time

challah . . . . Egg bread, eaten every Shabes (YIVO: *khale*)

charoset . . . . A sweet paste, made with apples and nuts, eaten at the Seder (YIVO: *kharoyses*)

chuppah . . . . Wedding canopy (YIVO: *khupe*)

chutzpah . . . . Courage; guts (YIVO: *khutspe*)

czardas . . . . Hungarian folk dance

daven . . . . Pray

doyne . . . . A semi-improvised musical display piece

dreydl . . . . Top used to play a gambling game on Hanukkah

dveykes . . . . Spiritual adhesion; the Hasidic concept that through song one can reach a spiritual sense of nirvana and adhere to God

fleysh keyz . . . . Headcheese in aspic

fleyshik . . . . Meat; made with meat; served with meat

fosiln . . . . Fossils

freylekhs . . . . Most common upbeat klezmer dance, in 2/4 time

frume . . . . Observant

gabe . . . . Trustee or warden of the synagogue

ganovim . . . . Thieves

gartlekh . . . . Sashes; belts

gelt . . . . Money

Gemore . . . . The part of the Talmud that comments on the Mishna

gleyzele . . . . Small glass

gnize . . . . A synagogue storeroom for unusable books and ritual objects *grogers* . . . . Rattles; noisemakers

Haggadah . . . . Prayer book for the Passover *seder* (YIVO: *Hagode*)

hakofes . . . . Circular procession with the Torah scrolls,
                    done several times on Simchas Torah

halakhic . . . . According to Talmudic law

hamantaschen . . . . Traditional pastry eaten on Purim; "Haman's pouches"
                    (YIVO: *homentashn*)

Hanukkah . . . . . . (Hebrew, dedication) A festival commemorating the
                    victory of Judah Maccabee and his followers, who
                    captured Jerusalem after defeating the Assyrian Greeks
                    who had defiled the Temple (YIVO: *Khanike*)

Hashem . . . . The name of God; an expression used to avoid the
                    disrespectful act of speaking God's name directly

Hasidic . . . . Drawing from the philosophy of Hasidism
                    (YIVO: *Khasidic*)

Hasidim . . . . Followers of a kabbalistic and spiritual philosophy
                    begun by the Ba'al Shem Tov in the eighteenth century
                    that garnered a huge following among Eastern
                    European Jews (YIVO: *Khasidim*)

"Hatikvah" . . . . . . (Hebrew, hope) Title of the Israeli national anthem

heymish . . . . Informal; cozy

hilke-pilke . . . . . . Baseball

hoyf . . . . Courtyard

hora . . . . Popular Romanian Jewish dance played in a
                    hobbling 3/8 gait

ish ha-tsadek . . . . . A pious person

Kaddish . . . . Prayer for the dead (YIVO: *Kadesh*)

kapelye . . . . Band; ensemble

kehile . . . . Jewish community

khakhshara . . . . . . Training farm

kharoyses . . . . A sweet paste, made with apples and nuts,
                    eaten at the Passover *seder*

khazer . . . . Pig

khazn . . . . Cantor

khevre kedishe . . . . . Burial society (Hebrew)

kheyder tehoyre . . . . Purification room (Hebrew)

kidesh . . . . Small meal served after daily morning prayers *kikhl* . . . . Egg and wheat sugar cookie

klezmer . . . . Ashkenazic instrumental folk music; a musician who plays such music (plural, klezmorim or klezmers)

kohanim . . . . High priests

Kol Nidre . . . . . . Reverent prayer recited on Yom Kippur (YIVO: *Kolnidre*)

kvitlekh . . . . Small notes from people to a rabbi

Lag B'Omer . . . . . Jewish springtime festival (YIVO: *Legboymer*)

Lamed Vovnik . . . . One of the thirty-six righteous souls

L'chayim . . . . "To life!"; a toast

marshalik . . . . Wedding jester or master of ceremonies

matzah . . . . Unleavened bread, traditional for Passover (YIVO: *matse*)

mazl . . . . Fortune, luck

megile . . . . Scroll; the Book of Esther, read on Purim

menorah . . . . Seven-branched candelabra (YIVO: *menoyre*)

meshuga . . . . Crazy person (plural, *meshugim*)

meshugas . . . . Craziness; nonsense

mezuzah . . . . Encased religious scroll, affixed to a doorpost (YIVO: *mezuze*)

mikvah . . . . Ritual bath (YIVO: *mikve*)

minyan . . . . Quorum of ten men (YIVO: *minyen*)

Mishna . . . . A collection of postbiblical laws and rabbinical discussions of the second century that forms part of the Talmud (YIVO: *Mishne*)

mitzvah . . . . Commandment of Jewish law; a meritorious or charitable act (YIVO: *mitsve*)

m'lave malke . . . . . . The evening meal marking the conclusion of the Sabbath festivities (Hebrew)

Mogen Dovid . . . . Star of David (YIVO: *Mogn Doved*)

mohel . . . . Circumciser

mumzer . . . . Bastard (plural, *mumzerim*)

neshome . . . . Soul

nign . . . . Melody (plural, *nigunim*)

Oi veys mir . . . . . . "Oh, woe is me"

oysgeputst . . . . Dressed up

oysgevarfn . . . . Rebuked, reproached

peyes . . . . Earlocks

Peysekh . . . . Passover, a springtime festival commemorating the Exodus of the Jews from Egypt after generations in slavery

pinkes . . . . Book of records; town register

rebe . . . . Hasidic spiritual leader

reydl . . . . Circle dance

Rom . . . . Gypsy

Rosh Hashana . . . . Jewish New Year (YIVO: *Rosheshone*)

roshekool . . . . Head of a Jewish community

sazshlke . . . . Pond

seder . . . . Ceremonial dinner held on the first or first and second evenings of Passover (YIVO: *sdor*; plural, *sdorim*)

sekund . . . . Second violin, playing only chords

sforim . . . . Religious books

Shabes . . . . Sabbath (plural, Shabeses)

Shabes goy . . . . . . Gentile employed to build a fire or turn on the light for observant Jews

shadchan . . . . Matchmaker (YIVO: *shatkhn*)

shaitel . . . . Wigs worn by Orthodox women (YIVO: *shaytl*; plural *shaytlekh*)

shaloshudes . . . . . . The third meal of the Sabbath

shames . . . . Sexton

Shavuos . . . . Jewish holiday celebrating the giving of the Torah (YIVO: *Shvues*)

Sheve Brokhes . . . . . Seven blessings said at the end of a wedding celebration

shlep . . . . Carry; drag

shofar . . . . Ram's horn (YIVO: *shoyfer*)

Sholom aleykhem . . . "Peace be unto you"; traditional greeting

shoykhet . . . . Ritual slaughterer (shoykihetim)

shpringers . . . . Grasshoppers

shtekh . . . . Stick

shtetl . . . . Small Eastern European town, predominantly Jewish

shtibl . . . . Small synagogue

shuklen . . . . Rocking; swaying

shul . . . . Synagogue

Simchas Torah . . . . Eighth day of the Feast of Tabernacles, celebrating the completion of a year's reading cycle (YIVO: *Simkhes Toyre*)

simkhes . . . . Celebrations

skhakh . . . . Branches used for covering a sukkah tabernacle roof

sukkah . . . . Booth constructed for Sukkos, the Jewish harvest holiday (YIVO: *suke, Sukes*)

tallisim . . . . Prayer shawls (YIVO: *talesim*)

tanc haz . . . . Hungarian dance house

tants . . . . Dance

taykhl . . . . River

tcholnt . . . . Traditional stew, slow-cooked and served on Shabes

tefiln . . . . Phylacteries

Terkishe Zogekhts . . . A Romanian plaintive display piece, with Turkish influence

Tisha B'Av . . . . . . Jewish day of fasting and mourning to commemorate the destruction of the first and second Temples in Jerusalem (YIVO: *Tishebov*)

tsimbl . . . . Hungarian stringed instrument

tsitsis . . . . Ritual undergarment with tassels

tsotskes . . . . Baubles; toys

Tu B'Shvat . . . . . . Festival of trees. In Yiddish, the holiday is referred to as *khamishoser*, literally "the fifteenth" because the festival falls on the fifteenth day of the Hebrew month Shvat

tuica . . . . Traditional Romanian liquor made from small prunes

tukhes . . . . Buttocks

yarmulke . . . . Skullcap

yartzayt . . . . Anniversary of a death

yente . . . . Gossip

yeshiva . . . . School for Talmudic study (YIVO: *yeshive*)

Yidishkayt . . . . Jewishness; Judaism

yikhes . . . . Lineage; pedigree

yold . . . . Chump

Yom Kippur . . . . . The Day of Atonement, the most solemn Jewish holiday (YIVO: *Yom Kiper*)

yontef . . . . Holiday
zhlob . . . . Hick; yokel; boor
zmiros . . . . Songs, particularly for Shabes
zogekhts . . . . A plaintive display piece

PLACE NAMES

The names on the map are as they appeared in the 1980s. In text, I use the name most commonly used by the Jews I met. Sometimes they called a city by its Yiddish name (such as Seylish for Vinogradov). Sometimes they referred to a city in the language of the country that influenced them most strongly. For example, Jews referred to Kosice by its Hungarian name, Kassa, but pronounced it in Yiddish as Kashoy. Here is a list of cities that are referred to by more than one name.

Yugoslavia
Split . . . . Italians called it Spalato.
Novi-Sad . . . . Hungarian Jews and gentiles said Ujvidek.

Czechoslovakia
Brno . . . . Jews called it in German Brunn.
Bratislava . . . . . . German/Yiddish-speaking Jews and gentiles said
                        Pressburg; Hungarian-speaking Jews and gentiles
                        said Pozsony.
Kosice . . . . Yiddish-speaking Jews said Kashoy; Hungarian-
                        speaking Jews and gentiles said Kassa.

Poland
Karkow . . . . Jews called it Kroke.
Auschwitz . . . . . . Poles and Jews called Oswiencim.
Wroclaw . . . . Jews and German gentiles called it Breslau.
Warsaw . . . . Jews called it Varshe.

Ukraine
Mukacevo . . . . . . Jews and Hungarian gentiles said Munkatsh;
                        Ukrainians said Mukaceve.

Vinogradov . . . . . Jews said Seylish; Hungarian gentiles said Nagyszollos; Czechoslovaks said Sevlus; and Ukrainians said Vinohradiv.

Salanka . . . . .Rom (ethnic Hungarians) said Salang.

Vylok . . . . .Hungarian Jews and gentiles said Tiszaujlok.

Romania

Suceava . . . . .Jews said Shutz

Iasi . . . . .Jews said Yash, as it is pronounced in Romanian.

Chapter One

YUGOSLAVIA

SAT ON MY BACKPACK in the narrow, hot, stinky, clamorous, smoke-filled corridor of the train, trying to get some sleep while other passengers walked into and over me en route to the bathroom and dining car. People had crammed themselves in every nook and cranny available—in the hallways, in the dining car, outside between the cars, even in the bathrooms.

It was June 1981. I was twenty-three years old and traveling from Vienna to Zagreb, Yugoslavia—the first stop in my yearlong journey through Eastern Europe in search of klezmer and of Jewish music, culture, stories, and life under communist rule. I would learn many things in the following year—both about myself and the people and places I visited—and I had just learned a very important and practical travel tip: in addition to the train ticket, you must buy a seat ticket if you want to sit on something other than your luggage.

It had never occurred to me that buying a train ticket in the Eastern bloc would not automatically guarantee me a seat. I was soon to learn that it was not uncommon for a railroad company to sell many more tickets than they had seats. What did they care? They wanted the revenue. Anyone from the West traveling from one country to another had to pay in U.S. dollars or German marks—usually at a much higher price than the locals paid. Most locals didn't have cars, so they were obliged to use public transportation, and the train was much quicker than a bus and cheaper than an airplane—in other words, the railroad company knew they could take advantage of the situation, and they did.

The upside: by the end of my trek, I had mastered the art of sleeping in a train hallway . . . standing up.

I resigned myself to a difficult journey and took out my banjoline. I had bought it for $20 from an old hunched-over man in a flea market during my four-hour train layover in Budapest earlier that day.

Banjolines were commonly played in 1920s dance bands, and now I used my droll new instrument to compose a klezmer tune called "Maestral Hora and Bulgar." The hora was originally a popular Romanian Jewish dance, played in a hobbling 3/8 gait; it was often followed by an upbeat *bulgar* in 8/8. Similar to a *freylekhs* (an upbeat dance, generally in 2/4 time), a *bulgar* was danced as either a circle or line dance; it was popular in Bessarabia and South Ukraine in the nineteenth century through the eve of World War II. The name probably refers to the Bulgarian minority in Bessarabia. I had fun playing counter-rhythm to the rhythm of the train over the tracks.

ZAGREB

My train arrived in Zagreb at 8:30 P.M. Exhausted, I gathered my gear and walked to the only address I had, 55 Bukovacka Cesta, the Jewish Home for the Aged. The home had been built in 1957 with funds from the American Jewish Joint Distribution Committee and from Jewish Material Claims against Germany. I had learned of the home (and other Jewish places I would seek out over the course of my journey) in *The Jewish Travel Guide,* published by the Jewish Chronicle of London. I was on a strict budget and hoped that I could get a free room in exchange for entertaining the residents with some Jewish music—I figured that Jewish music, like young Jews, was scarce and would be much appreciated. So I began the two-mile walk.

Although it was cloudy and drizzling, it was still excruciatingly hot and humid. Among all the negative things people kept telling me about the Eastern bloc before I left on my trip—that I was wasting my time searching for anything connected to klezmer, there were only a few Jews left and those who remained were all old, the communists forbade any kind of religious or Jewish cultural expression, food was scarce and one had to wait in long lines

"Maestral Hora and Bulgar"

Written by Yale Strom

The Jewish History of Yugoslavia

Of all the Balkan countries, Yugoslavia is the only one with a sizable Ashkenazic community as well as a Sephardic one. Yugoslavia was founded at the end of World War I in 1918 and comprised six republics—Bosnia-Herzegovina, Croatia, Macedonia, Montenegro, Serbia, and Slovenia; and two provinces—Kosovo and Vojvodina. Jews first settled in Yugoslavia during Roman times (third century C.E.), as evidenced by synagogue and tombstone inscriptions found near Split (Italian, Spalato) on the Dalmatian coast. Following their expulsion from Spain in 1492, Sephardic Jews started migrating to the Dalmatian coast from Spain, Portugal, and Italy. By 1521, this area of Yugoslavia was under Turkish rule, and the Jewish communities came under the authority of the chief rabbi of Constantinople.

In 1878, Serbia's Jews were granted complete civil, economic, and political emancipation by the Treaty of Berlin. The Jews in the other regions did not become full legal citizens until the end of World War I.

With an influx of Jews from the former Austro-Hungarian territories, Yugoslavia's Jewish population swelled to 76,654 by 1931. The Sephardim comprised about thirty thousand and the Ashkenazim about forty-six thousand, of which some twenty-two thousand were Hungarian. Until the 1930s, anti-Semitism had not been a part of Jewish life, but gradually it began to seep in from Germany. The Yugoslavian government initiated its first two anti-Jewish laws in October 1940. The first limited the access of Jews to high schools and higher education; the second stopped the granting to Jews of licenses for opening new businesses and restricted the renewal of licenses already granted.

On April 6, 1941, German forces, along with their Italian, Bulgarian, and Hungarian allies, invaded Yugoslavia. Eleven days later, the Yugoslavian government capitulated to the Nazis. Some five thousand Jews fought among the partisans. By the end of 1941, Belgrade became the first capital city in occupied Europe to be declared completely *Judenrein* (free of Jews). Those few Jews who were able to escape were hunted down by the Croatian and Serbian collaborators. Some sixty thousand Yugoslavian Jews perished in the Holocaust, many in the infamous concentration camps located in Nis (Macedonia), Sabac (Serbia), and Jasenovac (Croatia)—the largest camp. After the war, between 1948 and 1951, about nine thousand Yugoslavian Jews immigrated to Israel. In 1981 there were some seven thousand Jews in Yugoslavia. Today, there are 1,716 in Croatia, 3,300 in Serbia, and 1,000 in Bosnia.

when it arrived in the stores—I remembered being told that it was either damp or cold most of the time. Well, unless the Berlin Wall provided enough shade, it promised to be a hot, steamy summer.

Though overcast, it wasn't completely dark yet. The drizzle didn't bother me too much, because the poplars along the street provided a thick canopy. Most of the shops were closed and looked rather nondescript, except for the usual portrait of Premier Josip Tito hanging in each window. I hadn't eaten since lunch, but I was reluctant to go into any of the smoke-filled cafés. I was trying to detox my lungs from all of the cigarette smoke I had inhaled for eight hours, but more, I felt a bit uneasy. I didn't see any other tourists or backpackers like myself strolling the evening streets. I felt conspicuous and I sensed a lot of stares, especially from the young men who were just hanging out, drinking beer and smoking. I knew enough before I embarked on my trek not to display my being a foreigner any more than I had to. No flags, no buttons on my backpack, and just regular clothes except for the occasional T-shirt with a running-race logo. My Adidas running shoes even matched those of many of the guys hanging out.

Maybe my imagination was a bit overactive, but when I glanced at them they seemed to turn to each other with their roguish smiles to talk about me. Perhaps I was an easy target for someone to rob for a few dollars—currency that went a long way in the Eastern bloc. At five foot ten inches and 135 pounds (soaking wet), and carrying just about as much as I weighed, I was not an imposing figure. As it turned out, during my entire trip the only trouble I was to encounter would come from the police and border guards in each country.

A PLACE TO STAY

Three or four wrong turns later, I arrived at the Jewish Home for the Aged. The three-story building stood two hundred feet back from the street in a lush, tree-filled garden. A wrought-iron fence surrounded the compound. I was tired, famished, wet, and eager to get inside. Though it was past 9:30 P.M., I hoped someone would still be up to open the gate. I pushed and pushed the doorbell as the drizzle turned into a driving rain. Finally, an old man dressed in striped pajamas, bathrobe, and slippers shuffled down the path toward me. You can imagine the look on his face when he saw me. He unlocked the gate and opened it just enough to gape at me in utter amazement. He said something in Croatian, which I didn't quite understand, but the gist of it was "I am sorry we are closed and your grandmother is sleeping."

I answered him in Yiddish (my Croatian nearly nonexistent at that time), explaining that I was wet, hungry, and had no place to stay that night—and I was Jewish. Again he answered me, only this time, as he spoke, I gently pushed him to the side and walked into the yard. If nothing else, I hoped to sleep in my sleeping bag on the floor somewhere where it was dry. After a few seconds the old man scurried past me to get to the front door before I did. When he got there he yelled to me in German, "Wait, wait!" He then went inside, closing the door firmly behind him.

As I stood there waiting, I began to laugh at myself. I could just see trying to pull the same stunt at the Jewish Home for the Aged in San Diego. Needless to say, the police back home would have obliged me with a place to sleep, but here in Yugoslavia I was acting the same way I didn't want to be perceived: as the arrogant American. I realized I should not have assumed that I could stay there, but it was raining, late, I hadn't slept in over twenty-four hours, and I was desperate.

Four elderly women opened the door; three of them were wide awake, the other half asleep. They stood there for a moment in their nightclothes, dumbfounded by my presence. Then they all began speaking to each other at once. Finally one of them—a slender lady with an alabaster face, wearing a purple silk bathrobe and sleeping bonnet—pushed herself forward, shushed the others to be quiet, and said to me in perfect English with no trace of an accent, "Are you here to visit your grandmother?"

"Well not exactly. I'm here to—"

"Did you come to see your grandfather?"

"I'm sorry to be bothering you but I have no relatives here and I need a place to sleep for the night. . . . I am Jewish."

"As you can see, this is not a hotel."

"I'm from the United States and I'm researching Jewish folk music."

"We are all Jewish and some of us know some Jewish songs, but it is rather late for us."

"No, I don't mean to record you tonight. I just arrived from Budapest and I need a place to sleep just for the night. See my sleeping bag? I just need some floor space."

With a delicate smile, she gently pushed the women out of the way and closed the door on me. From the other side of the door I could hear her speaking to the other ladies, which prompted them to again all begin speaking at once. A minute went by, then the door reopened and the slender lady said:

"This is highly unusual, but since you have no place to stay tonight and you seem like a nice young man we have decided to let you sleep here. Please, what is your name?"

"My name is Yale."

"And I am Olga."

I walked in and followed Olga down a corridor that smelled of mothballs. There was room after room off of the corridor. We turned right, then Olga opened a door and showed me inside. The room was fully furnished with a bed, toilet, and bathtub.

"I hope you find this comfortable. There are towels in the cupboard and breakfast is at eight A.M."

"Thank you so much, Olga, I—"

"Please do come and join me at my table tomorrow. We will see what sort of Jewish music we might find for you."

I quickly got out of my dirty, sweaty clothes and took an enjoyable hot bath with the European-style flexible shower nozzle, washed some clothes, and dove into the cold, freshly laundered sheets. As my head sank into the soft goose down pillow, I remembered that I wanted to write in my diary religiously every night about that day's events. Not tonight, I thought, as my eyelids closed and I drifted off into a deep slumber.

Songs and Stories from the Past

The next morning I found myself eating breakfast with some eighty residents, mostly women, whose average age was probably around seventy-seven. The home was intended only for elderly Jews but there were seven non-Jewish residents; as they had been married to Jews, they were allowed to live there as well.

As a vegetarian, I appreciated the delicious food on the menu so much that I had double portions: plain white bread with apricot preserves, a kind of hot farina, fresh tomatoes, leeks, red peppers from their own garden, pickled hot peppers, brinze cheese (like feta, only drier and sharper), tea, and thick strong Turkish coffee.

I sat with Olga (who I could not believe was ninety-one); Moises, eighty-three; and Rut (Ruth), seventy-nine. I spoke English with Olga and some Yiddish and German with Moises; Olga translated our conversation into Serbo-Croatian for Rut.

I would soon learn that although there were Ashkenazim in Yugoslavia, a good portion of them had assimilated during the Austro-Hungarian Empire and thus had abandoned many of their cultural traditions—like speaking Yiddish as their mother tongue and playing klezmer music—in favor of adopting their host cultures. There was also a sizable Sephardic population in Yugoslavia, and their traditions, particularly their musical traditions, were very different from those of their Ashkenazim counterparts. So I was probably more likely to hear Sephardic folk music in Yugoslavia than Ashkenazic klezmer. Well, I shrugged to myself, I was here, I already had planned to visit a few other cities before traveling to Hungary, and there were *some* Ashkenazim living in Yugoslavia. I'd just have to work a little harder to find them.

As it turned out, I didn't have to look too far. Rut was Ashkenaz, from the small town of Senta near the Hungarian border. She remembered going to her cousin's wedding in Szeged, Hungary, at which Rom (Gypsy) musicians played both Hungarian and Jewish melodies. Rut actually remembered a Jewish waltz she and her father had danced to. She began to sing it, but I told her to wait just a moment, I wanted to record it. I ran back to my room, grabbed my tape recorder and microphone, and quickly set it up on the dining table. Wow! She sang a klezmer tune she remembered from seventy years ago. What better place than a Jewish home for the aged?

Rut had a pleasant voice and seemed quite proud to be singing for me. It was probably the first time in her life someone had recorded her singing. I asked her to sing it three times so that when it came time to transcribe the tune I would have enough examples of Rut's exact musical nuances. The melody seemed to have a Hungarian flavor that made perfect sense: when Rut had danced with her father at that Jewish wedding, she was living in the Austro-Hungarian Empire.

By the third rendition of the song, a group of twenty residents had gathered around the table to listen intently as Rut's voice rose in volume and confidence (as any good performer's would). After she finished singing,

"Waltz from Senta"

Collected by Yale Strom

several other residents pushed forward, volunteering to sing me some Jewish songs. I decided to take their names and room numbers so I could visit them individually and ask them a few questions about each tune and themselves. The fidelity would also be much better without the extraneous sounds from the others standing around watching.

Olga had become my surrogate grandmother, while I became the surrogate grandson for many of the residents. Olga (her Jewish name was Blumele) was born in Cepin near Osijek. She lived there with her first husband, a doctor. Then she moved to Demasuhara (today part of Romania), where she learned to speak Hungarian. She divorced and was remarried, to another doctor. Together they moved to Palestine in 1930. She was a strong Zionist and they lived at first in Jerusalem, but her husband couldn't make a living—too few patients—so after ten months they moved to Rabat, Morocco.

Olga loved Rabat, but life got harder for all the Jews in Morocco when Italy took control of the country. Finally, in 1943, Olga and her husband moved to New York City. There she designed and sold costume jewelry for Macy's. She got a second divorce (in Nevada) and remained in New York for six years. Then she went to Kalmar, Sweden, to visit her only child, her son from her first marriage. He wanted Olga to move to Sweden, but she was

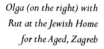

Olga (on the right) with Rut at the Jewish Home for the Aged, Zagreb

afraid she wouldn't be able to learn the language. Eventually she moved back to Zagreb. Olga was now a great-grandmother.

Olga so impressed me with her great health—no hearing aids, false teeth, or glasses—that I said, "To one hundred twenty you should live!"

"Anything too much is not good," she replied. "While I feel young everything is all right. When I will feel old then I will be ready to go and see my husbands."

Unfortunately, few residents were as cheerful and healthy as Olga. A sense of stark loneliness pervaded the home. There were elderly Jews who lived there because they'd never had children, or their spouses had died, or they had never married, and they needed some physical assistance in doing many of the mundane things of everyday life. Then there were other residents who could take care of themselves but wanted to live among their Jewish brethren. These people had lived their entire lives in small towns or even villages where the Jewish community had gradually disappeared from migration and death. This is what happened to Rut, who'd lived her entire life in Senta.

Though Rut and her husband, Ferenc, were the last Jews in the town by 1971, they chose to stay because they had a successful toy store. Rut had a cousin on her mother's side who had immigrated to the United States before World War II, but she lost contact with her, and the rest of her family perished in the Holocaust. Her husband was also the sole survivor from his family, except for a nephew who lived in Belgrade. Then in 1977, Ferenc died suddenly from a heart attack and Rut wasn't able to operate the store by herself. She sold it and moved to the Jewish Home for the Aged as soon as space became available. Rut only had to wait two years before she could move in; some other residents had had to wait as long as five years before being admitted.

Though the Jewish population in Yugoslavia was not large, most of its Jews were elderly. This was the only Jewish Home for the Aged in the entire country, and that created some real but morbid realities for those elderly Jews who were waiting to be accepted into it. Olga told me she received letters from friends who asked specifically about a certain resident who had been seriously ill. Was she getting better, or was death just sitting in a chair across from her bed, waiting for the precise moment to take her away . . . so others could fill the vacancy?

What bothered me most was seeing the residents' children visiting their parents, sometimes having to drag the grandchildren along. This reminded me of the times I had played klezmer music for the elderly Jews in the Home for the Aged in San Diego. The music occupied their minds for a while, but when I left many were once again overtaken by isolation. Before the Holocaust, in the shtetl (Yiddish, primarily Jewish town) the concept of a separate home for the aged was not known. Grandmothers and grandfathers lived with their children and helped to raise their grandchildren. I missed my grandma.

My intention had always been to stay a couple of days, maximum, before I left Zagreb for Split. I ended up staying another week with these incredible Jewish seniors. The night I left the home to walk to the train station, Olga

Burek Sasirom Spinat

Yugoslavian Spinach and Cheese Pies

Makes about 5 dozen

Yugoslavian *bureks* are close cousins to Greek pitas (as in spanikopita and tiropita). The difference is in the consistency of the dough and the flavor. The dough in the Yugoslavian *burek* is different from the phyllo used in the Greek version—it is more like our traditional pie dough. *Bureks* can be stuffed with spinach, potato, meat, or fruit. This filling will also work well for a Greek spinach pie. You can substitute one and a half 10-ounce packages of thawed, drained chopped spinach for the fresh spinach.

For the filling:

¼ lb. pot cheese or farmer cheese
⅓ lb. shredded Swiss cheese
¼ lb. feta, finely crumbled
1 large potato, boiled and mashed
4 medium eggs
2 Tbsp. finely chopped garlic
1½ lb. fresh spinach, washed well and
   finely chopped
Salt and pepper to taste

For the dough:

7 cups unsifted flour
1½ cups peanut oil
2 cups hot water
Extra oil for brushing *bureks*
1 egg yolk and 2 tsp. water, beaten together for an egg wash

and Rut came to say good-bye. And just like typical Jewish mothers, they didn't let me leave without taking some food for the train.

"Yale, you won't find any cheese-spinach *bureks* on the train as good as ours—and they are still hot," said Olga.

I said good-bye to everyone and thanked them profusely for their warm hospitality and generosity. Then, with a lump in my throat, I hugged and kissed Olga, telling her I hoped to be back to see her. (And sure enough, three and a half years later I found myself back in Zagreb once again with my buddy Brian Blue—this time, Olga welcomed us both.)

1. *For the filling:* Combine all the filling ingredients and mix well. Set aside.

2. *For the dough:* In a large bowl, place the flour and make a well in the center. Add the peanut oil and 1 cup of the water and mix with your hands. If necessary, dust your hands with flour to keep the dough from sticking. Add the remaining water and mix until the dough pulls away from the sides of the bowl; do not knead or overmix. Cover with a clean towel and let it rest for 30 minutes on the kitchen counter.

3. Preheat the oven to 350°. Dust the work surface and a rolling pin with flour. Pinch off an egg-sized piece of dough and roll into a 5-inch circle. Place a heaping teaspoonful of filling in the center and fold in half to form a half moon. Trim the excess dough from around the filling and press the edges together with the tines of a fork, being careful not to puncture the *burek*. Repeat with the remaining dough and filling.

4. Generously oil the bottom of a shallow baking pan (a jelly roll pan is best). Brush the tops and bottoms of the *bureks* with oil as you place them in the pan. Then brush the tops with the egg wash.

5. Bake until golden, about 45 minutes. Serve hot or at room temperature.

SPLIT

The houses and buildings of the coastal city of Split are made of white stone. Lush, decorative flowerboxes hang from nearly every window, and wooden shutters are opened in the mornings to let in the breezes off the Adriatic Sea.

On my first day there, I slowly traversed the cool, shaded narrow streets of the old city and ended up at the harbor. I walked the maze of smooth-worn stone passages, which led me to Zidovski Prolaz (Serbo-Croatian, Jewish alley). I waited at the foot of the stairs of the Jewish Community Center thirty minutes before the *roshekool* (Yiddish, head of the Jewish community) appeared. Roundfaced and moustachioed, he had a scar across his chin. His name was Eduard Toyb. In perfect English, he invited me inside for Turkish coffee and biscuits.

A Sacred Torah and a Soccer Game

Eduard took me to see the Ashkenazic synagogue, built in the eighteenth century. Large marble columns ringed the perimeter of the sanctuary. In the middle stood the bimah (Hebrew, elevated platform) and set into the eastern wall was the Holy Ark. Eduard opened it and handed me a small, beautiful Torah.

"My mother saved this Torah before she was deported to Jasenovac, the death camp. She never returned home. It had been in our family for three hundred years, so she hid it with a gentile neighbor she had grown up with. After the war the neighbor gave it back to the Jewish community. Now when I touch the Torah I feel as if I am touching my mother's soul, and when the rabbi reads from it I hear my mother's voice."

Unfortunately, the rabbi rarely read from this Torah, as he came from Belgrade only to officiate at the funerals of members of the Jewish community. The synagogue itself was used only on the holidays.

Though there were some Ashkenazim among the eighty-one Jews in the community, I didn't get the sense from Eduard that I was going to find any unknown Yiddish folk melodies or klezmer tunes.

Eduard invited me to a soccer game that night between the Jewish community's soccer team Maccabi and another local team. I sat with him and several young members of the Jewish community in a four-thousand-seat stadium. It was about half full. The Maccabi team was winning, and the delicious ocean breeze cooled the hot daytime temperatures. Although I had only just met the people I sat with, I felt a kind of warm familial feeling for them, a camaraderie. Though we were born in different countries in completely different circumstances, we were all Jews. We discussed what it meant to be a Jew in today's world, the importance of maintaining and celebrating one's culture, and what Israel meant to us.

I realized, as I sat with my new friends in that soccer stadium, that this trek was about more than just trying to collect some old klezmer tunes. It was about meeting the Holocaust survivors and hearing their incredible stories of their lives before, during, and after the Holocaust. After all, what was a klezmer tune without the human vessel to transmit it to others?

DUBROVNIK

Early the next morning I was on a bus on the road that followed the rugged and picturesque Adriatic coastline all the way down to Dubrovnik, home of the third-oldest existing synagogue. I was curious to meet the synagogue's *shames* (sexton); Eduard told me he was quite a colorful character.

The city was once an independent republic allied to Venice. It sits on top of a rock that juts out into the Adriatic Sea like a beautiful medieval Mediterranean fortress. Hills dotted with small houses surround the walled city. Its main section was built around a large boulevard known as the Placa. From this main square, many narrow, twisting streets and alleys extend out and up into the surrounding hills.

The Placa was wider than any boulevard I had ever walked on before. Well-tended shops lined it on either side. To my left, shops and homes began at the foot of the mountain and continued upward. To my right, I could see the Adriatic through gaps in the fortress wall.

The marble stones underfoot were large and worn to a fine smooth sheen. A short cloudburst had just ended, which left the stones even shinier and extremely slippery. Just then I saw some young kids running and sliding down the Placa on cardboard, as if they were surfing the stones. Then my stomach reminded me it hadn't had any food since the evening before, so I bought some hot cheese and spinach *bureks* from an elderly street vendor. He sized me up as a foreigner and addressed me in English:

"Where you from?"

"I'm from America."

"America, great country. You have big car?"

"No, I don't own one."

"Why you here, tourist?"

"Actually, I'm here looking for old Jewish folk music."

"Jews no more. Maybe you find something at synagogue. Very beautiful synagogue, over there."

He pointed to a street about a quarter mile up the Placa. But before I continued to the synagogue, I walked over to the sea wall and sat down, eating and gazing out at the calm Adriatic Sea. In San Diego I was accustomed to stunning views, but this one—with the high stone walls encompassing the medieval architecture, the flowering vines growing out of the wall's crevices, the little rocky islands that dotted the coastline, and the rainbow that swept over the horizon—was more spectacular than any view I had seen back home.

The Dandy and the Synagogue

As I was daydreaming, I spied a tall, lanky old man, wearing a yellow summer fedora and walking with a cane. He looked exactly as I'd imagined the *shames,* Emilio Tolentino, from Eduard's description. I figured that Mr. Tolentino would not look favorably upon a stranger's taking photos of him, but he was such a colorful character, tipping his hat to the ladies walking by, chatting with the open-air vendors . . . he was a regular Jewish dandy. I couldn't resist. I hopped down off of my perch and followed him, stealthily taking photos.

After walking down the Placa for half a mile, he turned left down Zudioska Ulica (Croatian, Jewish street). This was only the third city on my trek and already I had twice encountered a street named after the Jews. Of course, I knew that the original reason these streets were called Jew Street was out of a sense not of celebration, but of suspicion—a way to segregate the Jewish community from the non-Jewish. All of the former Jewish ghettos throughout Europe had Jew Streets, which, although created by the church, had been agreed upon by many rabbis. They too were worried about too much interaction between the Jews and non-Jews. Because the Jews were a very small minority, the rabbis knew all too well that it was easy and natural for many Jews to assimilate and adopt many of their non-Jewish customs.

This particular Jew Street was actually a tapered passageway that ended at the foot of a hill, with steep stone steps leading up to homes that overlooked the city below. After Mr. Tolentino had gone inside the synagogue, I waited a few minutes before I pushed the doorbell.

Three stories up, an elderly lady stuck her head out of the window and yelled down to me. I wasn't quite sure what she was saying, but I knew enough Croatian to say I was Jewish and wanted to see the synagogue. She disappeared, and another minute went by before the big heavy wooden door slowly creaked open. Mr. Emilio Tolentino stood there, next to the large mezuzah (engraved scroll). Without saying a word, he waved to me to come in and follow him up two flights of narrow wooden stairs. Later I found out that Mr. Tolentino was a mere eighty-three years old; the elderly lady, who was his sister, was eighty-two; and he had an older brother who was eighty-nine. Just walking up and down the stairs several times a day would keep anyone young and spry.

As soon as I walked into the synagogue's Baroque interior, I was transported back several centuries. Three arches, all paneled in dark wood, divided the space. From the main beam on the ceiling hung a stunning antique Florentine chandelier. The bimah, again in the center of the room, was made from ornately carved wood.

As I stood there, wide-eyed and amazed, Mr. Tolentino (he seemed too venerable for me to call him Emilio) opened up the Ark to show me the fourteenth-century Torah scrolls. He explained that one of the Torahs had been carried by a family member all the way from Toledo, Spain, to Dubrovnik. (His family name was Tolentino because of his ancestral roots in Toledo.) Next to the Ark was a magnificent Moorish tapestry. This was a gift from Queen Isabella to her Jewish doctor at the time of the expulsion.

Some minutes later Mr. Tolentino's sister brought us freshly baked rolls, stuffed with brinze cheese and olives, and Turkish coffee. Since Mr. Tolentino did not speak a word of English, we communicated through his German, my Yiddish, and a little Hebrew. Unfortunately, I didn't speak Spanish, which would have made communicating in Mr. Tolentino's mother tongue, Ladino, possible. Ladino, or Judeo-Spanish, is a Hispanic language, written in Hebrew characters, from the end of the Middle Ages. It had led to different dialects spoken by the descendents of the Jews expelled from Spain in 1492 in their different lands of settlement.

While we spoke, my mind wandered to the foreseeable end of this six-hundred-year-old Jewish community. Who would take care of the synagogue when Mr. Tolentino passed on?

SARAJEVO

This time I had a ticket for my seat, but the train broke down halfway to Sarajevo. There was not a cloud in the sky and the temperatures were in the mid-nineties with unbearable humidity. I sweltered in my couchette while the train stood still for two and a half hours, baking in the hot sun. Eventually passengers began to leave the train to sit under anything that offered some shade. I left everything except my violin on the train and went out to buy some soda water and sit under some tall shady trees.

With nothing better to do, I began to play my violin. This soon drew a small crowd. I played a couple of Serbian tunes I knew, along with some klezmer. Surprisingly, when I played the folk tune known in Yiddish as "Papirossen," a Rom woman joined in, singing some lyrics in Romani, and a young kid began playing the spoons. We had a regular hootenanny going in the middle of who knows where. After another hour the conductor blew his whistle and ordered us all back onto the train.

Split and Dubrovnik had offered intriguing architecture and, by virtue of being on the Adriatic coast, a natural beauty, but Sarajevo was even more breathtaking. The city sat in a valley surrounded by tree-lined mountains eight thousand feet high. A few scattered clouds hovered above the mountain peaks, letting in swaths of light that shone on the buildings below. The architecture was clearly influenced by the Austro-Hungarian and Ottoman empires, with the minarets of mosques dotting the skyline. As the train slowly wound down the hill, I could see some of the homes and shops, and people walking on the narrow cobblestone streets below. There was a kind of Alpine feel to the city that mingled strangely with the open-air Middle-Eastern market.

The Young and Old of Sarajevo

I walked to the only operating synagogue, Ashkenazic and built in 1902 on the banks of the Miljacka River, which runs through the entire city. Several men sat in the synagogue courtyard, playing cards and backgammon,

Emilio Tolentino,
Dubrovnik

smoking, and drinking Turkish coffee. They spoke Serbo-Croatian and Ladino. My walking in with all of my gear didn't make an impression on any of them except a man named Josip Stokic, who stood up and introduced himself in English.

He invited me to dinner that evening at his home. There I met his wife, Regina, and over a hearty meal, topped off with some homemade baklava, the Stokics told me of their experiences during the Holocaust. Regina had survived the Italian concentration camp on the island of Rab (the only concentration camp liberated by partisans), and Josip had survived as a POW in a camp near Nuremberg.

Before I left, Regina invited me back for lunch the next day. I would meet her son, David Kamhi (from her first marriage); he was a classical violinist but had learned some klezmer tunes before he began his classical studies in Odessa, USSR.

I left the Stokics' home in high spirits. The air was cool and smelled of the pine trees that dotted the mountainside. Finally—in, of all places, the heart of Bosnia-Herzegovina—I was about to hear some klezmer fiddle.

The next day, at the Jewish Community Center next door to the synagogue, I met Rosita. She was twenty-seven, had two small children, and worked as a secretary at the JCC. She had been trained as a journalist but it was difficult to find a steady job. She supplemented her meager earnings by writing an occasional article for Jewish publications throughout Europe. Rosita spoke excellent English and said she would gladly serve as my interpreter while I was in Sarajevo.

In the fall, she was going to Israel to take a course on becoming a Jewish youth leader and teacher of elementary Hebrew and Jewish history and religion. Though the Jewish community of Sarajevo was small, she was determined not to stand idly by and let it gradually disappear.

While we hung out at the Center, talking, eating pistachios, and drinking coffee, Rosita smoked, and pensioners, both men and women, played various games, read the newspaper, talked, and watched soccer on the television. They all spoke Ladino. It was fascinating to hear this old Jewish language. I had heard it only once before, at a meeting of Holocaust survivors at a private home in San Diego.

So far, the survivors and their children whom I had met during my travels had not only been very friendly but had freely given their time to me. It struck me that they had lived their entire lives there and didn't have to go to a museum to learn about the Holocaust. All they had to do was go out the front door to find the place where their friends and family had been murdered forty years earlier. They didn't take anything for granted, especially being Jewish.

As for the young Jews I met in Yugoslavia, I was beginning to see a pattern. The few who were interested in Jewish culture were, for the most part, interested not in religious Judaism, but only in secular culture. One cause for this was certainly the lack of religious infrastructure in their communities: if there was a synagogue, it was only open for the holidays, and if there were Shabes services, there was no rabbi to lead and to discuss religious issues with them.

The synagogue in Sarajevo was not open during the summer, because the few men who actually came to pray were at the seaside. Perhaps, I thought, after nearly four decades, the Stalinist-style regimes had successfully squashed most interest in religious Judaism by intimidation and propaganda. Or perhaps, because there was only one rabbi in the entire country (based in Belgrade), the younger Jews felt it was too difficult to learn Torah and Talmud without him. Or maybe religious Judaism just didn't seem practical in the scheme of their day-to-day lives.

Whatever the reason, the interest was still there among many that I met at the Jewish Community Center. One young man told me this:

"I would like to study Talmud but I only have a few free hours during the week to come here and study Hebrew. One day I will move to Israel and knowing the Talmud will not be a necessity for getting a job."

The King of the Orchestra

I invited Rosita to come along to lunch at Regina Stokic's. We took an electric trolley up and down the steep inclines of Sarajevo, past open markets, pedestrians, outdoor cafés, and historical architecture, and heard the muezzin call the Muslims to prayer. The trolley cost only fifteen cents, and it was the best "E" ticket ride I had ever had.

Regina's son, David, was solidly built, with dark hair and glasses. I was excited to learn that he had studied under my favorite classical virtuoso violinist, David Oistrakh, for two years in Odessa. Oistrakh was one of the greatest violin virtuosi of the twentieth century; my mother had taken me to see him perform when I was fourteen years old. What luck to now be sitting and chatting with one of his students! Even more exciting to me was that David knew first-hand of Oistrakh's connection to klezmer.

"My first two lessons with Oistrakh had nothing to do with any classical training," David told me. "He taught me a *doyne* and *freylekhs* with all the appropriate ornamentation." (The *doyne*—a rubato, semi-improvised melody— was the cornerstone of the Romanian klezmer repertoire. In this listening piece, the klezmer would show off his virtuosity through improvisation and *fioratura* [Italian, musical ornamentation], imitating the coloratura of the cantor.)

"Oistrakh's first violin lessons were from his father, who was a klezmer. This was probably about when he was seven or eight years old. By his twelfth birthday he could play all of his father's repertoire and some classical music he heard from other local musicians. Soon he was sent to study classical music with Stolyarsky in Odessa.

"Yale, after those first two lessons he never spoke about klezmer music again."

David went on explain that both his own parents were Sephardic and never spoke about the Polish Jewish world of the klezmer. However, he had read some Sholom Alecheim stories as a kid, and therefore wasn't completely ignorant about shtetl life.

"The violin was the instrument of the Jews and the king of the orchestra," he said. "This is why I chose to play it."

Regina had prepared leek, garlic, and red pepper soup, homemade bread, and lamb *shishlik* for lunch, which we enjoyed on the patio. The view was magnificent. Below was the entire city with its twisting cobblestone streets; above, we could see where some of the facilities for the downhill skiers and tobogganers were being built for the 1984 Winter Olympics.

After lunch, I took out my violin and began to play a Hasidic *nign* (Yiddish, melody). After a minute, David asked if he could take a look at my violin. I hadn't planned this, but it was a wonderful idea. He began to play. Wow! My violin, which had been given to me by my uncle, sang in a voice I had never heard. I quickly went to get out my recording equipment. David played the *doyne* he learned from Oistrakh, who had learned it from his father; now I would learn it.

While I listened to this graceful, haunting melody I felt connected and transported to a time and milieu that belonged to my grandparents. Watching David play so intently with his eyes shut, while his mother and stepfather glowed with pride, I knew why the violin was once known as the Jewish instrument.

Leaving Sarajevo, I had mixed feelings. I would miss my newfound friends, but I was eager to continue my trek: the last two cities I was visiting in Yugoslavia, Novi-Sad and Belgrade, historically had sizable Ashkenazic communities. Surely I would find lots of klezmer there.

Novi-Sad

In Novi-Sad (Ujvidek in Hungarian), as in the other Yugoslavian cities I visited, an old woman dressed in the typical all-black of a Balkan widow in mourning found me at the train station and took me to her home, which

Leek, Garlic, and Red Pepper Soup

Makes 4 servings

This soup is so healthy and easy to prepare. It is surprisingly sweet for a vegetable soup, as the sugars in the peppers, tomatoes, and garlic will come out in the cooking. It makes a great starter for a variety of meals or can be served as a light meal with a salad. I prefer the second method of blackening the peppers, as it makes them easier to peel; however, for both methods, placing them in the paper bag steams the peppers, which helps loosen the skins for easier removal.

4 sweet red peppers
¼ cup olive oil
1 whole head garlic, cloves separated,
    peeled, and chopped
1 lb. tomatoes, peeled, seeded, and
    chopped

4 large leeks, washed, white part only,
    sliced thin
7 cups chicken or vegetable stock
Salt and pepper to taste

1. Blacken the peppers:

Method 1: Preheat the broiler. Cut the peppers in half lengthwise, flatten them with your hand, and broil skin side up until blackened. Remove from the broiler promptly.

Method 2: With tongs, hold each whole pepper over a gas flame, turning until black all over.

Put the peppers in a paper bag to cool.

2. While the peppers cool, heat the oil in a large stockpot. Add the garlic and stir until lightly toasted; do not overcook, or the garlic will become bitter. Remove the pot from the heat.

3. Peel the skin off the peppers and remove and discard any seeds and membranes. Slice the red pepper into strips. Add to the stockpot with the tomatoes, leeks, stock, and salt and pepper. Return to the heat, bring to a boil, and simmer for 20 minutes or until the leeks are soft. Serve warm.

doubled as cheap accommodations for travelers like myself. This woman's only splash of color was the bright purple parasol she carried. She was one of the fastest walkers I have ever met; I could barely keep up with her while shlepping all my gear and instruments. She'd get a block ahead of me and wave her parasol above her head like one of those tour guides at the Louvre.

Novi-Sad's only synagogue is a beautiful Byzantine structure with a stained-glass dome. Built in 1906, it is the fourth largest in Europe, seating one thousand people. The synagogue has two large cupolas that flank the sides of the building. In the middle of these two sides is the central part of the synagogue, with a giant stained-glass flower patterned window in its center. This synagogue once belonged to the Status Quo Jewish movement, which arose after the Hungarian government allowed Reform Jews to splinter off from the Orthodox Jews and create their own synagogues in 1867. Those Jews who chose to keep everything as it had been and not go with either group became the Status Quo Jews. The former Yugoslavia, Hungary, and Transylvania were the only areas with Status Quo synagogues. By the late 1970s, the Jewish community of Novi-Sad could no longer pay for the synagogue's upkeep, so they sold the building to the city. In return, the city allowed the Jewish community to use it whenever they needed to. At the time of my visit in 1981, the city was refurbishing the structure so it could be used as a concert hall. One can only imagine what it had sounded like, fifty years earlier, when a thousand voices in unison sang the *Kol Nidre* (Hebrew, all our vows) in this synagogue on *erev* Yom Kippur (Hebrew, the eve of Yom Kippur).

When I was there, the town's four-hundred-strong Jewish community still gathered at the synagogue once a year on Yom Kippur, where they would listen to cassettes of the sonorous devotional voice of the great Yossele Rosenblatt (1882–1933) singing several of the High Holiday prayers.

The Shabeses and other holidays were celebrated in Novi-Sad's Jewish Community Center, located nearby in a prewar four-story residential building complex that surrounded a common courtyard. In Jewish neighborhoods before World War II, it was common to find a small synagogue, Hebrew school, and sometimes even a *shoykhet* (Hebrew, ritual slaughterer) occupying the ground floors off of these courtyards. There were still four Jewish families living in this apartment building.

The Klezmer 78 LPs

Mr. Pavle (Pincus) Sarfberg, the former *roshekool* of Novi-Sad, lived in a prewar apartment building on a shady, tree-lined boulevard downtown, within walking distance of the philharmonic, theaters, art galleries, and outdoor cafés. A fanatical historian—not only documenting Novi-Sad Jewish history, but collecting it as well—Mr. Sarfberg had found some old 78 LPs of klezmer and a piece of sheet music dating from the 1920s in the attic of an old Jewish woman, the widow of a choral director, who had died three years ago. He had invited me to his home to hear these LPs and to discuss what he knew of klezmer.

When I entered his home I felt as if I had stepped back in time into an art salon of the 1920s. The high, open-beamed ceilings provided enough wall space for hanging large pieces of art. From the living room I entered a music salon whose walls were lined with beautiful cherrywood cabinets that held hundreds of LP recordings.

I would have thought we would listen to the 78 LPs in the music salon, but the whole apartment had been wired for stereo, and Mr. Sarfberg's favorite goose down, crushed-velvet armchair was in the library. I walked softly along the Persian carpet runner leading directly to the library. Mrs. Sarfberg brought in some tea, soda water, and little almond sugar cookies and joined us.

I guessed that there were several thousand books neatly shelved from floor to ceiling. There were ladders on all four sides of the room that slid along a rail from side to side, enabling Mr. Sarfberg to reach the top shelves. The books were on many different subjects, but the largest selection was on Jewish history of Europe.

"My father was an avid book collector," said Mr. Sarfberg. "When I was fifteen years old he told me that books were the portals to mankind's soul.

"I remember my father telling me, 'When you open a book, Pinchas, touch the pages, and begin reading it is as if you have revived a person that has been in a deep, deep sleep. You are now entering the essence of that person. To throw away a book, any book, is an *aveyre* (Hebrew, sin), especially if it is a Jewish book.'

"Thus I have continued the tradition my father started and will bequeath this collection to [the Jewish community]."

An architect, Mr. Sarfberg had retired the previous year at the age of seventy-two to pursue in earnest his passion for researching and writing the history of the Jews of Vojvodina, and specifically of Novi-Sad. His intense interest in local Jewish history extended to his own family. He had traced his family's roots back two hundred years, where they originated from a small town in eastern Czechoslovakia. When I'd first met him, back at the Jewish Community Center, he had proudly showed me the *pinkes* (Yiddish, town register) that listed his great-grandfather's contribution to the previous Status Quo synagogue, when he made the pledge from the bimah on Yom Kippur in 1888.

I was amazed at the reverence that Mr. Sarfberg and other Jews I had met had for their personal family histories. It meant more to them than simply possessing a piece of Jewish memorabilia; they treasured these artifacts as a part of their ancestors' past, an integral part of the religious and cultural development of that specific Jewish community. These roots sometimes went back over five hundred years. And to think that one of the most common anti-Semitic diatribes used against the Jews of Europe for centuries prior to World War II was they were "rootless"—implying they had no deep commitment to their town and community and could therefore never really be trusted.

This endemic mistrust led to Mr. Sarfberg's being one of only two boys to survive the *aktion* of January 21 to 23, 1942. The Hungarian Arrow Cross fascists used a small labor-camp rebellion near the city as an excuse for the *aktion*. They searched and plundered Jewish homes and murdered the Jews inside. Fifteen hundred Jews and five hundred Serbs were rounded up in the main square, then marched to the Danube. There they were ordered to strip; then they were lined up and individually shot in the back of the head. Their bodies were thrown into the icy river. After that, the Hungarian fascists—the Arrow Cross of Budapest—ordered an end to the massacres and gathered all of the Jewish men between the ages of eighteen and forty-five. They were subsequently put into Hungarian labor battalions and sent to Hungary and the Ukraine. Most died from starvation, exposure, and beatings. Mr. Sarfberg's twin brother was killed and his body dumped into the Danube.

But now it was time to listen to music. Mr. Sarfberg put on the first klezmer 78 LP. Released by Odeon in 1923, it was called "Bay Dem Rebns Tish" (At the *Rebe*'s Table). It was scratchy but the melody was still quite discernible. While sitting there listening to this archival klezmer LP, surrounded by all these books (some over two hundred years old) in this magnificent home in Novi-Sad, I couldn't help but be excited and exhilarated. I felt as if I were an archaeologist finding a key piece of pottery that helped identify its maker, only instead of pottery I was finding archival sonic gems that other klezmer musicians back home would never find.

I had Mr. Sarfberg play both records (four tunes) three times each, for easier transcription when I returned home. Then he brought out the piece of old sheet music he had found along with the LPs. The title was faded, and one corner of the page, containing the last two bars of the tune, had been torn. The title was written in Yiddish: "Shimen's Ershte Valts" (Simon's First Waltz). The title intrigued me. Who was Shimen? Who had composed it? Did he or she write more than this one tune? I took out some staff paper and copied the tune, humming the melody as I read it.

When I left his apartment, my mind was racing about so many things, but especially about the success I had had in Yugoslavia with finding klezmer 78 LPs and sheet music and collecting field recordings from some of the least likely informants. What would I find in Poland or the Ukraine, where several thousand klezmorim had lived before the Holocaust? Maybe this was how the famous Jewish folklorist S. An-ski (1863–1920) and musicologist Moshe Beregovski (1892–1962) had done their field research before World Wars I and II.

The Jewish Soldier

In a pizza restaurant near Mr. Sarfberg's home, I recognized a man from the Jewish Community Center. I sat down and introduced myself. Zoran was on leave from his military duty, visiting his parents. Zoran's mother's grandmother had been Jewish before the Holocaust, but in the late 1930s she converted to Catholicism because she thought it would be safer for her and her family. After the war she converted back to Judaism. However, her daughter went to the baptismal font as a teenager and married a non-Jew. Both of Zoran's parents were in the communist party.

Zoran was like other young people I would meet later on in my journey who had Jewish blood, whether close or distant, but had been brought up with no connection to the religion and culture. Zoran had started going to the JCC two years before, as often as he could, so he could learn more about

Judaism. He loved Jewish music in particular, so he joined the Zagreb Jewish choir and participated with them when he was allowed off his army base.

Zoran ordered a round of plum slivovitz for himself and me. After we had both gulped our shots down, Zoran leaned toward me.

"Yale, I want to tell you something I have not told anyone else."

"Sure, Zoran, what is it?"

He poured himself another shot of slivovitz and knocked it back even faster than the first one.

"Seriously, I think you will understand because you're Jewish and from America. I am not ashamed to say I am a religious man. I am only just beginning to learn how to read Hebrew, but when I sing Jewish songs I know I made the correct decision despite what my parents may think. I feel something in my heart that I can't describe in words. I am going to be circumcised. I want to be a full Jew to all the 'goyim' in the world. Where and when I am not sure, but it will happen."

I could see he was quite serious; it wasn't the slivovitz talking. I told him it was his and only his decision to make, as well as a brave and important one. He was happy to see my approval and encouragement because he hadn't told any of his friends yet. He was going to wait to be circumcised after his military service ended. Zoran told me a story of one young Jewish man who had served in the Yugoslavian army. He was born in Subotica and was taken to Budapest to be circumcised because that was where the closest *mohel* (Hebrew, circumciser) lived. In the army his fellow soldiers could clearly see he had been circumcised, so he was hassled with many practical jokes and called names like "Jew boy," "dirty Jew," and "Christ killer." It was definitely the right decision for Zoran to wait until he was out of the army.

We hugged each other as we said good-bye. I walked back to my room, thinking about the strength and conviction Zoran had to make the choice to be a Jew to the world, a world that all too often didn't act favorably toward us. I wondered, if I had been in his shoes, would I have chosen to "pass" as a gentile or not?

Among the Graves

You can learn a lot from a cemetery. Specifically, you can learn a lot about the history of a particular Jewish community from the gravestone design and inscription. That's why I made a point of spending an afternoon wandering through the gravestones and overgrown paths of the Novi-Sad Jewish cemetery, with the caretaker's two dogs following me expectantly.

In the Novi-Sad cemetery, the oldest, pre–World War I gravestones were made from sandstone, with inscriptions carved in either German, Hungarian, Yiddish, or a combination of the languages. The gravestones dated after World War I were all marble, with inscriptions in Hungarian and German, and the post–World War II gravestones had inscriptions in Hungarian and Serbo-Croatian.

The language that was used on each stone indicated the primary language spoken by the deceased. From this you could surmise what kind of Jew the person was. Gravestone inscriptions in German most likely meant that the person was more assimilated or at least acculturated to a degree that caused them to move in social and religious circles that separated them from the more religious, Yiddish-speaking Jews. Conversely, inscriptions in Yiddish meant the primary tongue of the deceased had been Yiddish and the person was more religious, probably with ancestors coming from Galicia, Poland. The inscriptions in Hungarian on stones dating from World War I to the present meant these Jews considered themselves ethnically and culturally Hungarian and not Yugoslavian (even after the fall of the Austro-Hungarian Empire). These Jews were often not as religious as their Yiddish-speaking brethren but were not as assimilated as their German-speaking brethren.

I also learned that the various pictorial carvings in the gravestones each told a story as well. For example, the split-fingered palm indicated the deceased was a descendant from the *kohanim,* the ancient high priests; a pitcher meant the deceased was a descendant of the Leviim, who served the high priests in the temple with various duties including washing their feet; a charity box with money being put into it meant the person had been generous; two Shabes candlesticks meant the woman had been pious; and a limb of a tree cut off at an angle meant the person died in their youth.

After I had walked around in the cemetery for an hour, the caretaker invited me into his workshop for tea. The caretaker, who wasn't Jewish, was eighty-six years old and hard of hearing. He smoked but walked with a strong gait and had a firm handshake. His workshop—where he worked on cars, chopped wood, and made the occasional coffin—had been the *kheyder tehoyre* (Hebrew, purification room) where the deceased had been ritually cleaned and prayers had been recited by the *khevre kedishe* (Hebrew, burial society). Now the only evidence that this had once been a sacred Jewish building was the large sign on the wall displaying a Hebrew prayer.

He was Hungarian and had grown up in a Jewish neighborhood, so he'd learned to speak some Yiddish. With his little Yiddish and German we were able to understand each other rather well. Eventually I asked him if he had ever been invited to a Jewish wedding or knew any Jewish music.

"My mother was a very good seamstress and her best friend was a Jewish woman who was getting married. My mother made the wedding dress and then the whole family was invited to the wedding. This was in 1905 when I was ten.

"The wedding was in a village near Zrenjanin. When we arrived by wagon I remember hearing a melody" [I proceeded to take out my tape recorder] "that never left my head." He broke off and began to sing the melody, then continued. "In the group there were five musicians—two were Gypsies and three were Jews. I can't remember all the instruments, but one Gypsy played the bass and one Jew played the trumpet. This Jew was a kid not much older than I was. They played all kinds of music, but I only remember that one tune and the people shouting 'He's coming, he's coming, the groom, the groom is coming.'

"After World War I, my mother's best friend went to America and my mother never heard from her again. During World War II, I was sent to a Hungarian labor battalion and first sent to Transylvania, then Transnistria. In Transnistria I saw the Jewish boy who played the trumpet, but he didn't remember me. But when I sang him the song he had played at the wedding, he began to cry and so did I. Unfortunately he died a few months later from typhus."

I thanked him profusely for his time and said goodbye. I was really starting to get into the thick of my research. I was learning to ask the right questions and I appreciated the luck I was having in finding such fascinating informants. Who would have ever thought one could find an old klezmer tune, never before transcribed, in a Jewish cemetery?

On the way back to my accommodations, I walked down to the Danube and found a new Holocaust memorial on the riverbank: a statue of a mother, father, and child huddled together before they were murdered. It was a beautiful afternoon, breezy, sunny, with billowy clouds moving swiftly in the sky. It was hard to imagine those fateful days of January 21 to 23, 1942,

Prayers for the dead line the walls of the former burial chapel in the Jewish cemetery, Novi-Sad

"KHOSN'S MARCH" (GROOM'S MARCH)

Collected by Yale Strom

when the Hungarian fascists rounded up and murdered those Jews and Serbs. Standing before this monument made me appreciate my fate even more, in a way I had never thought of—having been born in America and not in pre–World War II Eastern Europe like Mr. Sarfberg, or like the young Jewish trumpet player the cemetery caretaker remembered from that long-ago wedding in a village near Zrenjanin.

BELGRADE

For me, going to synagogue is all about the music. If there weren't any singing I probably would rarely attend. Singing and *shuklen* (Yiddish, rocking, swaying) to the prayers helped me to better understand why I attended synagogue even though I didn't believe in the traditional Jewish concept of God. Was there something greater, more absolute than man? Most definitely, but I believed it was not only a Jewish deity but a puissance that ruled over all of humanity. Mother Nature, perhaps.

I learned to enjoy going to synagogue from being with my father. While sitting together we'd talk about sports, politics, and the Torah portion and sing the prayers loudly together, sometimes making up our own funny lyrics. It became a habit I relished. Now, when I go to the synagogue on my own, it is a kind of nostalgic trip back to my childhood, when everything seemed much simpler and I didn't have the cares and concerns I have today.

Of course, I also had a practical reason for going to synagogues on this trip throughout the Eastern bloc countries: synagogues were a good place to begin searching for informants who knew something about klezmer.

The Last Rabbi

In Belgrade's synagogue, I was able to meet Rabbi Zadeek Danon, the only rabbi in all of Yugoslavia. He had graduated from the yeshiva in Sarajevo before the war. During the services the rabbi would occasionally take out his pitch pipe, give it a little toot, and begin singing. He had a pleasant, soft, almost vaporous kind of voice and when he sang the prayers he closed his eyes and rocked from side to side.

I had attended the Belgrade service to say Kaddish (Hebrew, holy; a prayer said by a mourner for the dead) for the father of my new friend Julia. It was a good thing I came. I helped to make the minyan (Hebrew, quorum)—I was the tenth man. Without a minyan there wouldn't have been services and we wouldn't have been able to say Kaddish for her father.

I had met Julia the previous evening at a concert I gave at Belgrade's Jewish Community Center. I'd been invited to perform by Darko, the leader of Belgrade's Jewish community and organizer of a Jewish seminar that started the day after I arrived; the man originally scheduled to give the concert of Yiddish folk songs was ill.

"Do you know anything about klezmer, or anyone who might be from the Jewish community?" I had asked him.

"No, never heard of klezmer."

"OK. I'll give the concert."

The performance was part of the *m'lave malke* (Hebrew, the evening meal marking the conclusion of the Sabbath festivities). I was joined on guitar by one of the elder statesmen of the Belgrade Jewish community, Eugene

"Moshe" Weber. Professionally, Moshe had been an actor, but he was also nationally known as a translator from English to Serbo-Croatian of a number of well-known Jewish books. We played Hebrew, Israeli, and Yiddish songs that we both knew, and Moshe sang with great gusto.

After our set, some students who were attending the seminar joined us. Gradually our repertoire morphed from Jewish to Beatles, Simon and Garfunkel, and eventually the blues.

After the concert and jam session many of us, including Julia, went for some drinks. Julia, a dentist with two young daughters, was the sole Jewish representative from the Rijeka Jewish community attending the seminar. She had recently gotten divorced and was getting more involved in the Jewish life in Rijeka.

Like several other women I had met at the seminar, Julia had been married to a non-Jewish husband. Many of the women told me their husbands were completely indifferent to their Jewish culture, which invariably caused a strain on the marriage. This indifference, among other things, had helped end Julia's marriage.

On the day we said Kaddish for her father, she was to return home on an afternoon train. I would be taking the same train, only she would change in Zagreb for a train to Rijeka; I would continue on to Budapest.

After services the rabbi invited Julia and me for a Shabes meal at his home. As we walked, Rabbi Danon sang several Ladino songs. They were beautiful, but it wasn't klezmer.

The rabbi lived in a small, modest home, nothing like Sarfberg's, but crammed full of Judaica. The rabbi's wife was very gracious and didn't seem surprised that we were there. She served up a Shabes feast: baked beans, a kind of beef stew, bread, peppers, salad, and for dessert, the sweet syrupy cake called *hurmasice*.

After lunch we retired to the living room, where we had marzipan and tea and listened to some Ladino folk music. I casually glanced up at the clock on the mantel—and realized our train was leaving in thirty minutes! The rabbi called a taxi for us and we hurriedly said our thank-yous and good-byes and raced out.

When we arrived at the station, I saw a huge line at the ticket window; I knew I would miss my train if I waited. Julia had her train and seat tickets already, in first class. I decided the best course of action would be to get on the

Prebanac

BAKED BEANS

Makes 4 servings

2 Tbsp. olive oil

4 medium onions, peeled and chopped
   medium thick

1 Tbsp. paprika

1 20-oz. can cannellini beans, drained
   and rinsed twice

1 large carrot, peeled and thinly sliced

3 bay leaves

Salt and pepper to taste

Water

1. Preheat the oven to 350°. Heat the oil in an ovenproof skillet and sauté the onions until golden brown. Add the paprika, mix in well, and remove from the heat. Stir in the beans, carrot, bay leaves, and salt and pepper and add just enough water to cover.

2. Put the beans in the oven and bake until the top is dark brown, about 30 minutes. Serve hot or cold.

train and deal with the conductor later—after all, how difficult could it be to buy my ticket on the train?

Safely ensconced, I looked out the window at the winding Danube as we followed it upstream toward Budapest. I was happily surprised to have collected more klezmer than I'd anticipated in a country where it was not as prevalent in daily Jewish life as it was in Poland and Romania. I felt optimistic about what I would discover in Hungary.

As the train left the station, I thought about all the people I had met during my brief stay in Yugoslavia. I also kept thinking about a thimble I'd seen at Belgrade's Jewish museum when I visited one morning to see if they had some information on klezmer.

The music archives had contained nothing out of the ordinary, but I was struck by the museum's glass-enclosed cabinets filled with relics of the

Yugoslavian Chopped Salad

Makes 4 to 6 servings

Fefferoni are similar to the more commonly found *peperoncini,* but longer and thinner. You can substitute *peperoncini* if you can't find this Yugoslavian cousin—just make sure they've got some kick. The dressing is a simple red wine vinaigrette. Note that the salad must marinate for three hours before serving.

For the salad:

1 15-oz. can red kidney beans, drained, rinsed twice

½ white onion, finely chopped

2 stalks celery, peeled and chopped fine

1 large ripe tomato, finely chopped

4 pickled *fefferoni* or peperoncini, stems discarded, chopped

For the dressing:

2 Tbsp. red wine vinegar

4 Tbsp. olive oil

1 Tbsp. water

Salt and pepper to taste

1. Combine the beans, onion, celery, tomato, and *fefferoni.*
2. Combine all the dressing ingredients and shake or stir well. Add to the salad and toss to coat. Let chill for 3 hours before serving.

personal daily lives of Yugoslavian Jews before the Holocaust: eyeglasses, combs, shoes, pocket-watches, diaries, and the like. To me these were even sadder and more poignant than the photographs of wanton murder.

One thimble had grooves etched into it, providing a better grip—and on one side of the thimble the grooves were worn smooth.

Standing there, I'd begun to wonder about the person who had once worn this tiny thimble for sewing and mending clothes. Perhaps they were special clothes for a little girl or boy who got all dressed up to go to the synagogue with Mommy and Daddy on Shabes. During the Shabes services, the child went into the courtyard to play with the other Jewish children. While playing, the child tripped, fell down, and tore that nice Shabes clothing. But

Hurmasice

POUND CAKE IN SYRUP

Makes 8 to 10 servings

I first tasted *hurmasice* at a Yugoslavian restaurant and was so captivated that I immediately began dissecting it to figure out how to make it. The proprietor was kind enough to give me a few hints (I think it was kindness—I may have been making a mess), and I went home to create this recipe. To me, this dessert represents Yugoslavia—linking aspects of Eastern Europe, the Balkans, and the Mediterranean. I've baked it with both butter and margarine, and I prefer the former—after all, this is a pound cake. That said, if you're serving a kosher meat meal or watching your cholesterol, use margarine (if it comes in a stick, it'll be better suited for baking). Butter makes it a bit moister. Note that the cake must soak in the syrup for three hours before serving.

For the cake:

1½ sticks unsalted butter or margarine
1¼ cups granulated sugar
3 large eggs
½ tsp. vanilla
1 tsp. grated orange zest
1½ cups sifted cake flour

For the syrup:

1½ cups orange juice
¼ cup granulated sugar

1. Preheat the oven to 300°. Grease and flour a 13-by-9-inch cake pan. Line the bottom of the pan with cooking parchment.

2. In a large bowl, cream the butter with a mixer on high speed, gradually adding the sugar, for 4 to 5 minutes. Still beating, add the eggs one at a time, then the vanilla, then the zest. Switch the speed to low and gradually add the flour until the batter is smooth.

3. Scrape the batter into the prepared pan and bake for 35 to 45 minutes, until a cake tester comes out clean. The cake should be well done and firm. While the cake is baking, prepare the syrup.

4. *For the syrup:* In a medium saucepan over high heat, combine the orange juice and sugar, bring to a boil, and cook until the sugar has dissolved. Set aside.

5. When the cake is done, remove it from the oven and, keeping it in the pan, cut it immediately into 24 squares. Pour half of the syrup over the cake and let soak for 10 minutes. Pour the remaining syrup over the cake. Cover and let soak for 3 hours. Serve at room temperature.

the father and mother weren't angry because they knew it was an accident, and with their special thimble they would be able to mend that tear after Shabes.

The thimble had survived—but the child and parents were murdered just because they were Jewish. . . .

In 1981, no one could have imagined that a mere ten years hence Yugoslavia would once again be ripped apart, this time by civil war, which would be particularly devastating for the *kehiles.* Yugoslavian Jews, fleeing the conflict, decimated the already tiny Jewish population. Some joined their predecessors in Israel; others scattered to Western Europe and the United States.

Chapter Two

HUNGARY

We HAD TRAVELED for about an hour when the conductor came for our tickets. Julia explained how I had arrived late at the Belgrade station and hadn't had time to stand in the long line. Was it possible to buy a ticket now?

The conductor looked me over and pronounced that the ticket was $65, which had to be paid in American dollars. I knew that Julia's ticket to Rijeka had cost only $15, and although Budapest was farther than Rijeka, could it really be $50 farther? I instructed Julia to tell the conductor that I knew I was being ripped off. The conductor insisted I pay her the entire sum right then. I refused and she immediately asked for my passport. I gave it to her and she left.

My mind began to race. Where in the hell is she going? To the police? Where in the hell can I go without my passport? Certainly not out of this grand old country. What if she steals my passport? Or sells it? I bet American passports go for a pretty sum these days. There are so many desperate people wanting to leave the Eastern bloc.

Oy veys mir, I thought, why didn't I buy the ticket in Belgrade yesterday when I had the time?

Ten minutes went by, then twenty. I couldn't stand being passive, so I sprang up to look for the conductor myself. Four train cars down, in the dining car, nearly invisible in a thick haze of cigarette smoke, sat the conductor, flirting with a man drinking a beer and eating a shiny, grayish-pink pork sausage smeared with some heavy white sauce that looked like mayonnaise. When she saw me, she invited me to sit down as if nothing had happened. I decided being cordial and calm would help my cause a lot more than being angry and hysterical. I sat down and joined them with a beer. Then I asked her about my passport.

"*Oh pasaporta, nema problema.*" (Serbo-Croatian, Oh, the passport, no problem.)

She then pulled it out of her breast pocket. I checked it, of course, to make sure it hadn't been tampered with (maybe I had seen too many B spy movies). After another round of beers I got up to cordially and quietly excuse myself and return to my couchette. Maybe she was so inebriated she had forgotten all about the ticket situation. No such luck. As soon as I got up to go she asked for my ticket.

"*Bilet, bilet, gde e bilet?*" (Ticket, ticket, where is your ticket?)

I took out a folded twenty-dollar bill that I had in my back pocket, unfolded it, carefully grabbed the conductor's hand, and slapped it onto her palm.

"*Dvadeset dolari, hlava mnogo.*" (Twenty dollars, thank you.)

I resolutely turned around and walked away without looking back to gauge her reaction. She never came to my couchette. I had gambled correctly—$20 or $65, it was all destined for her billfold.

When I told Julia what had happened, she burst out laughing and said it was my chutzpah that had caught the conductor off guard.

Another experience and another lesson learned. Bribery was a local custom and would become very familiar to me, something I would have to deal with throughout my trek in the Eastern bloc.

BORDERLAND LAW

Another lesson I quickly learned on this trip was the best way to deal with policemen and border guards. It was a lesson I never mastered; I was young, impulsive, and, yes, at times a bit hotheaded—especially when dealing with abusive authority figures who messed with my camera equipment.

This lesson had begun back in Yugoslavia, when a young soldier who was sitting across from me, on his way to visit his girlfriend in Belgrade, was gruffly ordered off the train by a dour policeman—supposedly because he was missing a very particular, special piece of paper giving him permission to be there.

The policeman had given my visa and passport a cursory glance and then, without so much as a "good day," slammed the couchette door behind him. I had been lucky that time, but my luck would soon run out.

My first encounter at the Yugoslavia-Hungary border belied the future troubles I would face. A rather jovial Yugoslavian policeman stamped my visa and then asked in perfect English:

"Did you enjoy our wine, women, and weather?"

Caught off guard and not knowing the right answer, I replied, "Well, the weather was nice but a bit too humid, the wine was tasty but a bit too sweet, and the women were just fine—not too sweet and not too hot."

He laughed, shook my hand, and closed the couchette door. Maybe not all of these border guards are shmucks, I thought to myself. This is a tedious job and I guess if you come across an exotic American, all the more reason to have some fun.

My reverie was short-lived. The couchette door flew open with a loud bang. Standing there were two Hungarian border policemen (one with a goatee, the other with an enormous mole on his right cheek) and two young, baby-faced soldiers straining to hold the leashes of two very large, fierce-looking German shepherds. The first policeman asked for my passport and visa. He turned each page with his index finger with such force that the crisp new pages snapped audibly with each turn. He went back and forth through the entire passport at least five times looking for something. Each time he came to my photo page he'd stare at the photo, then look at me with a grimace, as if the photo didn't match my face. He threw my passport down on the seat and asked which bags were mine, although I was the only one in the couchette. Out of the corner of my eye, I saw the two young soldiers struggling to contain the anxious German shepherds.

The second policeman took my backpack from the top shelf and began rifling through its contents. Before I left each city I always repacked my backpack, clothes neatly folded, toiletries in my dop kit, my pocketknife in its sheath, and any *tsotskes* I had bought for my family and friends properly wrapped. My film, all two hundred rolls, was packed with my camera batteries in a plastic Tupperware container, and next to that, wrapped in a towel and buried at the bottom of the backpack, were my tape recorder and microphone. I laid out all the contents of my camera bag on the seat. Now everything was on display all over both seats as if we were at a flea market.

The goateed policeman spoke in Hungarian and his sidekick with the mole translated his questions into English.

"Why so much film?"

"I'm a folklorist and tourist and it's difficult to find Kodak Tri-X black-and-white film in Eastern Europe."

"Folklorist?"

"Yes, yes, see my instruments? I am collecting Yugoslavian and Hungarian folk music, like Bela Bartok."

The Jewish History of Hungary

Under fourth-century Magyar rulers, Jews from Germany, Bohemia, and Moravia were welcomed as they settled up and down the Danube River valley. The Jews showed a talent for commerce. This talent bred a strong Jewish community—and a strong community bred fear and mistrust among the gentiles. By the eleventh century, the first anti-Jewish regulations had been issued.

From the twelfth through the fourteenth centuries, anti-Jewish decrees tightened the bonds on Jewish life until badges became required—a precursor in red cloth of the Nazis' yellow Star of David half a millennium later.

The first medieval synagogue to be unearthed in Europe was found in Sopron. It was used from 1350 to 1526, when the Turks overran Hungary.

When the Turks came in 1526, they deported Jews to Ottoman territory. But two years later the Jews were back in Buda, building a peaceful, prosperous community that would flourish unimpeded for 150 years, based on finance, commerce, and certain handcrafts. The Budapest *kehile* grew to more than a thousand by 1660 and was the wealthiest and largest in Hungary.

During the reign of Empress Maria Theresa (1740–1780), the *kehiles* were under constant attack. Her son, Joseph II (1780–1790), improved conditions for the Budapest *kehile,* abolished special taxes, and permitted Jews to settle in royal cities. During this period the country's Jewish population swelled to more than five hundred thousand. Nevertheless, life for Jews under the Austrian Hapsburgs was always unstable until 1867, when Hungary became an independent kingdom ruled by

"But why the cameras?"

"So I can take photos of the people that sing for me and of the beautiful sights."

"Do you have friends or family in Hungary?"

"No, no, this is my first time and I am really looking forward to it."

"We have black and white film in Hungary."

"Yes, I know, and I hate to say this, but East German film just isn't the greatest quality."

"What kind of cameras are those?"

"Nikon FEs."

the Hapsburg and Esterhazy families.

The three most famous synagogues of Pest were all built prior to World War II: the Moorish-style Reform Dohany Temple, built in 1859; the octagonal Conservative Rombach Synagogue, built in 1879; and the Orthodox Kazinczy Synagogue, built in 1913. The Jewish Rabbinical Seminary, which today also houses the Anne Frank Gymnasium, was built in 1877.

After World War I, a short-lived communist government led by Bela Kun, a Jew, failed before the onslaught of the fascist regent Admiral Miklos Horthy. In November 1938 Hungary joined Germany in the dismemberment of Czechoslovakia. In August 1940 Hungary received northern Transylvania from Romania, and in April 1941 Hungary occupied the Backa basin in northeastern Yugoslavia. Thus by May 1941 anti-Jewish laws affected all 725,000 Jews in Greater Hungary. On June 22, 1941, the Hungarian army invaded the Soviet Union alongside the Germans.

On March 19, 1944, the Nazis occupied Hungary and deported the majority of the Jews living in the countryside to Auschwitz. The Jews in the urban areas were deported to the ghetto in Budapest. Some forty thousand of these Jews perished at the hands of the Nazis and Hungarian Arrow Cross soldiers. By the war's end, 450,000 (70 percent) of the Jews of Greater Hungary were deported or murdered, or had otherwise died under German occupation.

Immediately after the war there were some eighty to ninety thousand Jews in Budapest. Then after the Soviets and other Eastern bloc countries crushed the anti-Communist rebellion in 1956, some twenty-five thousand Jews left Hungary for the West. By 1981 the Jewish population was approximately one hundred thousand; today it is approximately one hundred thirty thousand.

"Oh . . . *Nikon*."

Then the *yold* (Yiddish, chump) proceeded to pick one up and put his grimy fingers all over the lens, the eyepiece, the flash—he even pushed the shutter and took a photo by mistake. As he and his distinguished partner continued to poke around, now with my instruments, I tried to distract the English-speaking policeman with some small talk.

"Sir, maybe you can tell me where I might find some of the best authentic Hungarian *tanc haz* [Hungarian, dance house] folk music?"

"Yes, I know, you should go to the Komarom region near the Slovakian border. There you'll hear some of the best musicians playing the violin, bass, tarogato, and cimbalom [hammered dulcimer]. And of course many of these musicians are the Gypsies. Those dirty, black bastards are good for only two things, music and fucking. You'll find them everywhere."

"Thank you for your suggestions."

"OK, pack everything up and step out for a moment so the soldiers can check."

I threw everything haphazardly into the backpack, deciding to wait until after I'd crossed the border to organize it all. The soldiers came in with flashlights and the dogs. First they picked up both seats and gave a quick cursory look while the dogs sniffed around. Then one climbed onto a step stool and lifted the ceiling grating.

Finally came the last question: "Do you have any Marlboro cigarettes?"

Now I understood why it took so long to travel short distances in the Eastern bloc. At every international border crossing you usually wasted two hours in travel with all the bureaucratic *meshugas* (Yiddish, craziness).

BUDAPEST

Budapest is divided in half by the majestic (albeit polluted) Danube River. Most of my research kept me to the Pest side, where the heart of the former Jewish ghetto is located and where I found my accommodations. When I did go over to the Buda side, I could see the marked economic difference between the two halves. The Buda neighborhoods were vastly better off economically than those on the Pest side. If you were wealthy, whether Jew or non-Jew, you tried to live in the Buda hills.

One of the main streets I walked down every day was Lenin Korut (today called Teresz Korut). Shops of all kinds—bakeries and music and clothing stores—lined the boulevard. Food was so cheap and the bakeries were so plentiful that it was hard not to succumb to the various delicious Hungarian desserts. Occasionally, following the sounds of someone practicing the violin or cimbalom, I would enter a courtyard. The back streets of Budapest were a veritable maze of alluring sights, sounds, and smells.

I was amazed at how many different options for public transportation were available at such a cheap price—the trolley, the electric bus, the regular bus, and the subway, each always packed with passengers. This showed me that not everything was better back home in San Diego, where the car is king. Occasionally I took the trolley or bus, but most of the time I walked. I loved the nooks and crannies, the courtyards and alleys that dotted the city. I wandered in and out of the city's many antique bookstores, looking for old Jewish sheet music. I probably walked six to seven miles every day.

Over the two months I spent in Hungary, its Jewish life—from the obvious to the obscure—presented itself to me, with Budapest's vibrant Jewish community as my focal point. Since there was so much to see and so many elderly Jews who were potential informants, I decided to keep to a specific schedule: *davening* in the mornings, having my lunch at a place called the Hanna Kosher restaurant (located inside the Kazinczy synagogue courtyard), and conducting my interviews in the afternoons.

Davening in the Mornings

The Orthodox shul, known as the Kazinczy, had seen better days. The large sanctuary, completely covered in scaffolding, was not open to the public. Instead, there was a *besmedresh* (Yiddish, small Orthodox house of worship) inside the shul courtyard. The *besmedresh* was connected to the larger synagogue. Across the courtyard was a three-story building. On the first floor was the Hanna kosher restaurant. Upstairs used to be classrooms for a yeshiva that had closed some years before. In the middle of the courtyard, next to the back of the synagogue, was a permanent chuppah (Yiddish, wedding canopy) made of iron. From the looks of it, it hadn't been used in a long time. A staircase led to other parts of the building; dirt, debris and broken glass littered the steps. This was an entrance to the women's section of the main synagogue, obviously not in use.

As soon as I walked in, the *shames,* Reuven, came over and with a hearty handshake asked me, "*Nu, Reb Yid, vilstu leynen tefiln mit undz?*" ("So, Mr. Jew, will you put on phylacteries with us?")

His gregariousness and his fluent Yiddish gave me great hope that I was going to find some klezmer tunes and memories in this city.

Inside the *besmedresh* were wooden benches and tables, around which sat about twenty-five men, each *davening* at his own pace. The tables were strewn with some Talmuds—and cake crumbs. I was struck by the Old World feel of the place, and the fact that several of the men wore the traditional Ortho-dox garb of Eastern Europe: the *gartlekh* (sashes) worn outside around the waist, the *tsitses* (undergarments that had four corners with tassels), and the wide-brimmed black hats and long waistcoats called *bekeshes.* In addi-tion, they all sported beards and curly earlocks called *peyes.*

At the Kazinczy, I met the first of the few Hasidic Jews I would encounter in all of my travels: the shul's rabbi, Marton Weisz, and two *shokhtim* (Yid-dish, Jewish ritual slaughterers), Yitskhok Weisz (no relation to the rabbi) and Mendel Shwartz. The *shokhtim* hailed from Satoraljauhely, a town in the eastern part of the country near the Slovakian border, and were followers of the Satmar *rebe.*

Both *shokhtim* worked not only in Budapest but also in all of the *kehiles* in Hungary, as well as in some in Transylvania, Romania, and Bratislava, Czecho-slovakia. Since there were no other *shokhtim* in these *kehiles,* both old men had important responsibilities in helping to maintain Judaism in these smaller communities. They were the link in the chain. When they died, would these Jews still be able to get kosher meat?

After the morning prayers were finished, the men, including the rabbi and the *shokhtim,* stayed behind to discuss the Torah portion of the week. The discussion was all in Yiddish and lasted twenty minutes. Then a small *kidesh* was served—egg cookies, called *kikhl,* and schnapps. Afterward, Rabbi Weisz began to sing a beautiful *nign.*

He started the *nign* slowly and softly. Gradually, one by one, the rest of the men joined in. Soon the *nign* went from soft and lilting to loud, almost shouting. Reuven then made me put the camera down and brought me to the table to sing as well. He told me this was a melody the Satmar *rebe* would sing before Tisha B'Av (a Jewish day of fasting and mourning to commemo-rate the destruction of the first and second temples in Jerusalem). After listening to the *nign* a couple more times, I raised my voice with the others. Since it was a hot day, all of the *besmedresh* windows were open and all the world—at least everyone on Dob Utca (Drum Street)—could see and hear us. Before long, several passersby from the neighborhood stopped to listen and watch this amazing spectacle.

Lunch at the Hanna Kosher Restaurant

The Hanna restaurant was the only kosher restaurant in Budapest open to the public. Most of the patrons were Jews from the Orthodox *kehile*; there were some Hasidic tourists from abroad, mainly from Brooklyn. The men dressed in their typical garb; their wives wore elegant clothing, simple jewelry, and fancily coiffed shaitel (wigs worn by Orthodox women). The locals were

Galuska

HUNGARIAN DUMPLINGS

Makes 4 servings

This is a quick and easy recipe, and a wonderful addition to soups and stews.

1½ cups flour
2 tsp. baking powder
1 tsp. salt

1 egg, beaten well
½ cup milk
1 Tbsp. butter, melted

1. Sift together the flour, baking powder, and salt.
2. Combine the egg, milk, and butter; add gradually to the flour, stirring until the dough is smooth and no longer sticks to the sides of the bowl. If the dough seems too wet, sprinkle with 1 tsp. flour and mix again.
3. Bring a large pot of water to a rapid boil. Break off 1-inch pieces of dough and drop them into the water. Cover and boil for 12 to 15 minutes, or until the dumplings have expanded and are firm. Drain.

Letcho

VEGETABLE STEW

Makes 4 servings

This is a simple but hearty stew.

2 russet potatoes, peeled and sliced

1 large onion, chopped

2 garlic cloves, minced

2 Tbsp. oil

1¼ tsp. paprika

½ tsp. caraway seeds

1 vegetable bouillon cube (1-cup size)

2 Tbsp. water

1 cup peas, fresh or frozen

½ tsp. black pepper

2 cups chopped fresh tomatoes

3½ tsp. marjoram

¼ cup olive oil

1. Combine the oil, garlic, and onion in the bottom of a stockpot and cook until the onion is translucent (do not burn).

2. Remove from the heat and add the tomatoes, onions, and all other ingredients.

3. Cover and cook over medium heat for 20 minutes. Just before serving, add the *galuska*.

mostly elderly, a few middle-aged; some were dressed nicely, others a bit shabbily. Some ate in silence, slowly and deliberately eating every morsel on their plates; others engaged in lively conversation. It was some sight: a microcosm of Jews, many weighted down with the memories of their survival of the Holocaust. Completing this scene were the heavyset, sweating gentile waitresses. Wearing short dresses, white aprons, and ankle-high, opened-toed work shoes showing unshaven legs above, they zigzagged among the tables, carrying large serving plates laden with steaming hot food.

Eating at the Hanna provided me with a delicious, hot home-cooked meal every day but Shabes. The menu at the Hanna was *fleyshik* (made of meat), but I got to know the chief cook, and she took a liking to me, so she cooked

Potato Paprikash

Makes 6 to 8 servings

This is a vegetarian variation on the famous Hungarian chicken dish.

½ cup olive oil

1 clove garlic, crushed

1 large onion, finely chopped

¼ tsp. caraway seeds

2 tsp. paprika

2 cups water

4 lbs. potatoes, peeled and sliced thin

2 green peppers, seeded and cut into strips

1 large tomato, peeled, seeded, and chopped

Salt to taste

1. In a heavy-bottomed casserole dish, heat the oil and fry the onion and garlic until golden, being careful not to let them burn.

2. Add the caraway seeds, paprika, and water and stir well to combine. Add the potatoes, peppers, and tomato. Simmer, covered, for 35 to 45 minutes. Season with salt. Serve hot.

me special vegetarian dishes like *letcho* with *galuska* (vegetable stew with dumplings), potato *paprikash,* or *lecso* (peppers with eggs).

Eating at the Hanna also meant I had the pleasure of eating with people in the community and getting to know them. Throughout my travels, I would always seek out the local kosher restaurant or kosher kitchen; invariably the people I met there would lead to new discoveries and friends. Once people learned of my search for klezmer, they were happy to share what they knew or put me in touch with someone who could help.

On one of my first days in Budapest, I was eating lunch at the Hanna when Moshe-Yehuda, the kosher butcher, asked if he could sit with me. He told me he was born in Bekes in 1931 and in 1954 moved to Budapest, where he apprenticed at a kosher butcher shop. He and his wife (with two non-Jews) had the only privately owned kosher butcher shop in all of Hungary, plus he

Lecso

PEPPERS AND EGGS

Makes 4 servings

This is a hearty and delicious dish for breakfast or brunch. The yellow peppers are traditional and provide both sweetness and heat. Whenever working with hot peppers, be sure to wash your hands carefully—and often—as the oils from the pepper are fiery hot. I once decided to chop one up, and then, without thinking, rubbed my eye. It was excruciating. Fortunately, I was able to flush the eye with water well enough to avoid a trip to the hospital. I won't ever do that again.

¼ lb. yellow banana peppers or yellow bell peppers

1 yellow Hungarian wax pepper (4 oz.) or 2 yellow Fresno chilis

1 firm ripe tomato

1 onion, finely chopped

2 Tbsp. oil

8 large eggs

Salt and pepper to taste

1. Stem and seed the yellow peppers. Cut into ½-inch pieces. Finely chop the Hungarian or Fresno chili peppers. (Now go wash your hands with hot water and lots of soap!)

2. Core the tomato and cut in half. Gently squeeze to remove the seeds and juice, then coarsely chop the flesh.

3. In a 12-inch nonstick frying pan over high heat, combine the oil, the onion, all the peppers, and half of the tomato. Stir often until brownish and all the liquid has evaporated, about 8 minutes.

4. In a bowl, beat the eggs with 2 Tbsp. water and salt and pepper. Add the egg mixture to the vegetables and reduce the heat to medium. Use a wide spatula to lift the cooked egg from the surface of the pan, allowing the raw egg to run to the bottom. Cook until the egg is set, 1 to 2 minutes.

5. Garnish with the remaining tomato and serve immediately.

had a monopoly on the making and selling of all smoked meats, salamis, and liverwurst.

The consensus in the community was that Moshe-Yehuda was a thief for his high prices. When I asked him about this, he replied, "*Azoy kalt miz men trinken a bisl.*" (As it is so cold, one must drink a little.) Moshe-Yehuda figured that if given the opportunity to make a profit (no mean feat in the Eastern bloc), one was justified in doing so.

You can only imagine the conversation between a vegetarian and a kosher butcher:

"Why are you a vegetarian?"

"Well, I don't believe man needs to kill animals to sustain himself."

"*Borkhashem* [thank God] there aren't many *meshugim* [crazy people] like you in our *kehile.* I would be out of business."

Shifting the subject, he said, "I heard you are looking for some old Jewish music. You should go to the *shtibl* on Teleki Utca and there you'll meet Shani Polnauer. He is a cantorial student at the Rabbinical Seminary and he too has a big interest in Jewish music. He can help you."

Exploring the Archives

I made my way to this *shtibl,* which turned out to be Sephardic. Most of the congregants were of Sephardic origin and the prayers were spoken and sung in the Sephardic musical style.

After I introduced myself to Shani Polnauer, he invited me to stay with him and his wife Edit in their small apartment. Though the accommodations I already had were quite comfortable and in the heart of the former Jewish quarters, I decided to take him up on his offer. They could use the dollars, and why not give my money to new Jewish friends rather than to a gentile stranger? Part of me was conscious of this as a bias against the non-Jews of Hungary, but after two months of meeting and talking to Holocaust survivors nearly every day, having walked the streets from which their families were murdered or deported, I didn't care to rationalize any of my biases and chauvinistic feelings. There were a lot more gentiles, and they had strength in numbers, while the Jews were a tiny and ever shrinking minority.

Shani and Edit's apartment was small and located in one of the poorest Rom neighborhoods in all of Budapest. They were newlyweds, poor and studying. Edit also worked in an office, while Shani was also a Hebrew schoolteacher. He was finishing his cantorial studies at the Rabbinical Seminary.

"Tomorrow, Yale, we'll go to the seminary. There you will meet Dr. Rabbi Scheiber, a brilliant man. Afterward we'll begin your search for Yiddish songs in the archives."

A rabbinical seminary with Jewish music archives? How did the communist government allow this Jewish institution to exist? The more I saw of life in the Eastern bloc countries, the more I realized nothing was completely black or white, just many different shades of gray. I knew from my research that officially all organized religion was frowned upon. Apparently, though, there was more religious activity going on during the communist years than I'd assumed. The government generally turned a blind eye, particularly to the Jews, because primarily only elderly or retired Jews went to shul. Those Jews who held professional positions had to be much more wary of being caught worshipping, for fear of being denounced as Zionist agents.

From the outside, the seminary was a nondescript brick building. A dark corridor led to a sun-filled courtyard. Surrounding the courtyard were five floors, with iron railings that enclosed each floor's inner hallways. Shani pointed out to me that this building housed not only the seminary but also the Anna Frank Jewish high school, a kosher kitchen available only to students and teachers, and apartments for some of the rabbis who taught at the seminary.

Although there seemed to be an air of vibrant student life, according to Shani the opposite was true. He explained to me there were only eleven full-time students, of which only two were Hungarian (one of the rest was from Czechoslovakia and another was from Romania) and seven part-time students. The stark reality was there were just not enough synagogues and Hebrew schools in the Eastern bloc countries that needed rabbis, cantors, and teachers, and fewer and fewer students were enrolling, so Shani was afraid that the seminary might be closed in a few years. (Ultimately, after the Berlin Wall came down there was a resurgence of Judaism in Hungary and in the rest of the former Eastern bloc, including the former Soviet Union. This revival has kept the seminary's doors open to this day.)

In Dr. Scheiber's office, we were met by his secretary and told to wait a few minutes. He was on the phone with someone from the government.

Looking down at the front of the Kazincy Synagogue, Budapest

From what Shani and others had told me, I had the feeling Dr. Scheiber wasn't just any old rabbi.

A few more minutes went by before we were shown into his office. The much-revered rabbi sat behind a large oak table covered with books, papers, and two telephones. He had a thin mustache and was wearing a dark blue suit and a blue and white yarmulke.

"*Sholom aleykhem,* Mr. Strom. How are you enjoying Budapest?"

"The city is great. How did you know my name?"

"Rabbi Weisz told me you were *davening* in his synagogue and you were interested in finding some Jewish music, specifically klezmer."

Apparently I had underestimated the novelty of an American's hanging out in the *kehile.* The Yiddish word yente (gossip) existed for a reason.

Dr. Scheiber handed me a monograph he had written a few years earlier on Jewish music in Hungary, and he gave me permission to go to the archives to search and photocopy whatever sheet music I found of interest.

This was the first set of archives I encountered on my trip. I had no problem getting permission and a copy machine was available. (Later in my journey I would realize that the availability of that copy machine in Budapest was the exception, not the rule; for most of my trip I would have to copy everything by hand.)

The archives for the seminary were in a kind of attic loft space. I climbed the stairs, pushed opened a trapdoor, and found myself in a room with boxes and boxes of books and manuscripts spilling out onto the floor. The space was quite small, with a low ceiling, and very hot. This became my workspace for the next week. Some days I was alone, sometimes Shani came along. He was particularly interested in old cantorial sheet music.

It was quite difficult to work more than two hours in a row because there was virtually no ventilation and it was a challenge to not drip sweat onto the fragile music I was finding. Most of the music I found was either cantorial (luckily for Shani) or Yiddish vocal music.

I did find a few sheets of klezmer, but the most amazing find was the sheet music of a *Purim Shpil* (a play commemorating Haman's defeat, performed on the festival of Purim) from the late eighteenth century. There were five pages with beautiful illustrations in the margins of each instrument to be played and Yiddish lyrics written underneath the notation. Unfortunately, Dr. Scheiber wouldn't let me photocopy this rare find, but he did allow me to photograph each page.

A Wine Cake and Wedding Song

Over the course of my stay in Budapest, I often ate lunch at the Rabbinical Seminary, where I had the pleasure of eating with several of the students and rabbis. It was there I met Rabbi Hochberger over an excellent cake called *flodni*.

Rabbi Hochberger told me he remembered a klezmer tune that he heard at a wedding in his childhood village in the Carpathian Mountains. He was born in Rat (today called Ratyici in Ukraine), which at the time of his birth was located in the Austro-Hungarian Empire. As a little boy he was fascinated with the wandering Rom musicians who came to his village and played for the Jewish weddings.

"When I was eleven years old I was invited to my best friend's sister's wedding. His sister was sixteen and she was marrying a young man from Munkatsh (Mukacevo, Ukraine) whose family owned some kind of shop there. In our village we had no klezmorim, but there were some very talented Gypsies that lived outside our village and they knew all the Jewish dances. The leader of the group was known as Reb Lajos because he could speak Yiddish.

"After the chuppah the fun began. I remember that during the dinner Reb Lajos stood on the bride and groom's table and played them a beautiful but sad melody we called a *Terkishe Zogekhts* [Yiddish, Turkish saying; this was a plaintive display melody]. Then there was more food and dancing until the morning sunrise. I slept all the next day until the celebrating began again with the *Sheve Brokhes* [the seven blessings said at the end of the wedding celebration; the seven days of celebrating the wedding]. The tune I remember had a few words and went something like this." And he sang the "Katarina Maladitse."

Fasting in Szeged

Shani and Edit were so hospitable toward me with cooking, helping me with my research, even giving me a key to their apartment, that when Shani asked me if I would travel with him and Edit to Szeged to help ensure a minyan for Tisha B'Av, how could I say no?

Even though I came from a traditional Jewish upbringing, the only fast day we observed was Yom Kippur. This Tisha B'Av fast, which entailed consuming

Flodni

Makes 10 to 12 servings

Two dear friends from Hungary, Vera Suranyi and Judit Ujvari, told me how to make *flodni*. The recipe calls for the addition of sweet dessert wine. Judit wrote me that *flodni* is often made with a local sweet wine called Aszu, which can also be drunk as a liqueur. I had asked her about Tokay wine and she told me the following interesting fact: At the end of the nineteenth century, Jews from Poland escaping from the pogroms came to Hungary and settled in the countryside. They started to cultivate vineyards . . . and so developed the famous Tokay wine region. Any sweet dessert wine, like a sauterne (or a sweet Passover wine), can be substituted for its Hungarian counterpart.

For the pastry:

1 ¼-oz. package of yeast
2 Tbsp. warm water
½ cup sugar plus 1 pinch
2 sticks butter
2 egg yolks
½ cup sweet dessert wine
2½ cups flour
Grated zest of ½ lemon
1 tsp. lemon juice
Pinch of salt
1 egg
1 Tbsp. cream
Confectioner's sugar, sifted, for garnish

For the fillings:

2 cups sugar
½ cup water

For the walnut filling:

1 cup ground walnuts
3 Tbsp. unseasoned breadcrumbs or
    matzah meal
3 tsp. sweet dessert wine

For the poppy seed filling:

1 cup ground poppy seeds
½ cup raisins
Grated zest of 1 lemon

For the apple filling:

1 ¼ lb. apples, peeled, cored, and thinly
    sliced
1 tsp. cinnamon
1 tsp. lemon juice

1. Put the yeast in a bowl with the warm water and the pinch of sugar. Meanwhile, cream the ½ cup sugar and butter until completely combined. Add the egg yolks, wine, lemon zest, and juice.

2. Combine the flour and pinch of salt. Stir into the egg mixture, one-third at a time, alternating with one-third amounts of the dissolved yeast. Work the dough well to fully combine. Divide into equal quarters and refrigerate for at least 3 hours or overnight.

3. *For the fillings:* Make a sugar solution in a saucepan by combining the 2 cups sugar and ½ cup water and bringing to a boil. Place the ground walnuts in one medium bowl and the poppy seeds in a second medium bowl. Pour one-half of the sugar solution over each. To complete the walnut filling, add the breadcrumbs and wine. To complete the poppy seed filling, add the raisins and lemon zest. In a third bowl, combine the apples with the cinnamon and lemon juice.

4. Remove the dough from the refrigerator and roll out each quarter into a large rectangular sheet, approximately 8 by 10 inches. The dough will be quite sticky, so liberally flour your board and rolling pin.

5. Lay one sheet on a greased baking sheet and cover with the poppy seed filling, leaving a border of ¼ inch on each side. Lay on another sheet of dough and cover with the walnut filling. Lay on another sheet of dough and cover with the apple filling. Cover with the fourth sheet of dough and gently pat the edges with your hands to even it out. Allow the assembled pastry to rest at room temperature for 30 minutes.

6. Preheat the oven to 350°. Combine the egg and the cream to make an egg wash. Brush the top with the egg wash and bake for 30 to 35 minutes, until the top is golden brown. Sprinkle with confectioner's sugar. Serve warm or at room temperature.

"KATARINA MALADITSE" (YOUNG KATRINA)

Collected by Yale Strom

Katarina maladitsa	Katarina, my young girl,
nem mayne hent.	take my hand.
Katarina maladitsa	Katarina, my young girl,
vilstu blaybn mit mir?	will you remain with me?
Du un ikh loyfn ibern berg,	You and I are running over the mountains,
Ikh hob dir lib shtark,	I love you strongly,
Ikh hob dir lib teef,	I love you deeply,
morgn mir velen geyen.	tomorrow we will go.

no food or water for twenty-fours hours, would prove harder than any fast I had ever endured for Yom Kippur. We took the 5:30 A.M. train to Szeged, 120 miles southeast of Budapest and close to the Romanian border. Though it was early morning, it was already 85 degrees. When we arrived in Szeged, we walked directly to the shul. My shirt was drenched from sweat and I was already thirsty, but there were still thirteen more hours of fasting to go.

The Szeged shul was built in 1903 and had a seating capacity of at least fifteen hundred. It was magnificent—at first glance it looked like a cathedral in the Moorish architectural style, with two large cupolas on either side of the building. The façade was pale pink and yellow brick. The day we came, there were only forty Jews, sitting on benches in their socks, reciting prayers from the Book of Lamentations.

Rabbi Tamas Raj, who had been a mentor to Shani, met us at the shul's entrance. He was of medium build, with dark hair and a beard. His skin was such a beautiful, robust olive color that one might have mistakenly thought he was a Sephardic or Arabic Jew. The communists had stripped him of the pulpit he had held from 1962 to 1971. He had been too charismatic and had a strong following among the Jewish students at the university in Szeged. His lectures were on many Jewish topics but always seemed to end up with how the Hungarian government was despotic and one day all Hungarian people would live in a free democratic country. Now he was a rabbi in a small, dilapidated *shtibl,* where the average age of the congregation was over sixty. He lived in Budapest, but came to Szeged once a week to conduct services.

Meeting Rabbi Raj made the shlep to Szeged worth it, even with the fasting on this hot and humid Tisha B'Av. His enthusiasm for learning, his friendliness, and his deep air of spirituality were the real qualities all rabbis should have (but unfortunately, often don't). After services, Shani, Edit, Rabbi Raj, and I walked to a nearby park and talked about all sorts of political topics, dealing with America, Hungary, the Soviet Union, and Israel. Rabbi Raj invited me to give a lecture and play some klezmer during the Talmud class he taught twice a week in his home in Budapest.

The train trip back to Budapest was slow and hot, with the temperature 95 degrees in the shade. I felt that I could relate in some small way to the suffering of my forebears in ancient times. Nothing could be sweeter than the gallon of ice-cold water I drank as soon as those three stars appeared in the sky.

A Brush with the Law

When I arrived at Rabbi Raj's on the night of the class, there was already a crowd of some twenty people sitting on chairs, the sofa, and the floor, listening intently to Rabbi Raj discuss something from the Talmud in Hungarian. Rabbi Raj smiled at me as I walked to a corner at the back of the room so as not to disturb the class.

After Rabbi Raj led forty minutes of teaching and discussion, I was introduced to the students (I spoke Yiddish and some Hebrew to the rabbi, but most of the students understood English) and it was my turn. I told them of my experiences in Yugoslavia and played several of the new klezmer melodies

I had learned so far during my trek. I was in the middle of the klezmer tune I'd learned from the cemetery caretaker in Novi-Sad when all of a sudden the doorbell downstairs rang several times. I looked at Rabbi Raj. He put his index finger over his lips, indicating we should all be very quiet. He went over to the window and cautiously looked out.

"Yale, it is the police. Go down by the steps in the back. Tomorrow, come early to the shul."

I quickly packed up my violin while the students quietly gathered their things and left by the front staircase. Some came up to me to thank me for the music and said, "Don't worry, this kind if interruption has happened in the past. The police are a real nuisance."

I wasn't really scared, but my adrenaline was pumping. I figured I could act like the naïve American tourist and play dumb. I mean, what the hell, how threatening could a lecture on Jewish life in Yugoslavia and my playing of some unknown klezmer tunes really be to the Hungarian regime? The back staircase was actually the fire escape. I had to go down as quietly as I could and not lose my balance while holding my violin. Did I mention that I am not fond of heights?

I made it down safely and walked back toward my apartment down some side streets. Everything was calm when all of a sudden a plainclothes police-man jumped out from a dark alley and yelled something at me in Hungarian. I pretended not to understand but showed him I was happy to oblige and gave him my passport. He shone a small flashlight on the passport, then flipped the pages, looking at the various visas, and said:

"American?"

"Yes, I was born and raised there."

"Why you have visas?"

"I'm a violinist, as you can see"—lifting up my case—"and I'm collecting folk music from these countries."

"Why these countries?"

"Oh, you mean the communist countries? I'm Jewish and I thought, why not visit Hungary, which has a wonderful Jewish history?"

"Why you at Rabbi Raj tonight?"

"Oh, the rabbi? I met him in the shul, I mean the temple, and he invited me to play some music for him."

"Is this truth? I think maybe also a Jewish class there?"

"Oh, sir, you mean this."

I then took a piece of paper from my back pocket and wrote some lyrics in Yiddish. Then I added a few musical notes.

"You see, we were discussing the origins of these Yiddish lyrics. Some think they might have come from eastern Hungary, like Kisvarda. You see in Kisvarda they say '*lokshn*' for the word money, but here in Budapest . . ."

The policeman's face went from being angry and suspicious to irritated and perplexed. It was all I could do not to start cracking a smile and laughing.

"Would you like to hear this song?" I knelt down on the sidewalk and began opening my violin case. "It's so beautiful, so Hungarian."

"Go home, it's late now. Enjoy your trip."

He handed me back my passport and walked off in a huff. As I leisurely walked home, I couldn't help but laugh: I felt like I had walked through a scene in the film *The Third Man*.

The next day I went to Rabbi Raj's shul and asked him about the night before. He explained that ever since he had been forced back to Budapest after having lost his pulpit in Szeged, he was periodically harassed by the authorities. Their biggest complaint was that he taught unauthorized classes (Jewish studies and Israel) in his home without permission from the police, which they needed for tax purposes. Plus he didn't have the permission from the leader of the "official" Jewish community (appointed by the government). Consequently, when this happened, he would stop for a few weeks, then start again—sometimes in his home, other times in the shul or in the homes of some of the students. It was a farcical cat-and-mouse game, and a prime example of how to live under a totalitarian bureaucracy.

Issacher Klein

Issacher Klein was the *shames* of a small *shtibl* that I stumbled upon one afternoon on Dessewffy Utca. I stayed for services, and afterward Issacher invited me over to his apartment for dinner.

Issacher's apartment was on the sixth floor of a prewar apartment building with an atrium courtyard. A patch of dirt served as the communal garden. Bicycles of all sizes and shapes leaned against the railings that edged each floor's hallway. Above me, clotheslines crisscrossed the sky, their arrays of colors and shapes flapping in the wind. Dozens of cats walked about the hallways and stairwells.

Issacher told me that before the war only Jews had lived in this building. Today Issacher and one other elderly couple were the only Jews.

Inside, his home was like a *gnize* (Hebrew, storeroom of a synagogue for books and ritual objects that had become unusable). There were old torn *sforim* (religious books) of all sizes, old and stained *tallisim* (prayer shawls), even a few tarnished and bent silver Torah breastplates, finials, pointers, and *tefiln* lying on shelves and falling out of boxes. If a volcano had erupted and completely buried his house, future archaeologists would have been able to learn a lot about Jewish life in Budapest just from these artifacts.

Issacher had promised to tell me a story about a klezmer he knew from before the war and sing a few of his melodies. First, however, he shared with me his memories of horror and loss.

Issacher was born in 1911 in Tribisov, which at the time of my trip was located in Czechoslovakia. In 1942, the deportations began. Issacher and his wife Zsuzsa escaped to a farm where they hid until a neighbor found out and exposed them to the local police. The peasant who had hidden them told them they had to leave immediately because he would be shot as well if they were found on his farm.

They ran through the forest in the dead of night, with police dogs chasing them. Issacher grabbed his baby daughter from his wife because she couldn't run as fast while holding her. Then he tripped and the baby fell out of his arms, hitting her head on a large rock. In shock and not knowing what to do, he picked up the baby, whose head was bleeding profusely, and tried to calm his hysterical wife. Then they began running again, deeper into the dark woods. Their baby did not survive the night. The next morning they buried her in a deep hole covered with heavy rocks so the wild animals wouldn't unearth the body and eat it. For the next three months Issacher and Zsuzsa lived in various underground bunkers, moving from day to day, focusing on just finding food and staying alive. Finally they found a peasant willing to let them get food from his field while they slept in the woods.

While telling me his story, Issacher had taken such care to prepare me dinner that I felt I couldn't refuse, even when it turned out to be his favorite dish, *fleysh keyz* (meat cheese), a mold of grayish pieces of meat and cartilage suspended in glutinous aspic. While Issacher finished in the kitchen, I pawned most of my aspic off on his cat, managed to swallow some bites of runny eggs and rice, and gratefully gulped down the glass of Hungarian Tokay wine he had set before me.

After dinner, Issacher told me about his Uncle Albert, a violinist who played in a klezmer band in Tribisov before World War I. Issacher never saw the band play but his uncle did come over to his home often to play klezmer tunes for the family. Issacher remembered them and sang them for me while I recorded him. His voice had a nice timbre, with a little vibrato lilt to it.

Before I left he asked me where I was going for the High Holidays (Rosh Hashana and Yom Kippur). He invited me to attend the Dessewffy shul so I could hear his rendition of Kol Nidre, the prayer recited on Yom Kippur eve.

As I stood up to go, Issacher gave me a big hug and said, "I haven't sung these songs to anyone since the war. Yitskhok"—he called me by my Hebrew name—"play these melodies back in America and remember who gave them to you. The Jews there should only know how beautiful Jewish life was before the war, and not forget those few who survived and stayed here."

I thanked Issacher for the dinner and promised him I'd be there to hear him sing the Kol Nidre.

MISKOLC

On the train ride to Miskolc, I met two young Hungarian Rom who carried guitars. For two hours we all jammed together, playing music that ranged from klezmer to some swing and blues. Their style of playing, with the crisp, staccato-like strumming they used under each chord change, reminded me of the great Rom guitarist Django Reinhardt. When we arrived in Miskolc, they walked me to the *kehile* offices since it was on the way home for them.

The *kehile* offices were located in the shul courtyard. The front doors of the large shul faced in toward the open courtyard. The back of it formed one of the ten-foot walls that enclosed the courtyard. During the next week most of my research was done inside these four walls. I wandered from the kosher kitchen, butcher shop, *shoykhet, besmedresh,* and *kehile* offices between *davening* morning, noon, and evening prayers every day.

Those few Jews who maintained some semblance of Jewish culture and religion came at least once a week to the shul courtyard. Some came to do business with eighty-year-old Lipot Klein, the head of the *kehile*. Some came to have their chickens, geese, or ducks koshered by seventy-five-year-old Yidl Weisz, a Satmar Hasid and the brother of Rabbi Marton Weisz in Budapest. Others came to buy their kosher meat from the Dojc brothers, Efrayim and Yankl (eighty and seventy-five years old). And a few young Jewish students came to study in the *besmedresh* with a Hebrew teacher who traveled from Budapest once a week.

After *davening* morning prayers, several of the men stayed after to study Talmud under the guidance of Yidl Weisz. This *besmedresh* was much larger than any of the ones I had attended in Budapest. All of the benches were arranged to the outside perimeter of the room with the bimah in the center of the room. This lent the room the feel and look of an old-time western saloon (minus the long bar).

Miskolc was the first city on my trek that had fulfilled the expectations I'd had of finding the pre–World War II shtetl of my imagination—a small community in which Jewish daily life was centered around one courtyard. When I was initially planning my trip, I had hoped to find a few Jewish communities that mirrored (even just a little) shtetl life at the turn of the century. And for ten days in Miskolc I experienced a little of that world.

Crumbs from a Rabbi

After the study session I followed Lipot Klein to an office for an interview. He was originally from Satoraljaujhely, near the eastern Czechoslovakian border. A bit dour and impatient, all Lipot remembered about klezmer music before the war was that at his bar mitzvah (the religious ceremony whereby a thirteen-year-old Jewish boy becomes a young adult in the Jewish community) a blind *tsimbl* player had performed at a party in his honor that Saturday night. (The *tsimbl* is a trapezoid-shaped stringed instrument known as a cimbalom in Hungary and thought to have originated in China.) I kept at him for the next half hour, hoping he would sing some Yiddish tune from his childhood, but all he said was, "This Jewish life is no more, and we are only like the shredded tassels on the prayer shawl."

I told him I disagreed and explained that I had found not just a few remnants but actual pockets of Yidishkayt in all of its permutations.

"These were crumbs, not remnants from a Hasidic rabbi."

Lipot's words struck me deeply. Perhaps what I saw as pockets of survival and revival were aspects of Jewish culture but not the essence of Yidishkayt. For Lipot, the essential part of Judaism was the religion, based upon learning and living the Torah. If the crumbs were from a *rebe,* there was some hope (in his mind) of spiritual growth. Now I realized that those who participated in these small Talmud and Torah study sessions early every morning were "the last of the Mohicans." These elderly Orthodox men represented a Hasidic world gone forever, and wouldn't be a part of any future Jewish revival here in Hungary.

During my journey I met many old men and women who either were still Orthodox or were raised this way before the war. Jewish life as they remembered it was gone forever. As I left his office, I couldn't stop thinking about Lipot's words, his forlorn face, and how I was to reconcile these sentiments with my unbridled enthusiasm. I began to have some doubts about my trek and my reasons for coming. Was I just a naïve researcher scavenging off a dying carcass?

The next day I was in no mood to go to shul. In fact, I was feeling a bit burned out after three intense months of hanging out with only Jews, mostly old Jews. I wandered listlessly through the streets until I came upon a movie

Morning prayers in the Miskolc shul

theater. I didn't care that the film was in Hungarian. I just wanted a diversion. It turned out to be a hilarious slapstick comedy, with explicit sex scenes thrown in. I laughed my head off at this ridiculous film and felt a bit more refreshed as I left the theater.

That's when I ran straight into the old Dojc brothers, who were also leaving. You could say they were as surprised to see me as I was to see them.

"We closed early today because—"

"Because we ran out of meat to sell."

"Ahhh, we do have some salami—"

"Yes, salami. Come by tomorrow and we'll give you some for free."

"Thanks, but I don't eat meat."

"Oh, that's alright, we have some smoked sausage as well."

"Did you enjoy the film?" I asked.

"Oh, the film, well it was funny—"

"Yes, funny and crazy—"

"Well, I'm going. I will see you both tomorrow. Maybe you'll remember a story about a klezmer or a *nign?*"

"Yes, a *nign* or perhaps a sexy joke."

We all laughed and went our separate ways. The rest of the day I laughed and laughed, thinking about how the Dojc brothers had looked when they saw me. Maybe it was fate that I had gone to the movies and met them. If nothing else, there was still a lot of life in these old "shredded, crumbly" Jews—a lot of life.

The next morning when I arrived at the *besmedresh,* the shul courtyard was humming with people, carrying bags with various kinds of fowl to be koshered. There were two peasant men selling fresh eggs and baby chicks from the trunk of their car, while two babushka-clad women sold freshly baked potato *kugl* sprinkled with paprika—pans and pans of it. The place had the feel of an old-time market day. What was all of the commotion about? Then it dawned on me. It was Thursday and Rosh Hashana was to begin Saturday night—everyone was preparing for the *yontef* (Jewish holiday). And like all Jewish holidays, it was centered on prayer and food. Prayer was the spiritual sustenance for the soul and food the nourishment for the body.

After morning services Efrayim Dojc blew the shofar (ram's horn), just as it had been blown during the entire month (except on Shabes) before Rosh Hashana . . . but this time it sounded different to me. It was a clarion call that reaffirmed to me that my research and what I had discovered was not a futile nostalgic pursuit for the past, but something that could be used to help teach others in the future that Yiddish culture was worth preserving—and was still evolving. After a shot of schnapps and several pieces of honey cake, I walked over to visit with Yidl Weisz, the *shoykhet*.

Yidl Weisz

This morning Yidl didn't stay to learn with the others. Instead he went directly over to his shop and prepared for the onslaught of people bringing their various birds to be koshered. I followed him with my camera, clicking away, trying to capture a scene out of a Sholom Aleichem story. Yidl took off his black *bekeshe,* put on his bloodstained work frock, and changed his black wide-brimmed hat for another, this one speckled with flecks of sawdust, dirt, and feathers. The line to get into the small shop stretched out the door. I was interested to see that not all of these people were Jewish; there were a number of non-Jews who came to Yidl as well. I asked him why the gentiles came to have their fowl koshered?

"They know that Jesus ate kosher meat too."

I couldn't tell if he was joking or not, but really it didn't matter why they came. It was good business for the *kehile*.

Inside his shop he had a little alcove where he did his finances. The rest of the space was taken up by the stone tiled trough, which had a drain and two faucets. One customer, a Jewish lady who had a small farm outside of Miskolc, brought two geese and three chickens. Yidl took out his special knife from its sheath and checked the edge with his finger. He was looking for any imperfections in the blade. If the blade had even one microscopic nick it was declared invalid and couldn't be used. The blade was so shiny that it reflected the sun that shone through the windows.

The woman handed him each bird one by one. They struggled at first, then seemed to resign themselves to their fate. Clutching the body, Yidl took hold of the neck, ruffled the feathers so he could see the skin and exact point of entry, then swiftly took the knife that was resting on the trough ledge and with one rapid, precise stroke cut the throat and poured the blood into the trough. After every bird, he rinsed off the knife with hot water.

Most of customers then wrapped their birds in newspaper, put them into plastic bags, and left. A few people took their birds to a fire on the other side

Yidl Weisz walking
in the synagogue
courtyard in Miskolc

of the courtyard. They pulled out all of the large feathers, then singed the skin, which made it easier to pluck the remaining pin quill feathers. Yidl's wife, a rather heavyset woman, was responsible for all of the food cooked in the kosher kitchen. On this day she cleaned eight chickens and one goose.

As she plucked the feathers she hummed a beautiful melody. When I asked her about it, she said she had learned it from Yidl, and that he knew other beautiful *nigunim,* but that that I should wait until just before afternoon prayers if I wanted to have any chance of recording him. She said he only liked to sing for himself and God.

Later that day, before prayers, as Yidl's wife had advised, I knocked on their apartment door in the shul courtyard, hoping my chance to record him had come. Yidl opened the door, wiping the sleep from his eyes, and said, "Mr. Jew, come in. What do you want from my life?"

I walked into his house, turning to take in all the *Gemores* (part of the Talmud) stacked neatly on the floor-to-ceiling bookshelves.

"Perhaps you can sing me a few Satmar melodies?"

"Sit and learn a page of *Gemore* with me, afterward I'll sing a few *nigunim* for you."

"OK!"

So I took a seat at a small table that looked like it doubled as the dining table as well. Breadcrumbs, pieces of apple skins, cherry pits, and egg shells were neatly piled on one corner of the table. Yidl went to another room and returned carrying a large book. I told him it had been some time since I last studied some lines from the Talmud, but he didn't want to hear any of it. He opened it and began reading out loud in a singsong, rhythmic voice. He would read a line and then explain it to me in Yiddish.

We continued this way for half an hour. Then, in earnest, he closed the book and said, "Mr. Jew, this melody I will sing for you is from my teacher. Always after learning a page of Gemore he sang this song."

Yidl pushed back his chair, closed his eyes, rested both hands on the table, tilted his head back, and began to sing in a low soft voice. His tone was so sincere it gave me goosebumps.

After the verse, he pushed himself away from the table, slowly lifted his solid body up from the chair, and began to sing another verse, this time in a loud searing voice. He grabbed my hand and began to slowly dance around the table, singing the chorus, which was only "bay ay day, day ay," repeated over and over in true Hasidic fashion. It was a beautiful melody and I eagerly joined in singing the chorus. The courtyard was completely quiet, so I'm sure our singing was heard by all those in their apartments and the *besmedresh* and kosher kitchen.

As we circled around the table, Yidl's sweaty hand gripped mine harder and harder, causing it to go numb. I wanted to pull away but didn't dare. Maybe reading some *Gemore* for the first time in many years, in Eastern Europe, with a pious Hasid before celebrating the coming *yontef* was all part of a predestined plan. Or maybe I was just in the right place at the right time, actively experiencing a Jewish melody with my whole body rather than just passively recording it.

A few more revolutions around the table and we finally stopped. Then Yidl took a towel from the kitchen, wiped his neck and brow, changed his yarmulke, and walked outside, closing the door behind him. Wow, what a scene. I actually saw a Hasid reach a spiritual high, a level of *dveykes* (adhesion, the Hasidic concept that through song one can reach a spiritual sense of nirvana and adhere to God) that I had never seen before.

"YISMAKH MOYSHE" (MOSES REJOICED)

Collected by Yale Strom

Vi hat men im gerufn?	How did we call him?
Ki eved ne'eman, ki eved ne'eman	They called him, they called him,
ki eved ne'eman, karatsa lo.	they called him thy faithful servant.
Vus hat men im gegebn?	What did they give him?
K'lil tiferets, k'lil tiferets,	Placing on his head, placing on his head,
k'lil tiferets, b'rosho nasata lo.	placing on his head a crown of glory.
Vu iz er geshtanen?	Where did he stand?
B'amdo l'fanekha, b'amdo l'fanekha	He stood before you, he stood before you,
b'amdo l'fanekha, al har Sinay.	he stood before you on Mount Sinai.
Vus hat er mit zikh gebrakht?	What did he bring with himself?
Ushnay lookhos avanim, ushnay lookhos avanim,	In his hand he brought, in his hand he brought,
Ushnay lookhos avanim, horid b'yado.	in his hand he brought down the tablets of stone.
Vus shtayt in zey geshribn?	What is written on them?
V'katsuv bahem, v'katsuv bahem,	Inscribed on them, inscribed on them,
v'katsuv bahem, shmiras Shabes.	inscribed on them is the observance of the Sabbath.

CHORUS

Yismakh Moyshe, yismakh Moyshe,	Moses rejoiced, Moses rejoiced,
yismakh Moyshe, b'matnas khelko,	Moses rejoiced at the destiny bestowed on him
b'matnas khelko.	at the destiny bestowed on him.

I sat down for a moment to collect my thoughts and then I realized I had forgotten to record the song. Damn it! Writing down the notes from memory just wasn't going to capture the song as it was meant to be sung.

Chaya Preisz

During my time in Miskolc, I stayed in the home of Chaya and Nahum Preisz. Their families were both originally from the Maramures region (today northwest Romania). Whenever there was a Jewish guest visiting Miskolc who wanted private accommodations and kept kosher, they were usually brought to Chaya's rather than to a hotel. Both Chaya and Nahum spoke Yiddish, loved Jewish music, and were very *heymish* (Yiddish, informal, cozy) toward me.

Chaya was a wonderful cook and one afternoon she made me fresh cucumber salad and mushroom soup with mushrooms she had picked herself in the woods.

In her wispy soprano voice, Chaya sang some typical Yiddish folk and theater tunes I already knew. I thanked her and was about to retire to my room when she insisted on telling me a little about her war experiences. She wanted me to record her because she was worried that when all the Holocaust survivors had passed away only those who denied it would be around, and future generations must know the truth. The focus of my research seemed to be broadening and taking on a mission of urgency, a race against time before these survivors in the Eastern bloc all died.

"We were nine children, five boys and four girls. I have one sister today in Brooklyn. She and I were the only ones to survive. The Germans came to Miskolc in March 1944. Immediately they made the ghetto. Since there was little food to eat, the children who were nimble, strong, and quick were secretly sent out of the ghetto to search for food in the nearby fields. Usually all I ever brought back were potatoes.

"One day, my older sister and I were gathering potatoes when another girl came running back to me screaming, 'Two German soldiers have your sister on the ground!' I ran as fast as I could, in time to see the two soldiers stand over my sister and shoot her in the back. I ran back to the ghetto crying the whole way. I blame myself for not having stayed by my sister. Maybe I would have seen or heard the soldiers before they came upon her? This scene still haunts me today."

Hungarian Mushroom Soup

Makes 8 servings

The Hungarian tradition calls for sour cream, but I prefer to use Greek yogurt, which you can find in specialty food stores—the flavor is full but not sharp. It also has the benefit of coming in a nonfat, no-cholesterol variety, which works perfectly well here. Crème fraîche is another delicious alternative. Add Hungarian cucumber salad and black bread for a perfect Hungarian lunch! (If you need to reheat the soup, do it over a medium flame, stirring constantly until just simmering—don't let it boil, or the soup will curdle.)

2 Tbsp. canola or other vegetable oil
1 medium yellow onion, chopped medium
1½ lb. mushrooms, washed and sliced
4 tsp. dried dill

1 tsp. sweet paprika
6 cups vegetable stock
Salt and pepper to taste
2 cups sour cream or plain Greek yogurt or crème fraîche

1. In a lidded stockpot, heat the oil over medium heat. Add the onion and cook, stirring, until translucent.

2. Remove from the heat and add the mushrooms, 2 teaspoons of the dill, and the paprika. Add enough stock to cover (all 6 cups if necessary; remember that the mushrooms will add liquid as they cook). Cover and place on a burner over a low to medium flame. Bring to a boil, turn down, and simmer for 30 minutes.

3. Remove from the heat and add the remaining 2 teaspoons of dill and salt and pepper. Stir in the sour cream. Serve immediately.

Hungarian Cucumber Salad

Makes 4 to 6 servings

This traditional Hungarian recipe is a wonderful side dish. The cucumbers make it refreshing, the sour cream is filling and satisfying, and the dressing gives it character. It should be made at least a few hours in advance—better yet, a day ahead. If you must steer clear of full-fat sour cream, try substituting nonfat Greek yogurt. But in this recipe, the creaminess of the sour cream really makes a difference.

2 large cucumbers, peeled and sliced thin

3 to 4 tsp. salt

1 Tbsp. white vinegar

1 Tbsp. sugar

¼ tsp. sweet paprika, plus extra for garnish

¼ tsp. ground white pepper

1 clove garlic, minced

2 Tbsp. finely chopped onion

1 cup sour cream or Greek yogurt

1. Combine the cucumber slices and salt in a bowl, stirring to evenly coat the slices. Chill for 1 hour.

2. In the meantime, combine the vinegar, sugar, paprika, pepper, and garlic and set aside.

3. Drain the cucumbers, pressing to squeeze out the liquid. Rinse, pat dry, and return the cucumber slices to the bowl and add the vinegar mixture, onion, and sour cream. Stir to mix well and return to the refrigerator for at least 2 hours.

4. Before serving, sprinkle with a light dusting of paprika.

After she told me the story Chaya wiped the tears from her eyes with a handkerchief. Then she went back to her lace making and said nothing more.

Playing with the Rom

One day, while buying flowers for Rosh Hashana for the Preiszes, I ran into one of the Rom boys I had jammed with on the train. His name was Tibi. He invited me to come to his house later that evening to meet his family and play music. His father was a bass player and knew many Jewish melodies.

I readily accepted the invitation, and that evening I took a bus to the outlying suburbs. As we rumbled over the potholed roads, fertile fields with rows and rows of sunflowers and corn gave way to new homes in various stages of being built. Often those who lived in the city wanted to eventually move to the country or have a second home, a kind of vacation home. They built these dream homes themselves, putting hammer to nail and brick to mortar. Sometimes they ran out of money and had to stop halfway into the construction.

In half an hour the bus reached Tibi's neighborhood. This was the *tabor,* as the Rom called it—the Rom neighborhood. At home we called it a ghetto. The Hungarian Rom were generally all of darker skin than their fellow Hungarians. They were less wealthy, less employed, less educated—and more discriminated against by the non-Rom, called *gaje* in Romani.

As I walked to Tibi's home, there were many barefoot Rom children running around and playing. By the time I got there I had an entourage of ragamuffin Rom kids tagging along and yelling random English words at me:

"Mister, gum?"

"Michael Jackson, love Michael Jackson."

"Pizza, Mickey Mouse, pizza, Mickey Mouse."

As I approached Tibi's door I could hear that the music had already begun. Tibi and his younger brother played guitar, their dad played bass, their uncle played mandolin, and a cousin played violin. The musicians were scattered throughout two rooms while other men, women, and young girls sat on chairs and the floor. Tibi introduced me over the din of the music, then motioned for me to take out my violin. They played some Hungarian and some Transylvanian tunes while I improvised around the melodies. Then Tibi's father asked me to play a tune, so I picked the Yiddish "Papirossen" (cigarettes), a melody I'd heard played in several different styles in Belgrade and Budapest. I started slow and played rubato, improvising around the melody. Then Tibi set a churning syncopated rhythm while his dad plucked the bass on the off beats. The tune went from rubato to vivace and then into the stratosphere melodically.

From "Papirossen," we segued to ten different Jewish melodies—all of which I knew. In fact, I was a bit surprised that all the tunes they were playing were standard Jewish repertoire, like "Heyveynu Shalom Aleykhem" and "Hava Nagila." Finally, I asked Tibi if any of them knew a Jewish hora that might have been played at a Jewish wedding before the war? After a minute of discussion a woman went up to Tibi's father and whispered something in his ear. He nodded and began to sing a beautiful hora while he plucked the harmony out on his bass. Soon the other musicians joined in but not me. This time I remembered to take out my tape recorder. Throughout the evening there was very little conversation; it was all about the music.

Finally around midnight I was too exhausted to play anymore. The last bus back to town had left at 11:30 P.M., so Tibi and his girlfriend took me back in his horse-drawn wagon, through the moonlit fields of sunflowers.

Rosh Hashana

The next evening I went to the Rosh Hashana services and brought my tape recorder just in case I wanted to catch a bit of the *davening*.

Because it was Rosh Hashana, the services were held in the cavernous main shul, built in 1860. Every Jew I had seen over the last week was in attendance, plus a few I didn't recognize. Even though the minyan was much larger—about 150 people—than on the typical weekday or Shabes, that number seemed to be swallowed up in the immense shul, which had once held 1,500 people all singing in unison the beautiful *Unesane-Tokef* prayer on the eve of Rosh Hashana. On this night, the services were led by Yidl Weisz.

I was leaving the next day for Nyiregyhaza, so I got to the *besmedresh* early with all of my gear. I wanted to say goodbye to all of those who never seemed to mind having a microphone stuck in their face and answering my unceasing questions. As I was walking out, Yankl Dojc yelled, "Next year in Miskolc at the movie theater!"

"Tibi's Hora"

Collected by Yale Strom

NYIREGYHAZA

The autumn weather was perfect, with a hint of color in the trees and a cool breeze in the air. The downtown area was similar to Miskolc, but smaller, with less traffic. There were fewer tall buildings, and the residential neighborhoods were a mix of single-family homes and apartment buildings. Nyiregyhaza made Miskolc seem like a metropolis, and its shul, although large, was not nearly the size of the one in Miskolc. It stood next to the *besmedresh* and kosher butcher shop. It was padlocked and it looked like no one had been there for a few days.

Breaking and Entering

I decided to explore the back of the yard behind the shul. Maybe there was a back door I could somehow get through so I could see the interior and get some photos. I planned on spending only a few days in Nyiregyhaza, and from the looks of this city, the *kehile* probably only met for prayer services on Friday nights and Shabes.

There wasn't a door, but there was a window I was able to pry open with my pocketknife after I chipped away layers of green, ochre, pale yellow, and black paint. I pried open just enough so I could slide half my body in and use the force of my weight to push the window open farther. It had obviously been painted shut for a long time. It went up only three-quarters of the way, but I was skinny enough to climb through. I left my camera bag outside, taking in only one camera and a flash.

Once inside I found myself on a ledge, a kind of catwalk that stood above the mikvah (ritual bath), a sunken rectangular tiled box filled with about two feet of stagnant water. A staircase led down into the mikvah and a wrought-iron railing surrounded it. There were two changing rooms where men and women would hang their clothes before they went separately into the mikvah. An old faded mirror hung on the partition between the two changing rooms, reflecting the stagnant water. Another staircase led into a dark hallway that dead-ended into another staircase going up. I ventured up the stairs and opened the door. Suddenly I was standing in a beautiful shul sanctuary with a vaulted ceiling surrounded on all four sides by beautifully painted murals of the twelve Zodiac symbols.

I took photographs for a few minutes, then decided to leave. It wasn't that I felt I was trespassing in this long-abandoned building—it was the emptiness and lifelessness that were disturbing. Every time I heard a noise from within the shul, it sounded as if it were breathing, or as if the ghosts of those who used to go to this shul were watching me. I went back downstairs to the mikvah, climbed the catwalk, and shimmied myself through the window. I was happy to get outside.

As I rounded the corner and began to walk down the street, a car stopped and the driver rolled down his window. It was a young man who spoke German. He identified me as a tourist—who else would be coming from behind the shul with a camera bag?

His name was Andras and he was Jewish. I explained why I was in Nyiregyhaza and he invited me to his home. It turned out my guess about the frequency of the minyan was correct. They only *davened* on Friday nights and Shabes mornings. So instead of spending all my time at the shul, I hung out with Andras for the next few days.

Before bringing me to his home, Andras took me to Nagykallo to visit the grave of the *rebe* who brought Hasidism to Hungary, Rabbi Yitskhok Isaac Taub (1751–1821). He is still revered by many Hasidim throughout the world today for his teachings, moralistic stories, and beautiful songs. He wrote the lyrics to "*Szol A Kakas Mar*" (Hungarian, The Rooster Is Crowing Already), a peasant song that is considered the most famous Hungarian *nign,* known by all Hasidim as well as most Hungarians today. Every year on the anniversary of Rabbi Taub's death, Hasidim come to visit his gravesite to light candles, say prayers, and leave little notes on his tomb.

The key to the cemetery was kept by a gentile; he was not home but in some bar. We couldn't find the bar and the sun was going down quickly, which meant I was losing most of the available natural light I needed for my camera. The whole cemetery had only seven stones and was surrounded by a low barbed-wire fence. I carefully climbed over the fence and took my photos. I was quickly developing a knack for breaking and entering.

Magda and Elizabeth

Andras lived in a spacious, extremely clean home with his mother, Magda, and his aunt, Elizabeth. They were delighted to see that Andras had met a young Jew and were glad to have me hang around for the next few days.

There were only seventy Jewish families in the entire city, with about a dozen or so young children. A teacher from Budapest came every other week to teach four or five kids Hebrew and Torah. The kosher butcher shop was only open once a week, when Yitskhok Weisz (the *shoykhet* from Budapest) came and koshered some cows and fowls. Elizabeth, who spoke English well, was worried Andras wouldn't find a Jewish girl in Nyiregyhaza to marry. She lamented that there was so much intermarriage in Hungary today, the Jews were finishing off what Hitler had begun.

I told Elizabeth that I had met a number of nice attractive single Jewish women in Budapest and I'd give Andras their names, addresses, and telephone numbers. She was so pleased to hear that there was the remotest possibility that Andras might meet a nice Jewish girl; she immediately made me write down all of the information, plus a line describing each of them. From a wandering klezmer, somehow I had morphed into being a *shadchan* (marriage matchmaker) as well.

While Elizabeth was talkative, Magda was quiet, a little hunched over but active, scurrying from one room to the next doing various chores. Occasionally she stopped and stood behind her sister to listen to our conversation. Then she'd whisper something in Hungarian to Elizabeth, wait for the reply, and then scurry off to another room.

What fascinated me about Elizabeth and Magda was they had grown up upper-class before the war; so far I hadn't met anyone like them on my trek. They had lived on a large farm of two thousand acres, forty kilometers outside of Nyiregyhaza, with sheep, cows, and apple and cherry orchards.

Elizabeth recalled, "When I wasn't helping in the house, studying, or practicing piano, I was out in the orchards, lying under trees reading and writing poetry. My favorite writer was Robert Louis Stevenson. Our home was like an oasis of calm.

"I got married in 1931 to a young man I met at the synagogue. We were so in love and happy but this all changed in 1940 when the Hungarian fascists came to power. I urged my father that we should leave while we still had our lives, but he believed Hungary would remain a peaceful island in a burning hell.

"My two brothers, my husband, and two brothers-in-law were all taken by the Hungarian army to Russia. None of them came back. Then my father died on January 31, 1944, of a heart attack after he heard an inflammatory speech by Hitler condemning the Jews. On March 19, 1944, the Germans entered Nyiregyhaza and on April 19 we were all driven into the ghetto. The deportations to Auschwitz began immediately afterward. On June 4, the last day of the deportations, my mother was in total despair so she took poison and killed herself. She wanted to be buried next to her husband but we had no time to bury her. A Christian doctor said he would bury her. To this day I have no grave for my mother."

For a year after that, Magda and Elizabeth were marched from one hellish camp to another, constantly kept one step ahead of the advancing Allied armies.

"In March 1945, we were liberated by the Americans. I never gave up because I thought if I am alive, surely my husband is alive. I always was waiting but he never came back. I am a Jew and I will never forget that I am one because of this number on my arm. I hate the Hungarians as much as I hate the Germans. I never go to synagogue today because I only want to remember my happy childhood memories and not when I was deported from there.

"Remember when you collect your Jewish songs, you must not forget to collect the stories of these survivors. These are just as important, if not more, because if we hadn't lived through this nightmare you wouldn't need to collect these songs."

On the day I left Nyiregyhaza, all three of them came to see me off at the train station. I hugged them, then got into the train and found my couchette. I opened the window to say goodbye once more.

Elizabeth said in her soft but firm voice: "Don't forget us. We are family and only have each other."

Elizabeth was so small in stature but so strong in conviction.

DEBRECEN

Since Debrecen boasted the second largest *kehile* in Hungary, I hoped to find some klezmer material in this city. The kosher kitchen was quite a lively place, with a number of young people eating alongside the usual pensioners. Yankl Weisz, the *shames* of Debrecen's Orthodox shul, told me that even though they didn't have a rabbi, there was a Hebrew school that met every

Shabes just before lunch. The Jewish youth of Debrecen joined their brethren
from Budapest every summer at the Jewish camp in Szarvas.

Although each *kehile* in Yugoslavia and Hungary was independent of the
others, they all were still very interconnected. They had to be. Jews were already a small minority, and those Jews who were in any way connected with
their Judaism were an even smaller percentage. They had to be supportive of
each other to survive.

Yankl Weisz was a jovial man in his mid-sixties with a ruddy complexion
and streaks of red in his mostly gray hair. He had been born in Beregszasz
(Berehovo, Ukraine) and had planned to immigrate to Israel but he couldn't
get the visa, so instead he came to Debrecen in 1964. He was one of ten children. All his siblings, his parents, and both sets of grandparents were gassed
in Auschwitz.

I heard Yankl's lovely voice during morning prayers, and I tried to get him
to sing for me several times, but either he was too busy or he couldn't remember any Yiddish folk songs from his childhood. Then the day before I
was to travel back to Budapest, Yankl said, "Come with me to gather some
skhakh, then I'll sing you a song from my father." (*Skhakh* are the branches

used to cover the tabernacle roof for the Jewish festival of Sukkot—from the Hebrew sukkah, booth. The holiday commemorates the forty years in which the children of Israel lived in the wilderness after they left Egypt.)

We drove to a field where we gathered hay and dried corn stalks and picked some pears and apples in a nearby orchard to use as decoration in the sukkah. At home in San Diego we had always planned to build a sukkah. Every year we had promised ourselves we would do it that year for sure. I had traveled all the way to Debrecen to build my first sukkah.

Yankl explained that his father had been a coachman, ferrying people and goods between Beregszasz (Berehovo, Ukraine) and Munkatsh (Mukaceve, Ukraine).

"Once he picked up a klezmer who was walking with his bass. My father offered to take him to Munkatsh, but the klezmer didn't have any money to pay him. Instead the klezmer said he would compose a song about a coachman for him. And sure enough, several weeks later my father received a letter from this man with a poem about a coachman. My father then added some music to it."

As we sat under the pear and apple trees, enjoying the bucolic setting, Yankl sang and I recorded this unique song.

GOOD-BYES IN BUDAPEST

I arrived back in Budapest in time for Yom Kippur, and I planned to squeeze as much as possible into my last week in Hungary before leaving for Prague.

I stayed again with Shani and Edit Polnauer, who were very excited to hear all about my travels, specifically about the kehile in Debrecen, where Shani was going to become the rabbi of the Orthodox shul after graduating.

On the eve of Yom Kippur I went to the Dessewffy shul to hear Issacher sing the Kol Nidre. It was something to hear. As he sang, the congregation joined in. The unison clarion sound was emotionally piercing, causing some to cry. In fact, every few bars of the melody one young woman repeated the last phrase, wailing in her soprano voice. It was as if she were pleading directly to God to lessen the burden the Jews have carried for so long. The atmosphere was so spiritually heightened I began to cry too.

OnYom Kippur I fasted with the Polnauers (a breeze compared to my last fast with them on Tisha B'Av) and played klezmer tunes at their break fast party after the holiday.

On my last Shabes in Budapest, I went to the rabbinical seminary. After services, the congregation of 150 crowded upstairs in a room where Dr. Scheiber made the blessing over the challah. Afterward he tore off pieces with his hand and threw them to anyone in the audience who wanted a piece. Apparently this was an old custom of his and the congregants really appreciated catching a piece of challah from their revered spiritual leader. Then he introduced me as the "wandering Jew with his fiddle" and I played some *Shabes zmiros* (songs specifically for Shabes) to everyone's delight.

On my last night in Hungary, I celebrated Simchas Torah (the eighth day of Sukkot) at the Desseffwy shul. We danced the first three *hakofes*—a circular procession with the Torah scrolls done seven times on Simchas Torah in celebration of the completed year's reading cycle—inside the shul, then we all went outside into the cool evening and danced and sang the last four in the courtyard.

I decided to forget about photographing this joyous event. I put a two-hour cassette into my tape recorder, set it in a corner with the microphone, and forgot about it. Whatever I got, I got. I was feeling a little sad about my departure, so I danced and sang until 2 A.M. Then a few others and I went back to a friend's home for an early morning breakfast of bread, *lecso,* and some delicious Hungarian pastries. Afterward I went back to Shani and Edit's apartment and quietly gathered my belongings. I watched the sunrise as I meandered to the train station with my load (which was a little heavier after each city). Next stop: Prague.

Chapter Three

CZECHOSLOVAKIA

ROM THE TRAIN WINDOW, I admired the countryside: the fall harvest mirrored in the fields and autumnal colors. The peasants working in the field seemed to have stepped out of a Tolstoy novel. I realized one should never romanticize peasant life, but this bucolic and pastoral setting filled me with longing. Urban life could be overwhelming at times.

I usually took a night train to save money on a hotel; thus I never got to see much of the topography and buildings, so this train trip was rather special.

At the border it would become more "special" than I could have ever imagined.

The Hungarian border guards asked if I had bought anything. I showed them a tablecloth, shirt, and music cassettes. He then took a cursory look at my violin and banjoline (he didn't even ask about the cameras) and stamped my visa.

A few minutes went by. The door opened again. This time there were three Czechoslovakian border guards, two officers and one soldier, waiting to enter for inspection. They examined my passport thoroughly, flipping back and forth from the photo page to the visa, and casting furtive glances at me. Then it was time to check out the violin:

"Stradivarius?"

I wondered if he was attempting a joke.

Then they asked why I was traveling to Prague. My patience was getting thin and my twenty-three-year-old smart-aleck streak kicked in:

"I'm traveling to Prague to see your grand seventeenth-century capital and spend lots of money, my U.S. dollars, which will help your weak economy."

They didn't seem to like my answer. Whispering something to each other in Czech, they left with my passport. After twenty minutes one of the guards returned with my passport in his hands.

"Please come, we must ask you a few more questions."

"Come? Come where? Is there a problem?"

"Yes, a problem, but we can discuss this in the station."

"Bring your superior officer to me right now. I'm going nowhere and my visa is valid!"

"Sir, come now, this is an order from my superior."

My first thought was not to budge, but that plan backfired when he threw my backpack out of the window and onto the tracks. I grabbed my instruments and camera bag and ran outside.

The next thing I knew I was being escorted alongside the train by three soldiers, rifles drawn. I was nervous and annoyed, but those emotions soon gave way to a rising embarrassment. As we walked past the long train, the passengers leaned out of their windows to gawk at me. A few kids pointed, wide-eyed. Perhaps they think I'm some sort of spy, I thought.

If I had spoken fluent Czech I would have been tempted to yell something ridiculous: "Yes, they caught me! The notorious klezmer from San Diego with my secret cache of klezmer tapes! If you play them backward you will hear the voices of Jews plotting against your national football [soccer] team at the next World Cup match!"

Of course, I seethed in silence as we walked the frigid, windy quarter mile to the border guard station, located smack dab in the middle of No Man's Land between the two countries. To one side was the barbed wire fence representing the Czechoslovakian border, and to the other, the barbed wire fence representing the Hungarian border. I was walking on the thick black line that represents the border on a typical map.

Once inside the station, they instructed me to open my backpack and put all of its contents on a long wooden table. I scanned the nondescript room—there were a few folding chairs, a couch, some empty vodka bottles lined up in a corner, cigarette butts strewn all over the floor, and magazine center-folds of nude women taped to the wall.

I took each thing out of my backpack slowly and methodically. They immediately pushed my clothes aside and went directly for the two Tupperware containers of film.

I had written some identifying words in Yiddish on the caps of each film roll; these told me what it was but obviously left them clueless. They took out the tape cassettes and started to play them randomly. What a sight to behold: five Czechoslovak guards sitting around a table listening to the tape of Mr. Sarfberg's 78 LP that I'd recorded in Novi Sad. They listened to a few others, then tired of this and started to look at some of my books. One was the history of the Jews in the Austro-Hungarian Empire. When they came upon the map of the entire empire, it was as if they were looking at such a historical fact for the first time—Central Europe with no Czechoslovakia. They all had quizzical looks on their faces, as if someone had played a prank on them.

Then came the barrage of questions: Why did I carry so much film? Why did I have a tape recorder? Who was I seeing? Where did I stay in Hungary? Where was I going to stay in Prague? How much money did I have? As I was answering, a guard took all my film and cassettes—plus my tape recorder—to another room and shut the door behind him.

Then in walked two young, baby-faced soldiers from outside. Their cheeks were rosy red. They sat down on the folding chairs around the table.

Now I was mad. In fact, I was fuming. What if they confiscated my film—or perhaps, even worse, exposed it? Worse yet, what if they confiscated all the cassettes of the fantastic oral histories and klezmer and Yiddish music I had collected and ruined those? All my field research! Would I return immediately to all the places and people I had been to while it was fresh in my memory? (Impossible!) Could I somehow convince the U.S. embassy to intervene? (I somehow doubted it.) Or, would I just go home depressed, angry at the world, and ready to kill myself? (Much more likely.)

As I paced the room, cursing them all under my breath, the young soldiers—supposedly guarding me—offered me tea, crackers, and chocolate. They tried to engage me with their broken English, but I was having none of it!

Ninety minutes of pacing and hearing my cassettes being played behind the closed door made me decide that I finally had to do something. I spied a telephone in another room and hatched what turned out to be a very ill-conceived plan. I ran to the phone and quickly dialed the number of the U.S. embassy in Prague. The two soldiers, at first taken aback, ran over, yelling for me to put the phone down.

One ring, two rings . . . *pick up the damn phone!* One soldier grabbed my arm, but I refused to let go of the telephone. On the third ring, someone answered.

"Hello, American Embassy."

"I need help. My name is Yale—"

Before I could say anything further, one soldier pulled the receiver out of my hand while the other put me in a half nelson.

He dragged me to a jail cell, still holding my arm in a half nelson, threw me in, and slammed the cell door shut.

My heart was pounding, I was sweating profusely and it felt like my left arm had been torn off at the shoulder. There was a bench, but I sat on the floor and leaned up against the wall so I could stretch my legs out. Gradually, I calmed down and took stock of the whole situation.

OK, what's Plan B, Yale? I asked myself, and I couldn't help but chuckle.

An hour later, the pain in my arm had lessened, so I stood up on the bench and looked out through the small dirty windowpane. I saw the train tracks that led into Czechoslovakia, peasants in the field baling hay, and some soldiers smoking and kicking around an old soccer ball out of boredom.

Finally, the same two rosy-faced soldiers who had thrown me into the hoosegow brought me some black tea, poppy seed cookies, and my violin. The one who had put the half nelson on me apologized for his roughness. Then he asked if I would play my violin. But I insisted that before I played I would need to know what was happening to all my stuff and when was I going to be released. His reply was so benign and earnest, I almost began to feel sorry for him: "Wait no problem, train to Prague, later."

After I wolfed down the cookies and drank the tea, I got out my violin. I couldn't think of any appropriate prison blues tunes I knew, so I played "Stormy Monday." I followed it with some bluegrass and klezmer tunes. After thirty minutes of music I was feeling a bit more emboldened, so for a lark I ended my jailhouse concert with a rousing rendition of "Dire Gelt" (Rent Money) in Yiddish. This had to be a first at this border crossing.

At last, several hours after taking me to the station, the officers reappeared (they had taken so long they could have transcribed by hand every

The Jewish History of Czechoslovakia and Prague

In the tenth century Jewish merchants plied the trade routes from the Rhineland to the Near East. By 906 there was a settlement in Bohemia and by 1091 a permanent *kehile* in Prague, its capital.

In 1096, the First Crusade pillaged and killed many Jews and forced others to be baptized. In 1142, the Second Crusade drove the Jews out of the city. But they returned, settling on the bank of the Vltava River (more commonly known by its German name, the Moldau) in what later became Prague's Jewish quarter. Throughout the twelfth and thirteenth centuries, Jews settled all over Bohemia into Moravia and further east into Slovakia.

In 1270, in the Jewish quarter of Prague, the Alte-Neue Shul (Old-New Synagogue) was built. It is the oldest shul still in use in Europe today. By 1600, the *kehile* in Prague numbered two thousand. A Jewish Golden Age began, which lasted into the eighteenth century. The Prague ghetto became virtually an autonomous Jewish town, with independent police and fire departments, and its own judges, town hall, mayor, and flag. Many shuls were built, a Hebrew printing house was founded, and Jewish craft guilds, including a guild of Jewish musicians, added splendor to the vibrant *kehile*. Between 1576 and 1619 this self-contained *kehile* became a major center of European Jewish life and the home of many scholars and financiers. Meanwhile, Bohemia, Moravia, and Silesia became part of Austria, linking the history of Prague's Jews with that country.

Many exiles from the Chmielnicki pogroms in Poland (1648–1649) settled in Bohemia. By 1709, Prague's twelve thousand Jews constituted the largest Jewish community in Europe outside of Turkey.

In 1745, Empress Maria Theresa expelled all of Prague's Jews, but the ban was lifted within three years because it had created economic havoc and increased the taxes on the non-Jews. In 1781, her son, Joseph II, issued an edict that enabled Jews to live outside the ghetto walls for the first time. However, the emperor also forced the Jews to adopt family names, establish secular schools, and cease using Hebrew and Yiddish in business transactions.

By 1848, the ghetto was abolished and in 1867 Jews achieved full legal emancipation, which encouraged secularization and assimilation for many.

As the nineteenth century came to a close, Prague was one of the leading centers of German Jewish literary and intellectual activity, rivaling Berlin and Vienna.

By 1900, 44.4 percent of Prague's Jews declared themselves to be German. This inflamed anti-Semitism among the Czechs. Jews were looked upon as purveyors of Germanization. In 1918, the republic was born and led by Thomas Masaryk, the father of Czechoslovakian independence. At this time there were nearly 280,000 Jews in the country who were completely free for the first time. During the inter-war period, Czechoslovakia's Jews were the best treated in all of Central Europe.

The Nazi takeover of Germany in January 1933 caused a constant surge of Jewish refugees to pour into Prague over the next six years—first from Germany, then from Austria after the Anschluss of March of 1938, and finally from the Sudetenland. By 1939 the Prague *kehile* had swelled to 56,000 Jews.

As early as October 1939, Jews were arrested and deported from Prague to concentration camps in Poland and Germany; once the Nazis fully occupied all of Czechoslovakia in March 1940, this became a systematic campaign. By the time emigration was halted in October 1941, half of the *kehile* had fled the growing Nazi terror, many escaping to Palestine. Unfortunately, between October 6, 1941, and March 16, 1945, 46,067 Jews were sent from Prague to Theresienstadt (Terezin), Buchenwald, or other concentration camps. In all, some 155,000 Czechoslovakian Jews were murdered in the Holocaust. Only some ten thousand returned to Prague after the war. They were able to reconstitute some semblance of a *kehile,* but by 1948, the Communist takeover marked another turning point for the *kehile.*

The first formal blow against the Jews was the 1952 anti-Semitic trial of Rudolf Slansky, the Jewish Communist first secretary. Purges followed during which eleven Jews were accused of being Zionist agents. Jewish religious and secular activities began to stagnate, with occasional spurts of legal emigration to Israel and the West until 1967. Then after the Israeli Six-Day War and the Russian invasion of the country in August 1968, a new purge of Jewish intellectuals began. In 1981 there were about seven thousand Jews. In the Czech Republic today there are 2,700 Jews registered but probably around 8,000 to 10,000, and in Slovakia there are about 2,600.

one of my cassettes), accompanied by a man I hadn't had the pleasure of meeting yet. He was in his early thirties, clean-shaven, and short, and had so many medals pinned to his breast pockets I was sure if you gave him just a little push from behind he would have toppled over. In perfect English he said, "I am sorry for the inconvenience we caused you. The problem was your visa had expired two days ago and with all of your films and tapes we became just a little suspicious. But everything is in order now. We wrote an extension on your visa and you can go."

One of the young soldiers opened the jail door and accompanied me back to the room, where everything I had been carrying was laid out nice and neat. I carefully looked through it. Nothing seemed to be missing, all the cassettes were in their marked cases, and none of the used film had been tampered with. While I packed, a soldier gave me back my passport with the extended visa. Then I was told I had to pay fifty dollars for the new visa and their hospitality.

Ganovim! (thieves) I thought to myself as I walked back to the train station.

The next direct train to Prague wasn't for several more hours, so I caught one to Streda; from there I would transfer to Prague.

This was a commuter train, in this case meaning that it consisted of only one car and the engine. The car was packed with coal miners going home after a long day's toil. Here I was with all of my gear, standing among sixty or so miners covered in coal dust from head to toe. They all wore thick cotton blue-gray jackets, denim overalls, and miner's helmets with lamps. They looked at me as if I had just dropped from outer space. I wonder what they would have thought if I'd told them I was Jewish.

After a minute of whispering among themselves, one miner, a kid about seventeen years old, pulled a harmonica out of his pocket and started to play. Then this bearded older man took my violin case from the floor and opened it. I got the message, grabbed my violin, and began to play a polka.

The kid with the harmonica joined me, then all of the miners pushed back against the sides of the train wagon to clear a small space, which was immediately taken up by four guys dancing to the music. After another polka, I went into a *kolomeyke* (Carpathian circle dance), followed by a *freylekhs* and *bulgar.* Soon the car was filled with cigarette smoke, rounds of the local schnapps, and clapping and laughter. Too bad I had to get off at Streda.

I waited in Streda for three hours to get my train to Prague. Finally my adrenaline could not fend off my fatigue. I slept during the entire four-hour trip to Prague.

PRAGUE

I walked from the all-glass, modern-looking train station through a park that surrounded the station for a half-mile. Once out of the park, I stepped back into the seventeenth century. It was amazing. The buildings in Budapest had been nice, but here in Prague it was something completely different. I got a stiff neck just from tilting my head back to gaze at the stunning architecture.

Prague's Jewish quarter is the best-preserved in all of Central Europe. It is located in the Stare Mesto (Czech, Old Town), and most of its buildings—the Jewish Town Hall, the different shuls, and the famous old Jewish cemetery—center around Maiselova (Maislova) Street. Even during communist times, the former Jewish quarter was the most visited tourist location in the whole country.

A view of the medieval Jewish cemetery in Prague from outside one of its walls

The Cantor in the Attic

I first met Leybl in the attic chamber of Prague's hauntingly beautiful five-hundred-year-old Jewish Town Hall. The Hall was built at the end of the sixteenth century by Marcus Mordecai Meisel, the banker of the emperor of Bohemia. It was rebuilt after a fire burned a large section of it in 1754. At that time, a unique clock with Hebrew characters for numerals and with hands that ran backward was added.

The day I arrived, all of the curtains were drawn, and as a cost-saving measure the lights were either quite dim or not turned on at all. I felt as if I were walking in a haunted house, through the dark hallways that lead to even darker staircases, closed doors that opened to room after room, and always, always, the squeaking, scratching, and muffled sounds of disembodied voices filtering through the walls. Perhaps the legend of the golem is true, and the creature still creeps at night through the buildings in the former Jewish ghetto.

After several hours of perusing some old dusty books in one of the anterooms off the main archival room, I heard some singing that sounded cantorial coming from a room above me. I wanted to meet whoever was singing, but first I had to locate this room. I thought I was on the top floor . . . so where was the staircase that led to this attic chamber?

Down the hallway, a left here, a right there, and finally I found the elusive staircase. This part of the building had once been a shul known as the High Synagogue—an appropriate name. At the top of the staircase the music emanated from behind a closed door. I sat down in the narrow hallway. I wanted to just listen to the pure singing, afraid if I interrupted or distracted him he would stop.

There was a window at eye level, where just a touch of the autumn afternoon sunlight shone through and spread itself across the wooden floor where I sat. Through the glass I saw the tops of the ornately carved gables of the buildings on the horizon and below me. In the distance geese were flying in formation south. With this scenery, the light, and the beautiful cantorial singing, I felt as if I had just walked into an eighteenth-century landscape painting of Maiselova (Maislova) Street in the heart of the Prague ghetto.

After some twenty minutes I carefully opened the door and spied a short, nondescript, balding Jewish man wearing a faded red yarmulke, pacing the room while holding a prayer book behind his back. He glanced at me for a second, barely breaking his stride, and continued his singing. The room looked like it had been a *besmedresh* at one time. There were a few wooden chairs, benches, and shelves full of various religious books. Another minute went by before he stopped singing. Then suddenly in Yiddish he said, "*Sholom aleykhem.* Are you a Jew?"

"Of course I am a Jew. I am researching klezmer music."

"Not cantorial? I am the cantor of the Alte-Neue Shul."

"When do you *daven?*"

"Every morning at 7:30 A.M. and on Friday nights at 6 P.M."

"I'll come tomorrow."

"Can you *daven?*"

"Yes, of course."

"Good, you will help us make a minyan and I can tell you something about the klezmers in my shtetl. Now I have to practice, please leave now."

And with that he began pacing the room and singing again. At this first meeting I didn't get his name or where he was from—though he sounded eastern Czechoslovakian. I wanted to take some photos of him in this quaint hidden room, but he was rather emphatic about my leaving and his need to practice.

I saw him *davening* at the shul the next day, but he left so quickly after services I had no chance to speak with him again. It wasn't until later that afternoon, in the *kehile* archives in the Jewish Town Hall, that I finally met and recorded this mysterious cantor.

I had spent the afternoon at the archives looking for anything on klezmer. The room was small and stuffy, and had only one window, which I couldn't open. After some time in the warm stagnant air, with the numbing sound of the constant raindrops falling on the windowsill, I fell asleep.

I woke up after an hour or so. I had had a strange dream about a cantor who sang while sitting up in a tree in Prague's old Jewish cemetery. I soon realized that the singing part hadn't been a dream but a reality. The cantor from the Alte-Neue Shul was practicing to himself again. I decided to venture up to the garret to visit him.

This time, instead of just listening to him sing, I set up my tape recorder. If nothing else, I thought, I will have managed to tape some beautiful singing and melodious *davening.* After about fifteen minutes I got up the nerve and walked in. This time he stopped and said to me in Yiddish, "I was hoping you would come again. I didn't see you in shul this morning. I thought you had left."

I explained to him that I tried to talk to him after morning services but that he'd disappeared so quickly.

"I had an appointment with an old friend."

I introduced myself and he told me his name was Leybl. Lebyl was a Czechoslovak Jew from Michalovce, in eastern Slovakia at the foothills of the Carpathian Mountains. His father had been the *bal-tfile* in their small synagogue in the mid-1930s, and had been an itinerant cantor for the outlying villages. Leybl sat down, put his prayer book away inside the drawer of the small wooden lectern, pulled over a wooden bench, leaned backed on his oversize red plush velvet armchair, and put his feet up. Now quite comfortable, he let out a high-pitched sigh, folded his hands on his ample midriff, and began telling me about his father and a wedding he played at long ago.

"My father was well known in the region and a friend to everyone. Besides being an itinerant cantor, he was a barber. He always carried his scissors and other barber tools with him just in case someone he met needed a haircut. Even if they had very little money my father would cut their hair. He would say 'Your God, my God, everyone's God likes a clean-looking man.'

"One day my father was walking back to Michalovce—he liked to walk. He said it gave him the time to practice his cantorial music and stay healthy. He soon met a shepherd standing alongside of the road with his goats. The man recognized my father and asked him if he would give him a haircut right then and there.

"The shepherd had no money but said that that very evening his daughter was getting married and he would pay my father to come and sing some songs. Never one to turn a singing job down, he accepted. He proceeded to give the shepherd a haircut surrounded by all his goats.

"My father was the only Jew at this Hucul [Carpathian highlander] wedding, and many of the guests applauded him because his repertoire was large and he knew songs from all of the various people's folk music traditions. He even sang some Yiddish folk songs that the guests knew, like "Malke Zhote." But this wedding was not an easy job for him. He had to sing for four hours, accompanied only by a non-Jewish friend who played bass. They rested only a few minutes every hour with some hot cherry tea and cherry schnapps.

"MALKE ZHOTE"

Collected by Yale Strom

Malke Zhote,
es toot (teet) in hartsn brenen!
Malke Zhote,
loz zhe zikh derkenen.
Malke Zhote,
Ikh ken on dir nisht zayn!
Ikh tsu (tsi) dir,
du tsu mir,
lomir tantsn ale fir.

Malke Zhote,
my heart is burning!
Malke Zhote,
reveal yourself.
Malke Zhote,
I cannot be without you!
Me and you,
you and me,
let all four of us dance.

"I inherited the love and appreciation for Jewish music from my father. When I *daven* in the shul I have to *daven* in the style the congregants are used to, but up here I *daven* for myself and for my father. He loved everyone and gave his music to everyone. He sang songs to his fellow prisoners at Auschwitz until the very bitter end. Here is a Yiddish song my father sang when he was cutting someone's hair."

After singing, he excused himself. He had to go *daven* the afternoon and evening prayers. I thanked him as he walked out of the room; he just gestured with his hand and waved good-bye and nothing more.

I sat down in his big comfortable chair, rewound the cassette, pushed play, and relived the whole incredible story that Leybl had just told me.

As I listened, I realized that it didn't matter whether I used the tunes I had been collecting to form the repertoire for a band. All I knew was that every one of these survivors' stories and their music had become a part of me and I was a changed person forever. I could never go back to the way I was before I had left San Diego—never.

These people had cheated death and now I was the fortunate recipient of their having survived the Holocaust. They were true carriers of what had been Yiddish culture before the war.

The Nign *That Came to Me*

The Alte-Neue Shul is an awe-inspiring Gothic edifice. One of the first things you notice is that it is sunk below the street level. The Catholic church had dictated that no shul could ever be higher than a church, so by lowering the foundation of the building, the Jews were able to have a high ceiling. It was dimly lit with twelve narrow windows. On the bimah hung a scarlet flag embroidered with a Mogen Dovid and a Swedish hat. The banner was presented to the Jews of Prague by Ferdinand III in 1648, in appreciation of their role in the defense of the city against the Swedes. There was an empty chair on the bimah, which I was told used to be the famous Rabbi Loew's chair, from which he preached in the sixteenth century.

There were exactly ten men the morning I arrived. The *davening* was Ashkenazic but with a German slant to the melodies. I'd heard Leybl singing the same prayers in a more Jewish Polish style. Services were perfunctory and over in an hour. There was no *kidesh,* no conversation, no Talmud studying; everyone just went his own way.

Alone, I sat down in Europe's oldest shul still in existence. Within these thick stone walls, thousands of Jews once worshiped, sung, cried, and laughed. A believer in the twelfth-century kabbalistic doctrine of the transmigration of souls could imagine that these thousands of souls were floating in and around me.

As I sat there with my eyes closed, a melody came to me. It was as if it had been floating in the shul for centuries and had suddenly found its host. I quickly took out my violin and paper and pencil and began to transcribe the melody playing in my head. This had never happened to me before, and I knew I wasn't hearing the melody from outside the shul. In twenty minutes I composed the entire melody, which I called "Der Praguer Shayd" (The Prague Ghost).

I played the tune several times from the bimah, enjoying the fantastic acoustics. Then I gathered my gear, left the darkened shul, and walked outside into the bright sunshine. I waited a few seconds for my eyes to adjust, then went on the Charles Bridge. I had found a melody, a melody that was hidden in the deep recesses of my mind; it had taken sitting all alone in the Alte-Neue Shul for it to reappear. I had experienced a true moment of *dveykes.*

Klezmer in the Street

The historic Charles Bridge crosses the Vltava River and links the Old Town and the main part of the city. The early morning light and brisk air were invigorating. On the river, kayakers engaged in their morning exercise regime, and several flocks of swans nestled tightly together with their bills burrowed under their wings.

Feeling rather proud of my Jewish heritage at that moment, especially after the spiritual experience I had just had at the Alte-Neue Shul, I decided to express it to everyone who traversed the bridge that morning by playing my violin.

I started with "Hatikvah"—Israel's national anthem, whose title means "hope." Coincidentally, the same melody—originally a Bohemian folk tune—is used in "Vltava" (The Moldau), a symphonic poem about the river by Czechoslovakia's favorite son, composer Bedrich Smetana (1824–1884). Sure enough, people stopped to listen (they probably thought I was playing Smetana's composition), and some even threw money into my case.

I then played what I had composed in the Alte-Neue Shul. The haunting melody seemed to grab people and make them stop and listen. I continued playing Yiddish, klezmer, bluegrass, and swing. I had a great time—it was like being paid to practice.

As I played, a beautiful woman about my age, around five feet ten, with long brownish-red hair and a beguiling smile, stopped to listen. Luba was a philosophy student at Charles University. She came from Kolin, a small city east of Prague. She asked me where I was from and what I was doing in Prague. After I told her about my research, she told me she knew of one Jew in Kolin, an old man who had been a music teacher and musician, who had played Jewish, Czech, and Slovak folk songs at parties and dances years ago in her town. Wasting no time, I asked Luba if we could have dinner together that evening.

Meeting Ondre at the Kosher Kitchen

It was lunchtime, so I walked to the kosher kitchen to get a bite. Maybe, as in the other cities I had visited, in Prague's kosher kitchen I'd meet some older folks with invaluable information and stories.

This kosher kitchen was unlike any I had seen in Hungary. It was really more like a restaurant, because besides tourists many non-Jews that worked in the neighborhood came there to eat. The food was kosher, good, and inexpensive, and throughout my stay in Prague I ate nearly all my meals there. One of my favorite dishes was their sweet *lokshn* (noodle) kugel with raisins.

When I walked into the kosher kitchen, I saw a young man with curly black hair, about five feet six, olive-complexioned and solidly built, with a banjo case sitting on the ground by his table. I walked directly over to him, introduced myself in English, and asked if I could join him for lunch.

In equally good English he replied, "Of course you may join me, but first may I have a look at your violin?"

This is how I met Ondre, who became a dear friend of mine and remains so to this day. Ondre was a banjo player and leader of a Dixieland jazz band, but he earned his main bread and butter as a highly regarded and sought-after piano tuner. He tuned all the pianos for the symphony, opera, and ballet and for some private individuals, too. He didn't know any klezmer tunes. However, when the *kehile* held celebrations for Hanukkah and Purim, Ondre and a few members of his band played Hebrew and Israeli tunes.

Sweet Noodle Kugel with Raisins and Almonds

Makes 8 to 10 servings

This kugel is so fast and easy to make, and everyone loves it. You can easily substitute other dried fruits and nuts, to your taste. It makes a wonderful side dish for meat and chicken and is also great for brunch.

2 cups cottage cheese	½ cup dried raisins
3 eggs	1 cup slivered almonds
⅓ cup sugar	10-oz. package egg noodles, cooked
Dash salt	¼ cup melted butter

1. Preheat the oven to 325°. Combine the cheese, eggs, sugar, and salt in a large bowl. Add the raisins and nuts. Add the noodles, and toss thoroughly to combine.

2. Using roughly half the butter, coat the bottom and sides of a casserole dish. Pour any excess butter back into the remaining butter.

3. Place the kugel mixture in the buttered dish. Pour all the remaining butter over the top. Bake for 1 hour.

Ondre was very friendly and had an acutely sardonic wit, especially when it came to cracking anti-Reagan quips. We hit it off immediately. He invited me to his home for dinner the next day, and I gladly accepted. My social calendar was filling up rather nicely.

Ondre was married to Marta, a nurse, and they had two young girls. They lived in a spacious, yet cozy attached house with a large backyard vegetable garden. The children had their own bedroom, filled with toys; the hallway, living room, and den were filled with paintings, photos, records, cassettes, and musical instruments. Because Ondre played the banjo, he was partial to plectrum instruments and he had all kinds: banjo, mandolin, balalaika, cobza, bandura, guitars, lute, oud, and an old upright piano.

Bramborove Knedliky

POTATO DUMPLINGS

Makes 4 to 6 servings

These dumplings are fully cooked after being boiled, but traditionally the Czechoslovakians brown them in butter.

6 medium potatoes, peeled
1 egg yolk
1½ tsp. salt

½ cup all-purpose flour
Butter for sautéing, about ½ stick

1. Boil the potatoes in just enough water to cover. Drain thoroughly and rice with a hand-held masher or ricer. Let cool.

2. On a floured board, add the flour and egg yolk to the potatoes, working the mixture into a dough with your hands. Shape the mixture into a roll and cut into 10 slices.

3. Bring a large pot of water to a boil. Drop in the dumplings and boil gently for about 5 minutes.

4. Drain the dumplings on a paper towel.

5. In a heavy frying pan, melt the butter and fry the dumplings until they are lightly browned on all sides.

We ate, drank, and played some music; then Ondre told me his story:

"I was born in 1944 in England. My parents were lucky and got out of Slovakia in March 1939. They lived in England during the war, through 1946.

"Anyhow, like many Jews, my parents returned to Czechoslovakia after the war out of hope of building something new. I think my father felt that because he had not stayed, like many in his family did during the war, and suffered like they did, he couldn't run anymore. He needed to stay and fight this time.

"I was able to travel and live in England during our famous 'Prague Spring' of 1968. I was confused at the time, not sure where I wanted to live, and I was tired of the politics of my country. I learned the trade of piano tuning in England and then sent for Marta. We both began a new life in England, made some good friends, and did well financially, but . . . we were always a bit homesick. Then in the 1970s we encountered some bias against foreigners and I think also because I was Jewish. We got tired of the racial slurs and decided to move back to Prague.

"We both understand the irony of having moved back to a country that has Soviet soldiers based in it, but we wanted to raise a family in the land and culture we knew best, Czechoslovakia. Marta is not Jewish but the children are being brought up as Jews. What is a Christian but a lapsed Jew? Our moral compass is humanism, whether Jewish, Christian, or Muslim. And in terms of my Judaism I do what I can. I have hope for our tiny *kehile*."

The children went to bed and we stayed up into the early morning hours, eating, talking, and playing music together. It had been a full day for me, having experienced an array of emotional lows and highs, so I decided to extend the "high" by walking back to my hotel. I wanted to observe the city as dawn engulfed the home of the golem.

The Wedding and the Priest

I met Luba early one morning at the central bus station. On our dinner date we had made plans to travel to her hometown of Kolin, only thirty-five kilometers west of Prague. I was eager to meet this old Jewish friend of hers who had been a musician. His name was Arye and he was probably the last Jew in a city whose Jewish history began in the late fourteenth century.

The view from the bus window was of flat land as far as the eye could see. Field after field, dotted with a few trees, farm houses, sheep, and cattle, whizzed by.

When we arrived in Kolin, we first went to Marta's home. Her mother was an elementary school teacher and her father a journalist for the local newspaper. They served a huge breakfast of berries, homemade kefir, eggs, toast, and a berry tart.

After our gourmet breakfast we went to visit Arye. We'd called ahead before we left, so he was waiting for us at the door. He was very tall, probably six foot five, bald, and lanky, and had a smile full of gold teeth. Arye spoke German and a little Yiddish so we could communicate directly with each other.

Kuba

BARLEY DISH

Makes 6 to 8 servings

6 Tbsp. butter or margarine

1 cup finely chopped onion

2 cloves garlic, chopped fine

2½ cups dried mushrooms, reconstituted
   with boiling water, well cleaned, stems
   removed, chopped medium

1½ cups pearl barley

Salt and pepper to taste

1 tsp. dried marjoram or mint

7 cups vegetable stock

1. In a large saucepan, heat 4 tablespoons of the butter and sauté the onion and garlic until translucent.

2. Stir in the mushrooms. Add the barley, salt and pepper, marjoram, and stock.

3. Over medium-high heat, gently simmer, uncovered, approximately 10 to 15 minutes until almost all of the liquid has evaporated and the barley is plump. It should still be a bit moist and runny. Stir well.

4. Preheat the oven to 350°. Transfer the mixture to a greased casserole and dot the top with the remaining butter. Bake uncovered for 30 minutes. Serve warm or at room temperature.

After ushering us into his home and offering us sugar cookies, preserves, and black bread, he took out my violin and began to play a melody that sounded like an *oberek,* a spirited, acrobatic Polish dance in 3/8 time, popular among the peasants. He had learned this piece in Slovakia in a village called Palota, near the Polish border.

It turned out Arye wasn't just a musician but also a klezmer. He had played in his father's band during the 1930s. After Slovakia was separated from the rest of the country and became a fascist German puppet state in March 1939, Arye's father saw the writing on the wall and took his family to Stryj, in the Ukrainian Soviet Socialist Republic. When the Germans at-

"Oberek Palota"

Collected by Yale Strom

tacked the Soviet Union, the family was sent farther east to Samarkand, in the Uzbek SSR. The family returned to Palota in 1946.

Before I began to interview Arye, he said he wanted to make a toast with some pear wine he had made. He toasted to us, to himself, and to the hope that Jewish music should resound once again in Kolin. I couldn't help but think that if he didn't start teaching his Jewish repertoire to others very soon, the last part of his toast would never happen.

"My father's family originally came from Sanok, Poland, but they fled in the 1870s to escape the constant pogroms in the area. My father was a Polish teacher at the local high school, and also played music on the weekends at weddings and dances. My grandfather owned an inn in Palota. There my father met a man who played the mandolin. He learned from him and eventually taught me as well. In high school, I learned to play the violin because I wanted to be a soloist and not only play *sekund* (Yiddish, second violin playing only chords). Our band played Jewish, Slovakian, Polish, and Hungarian music.

"Once in 1937, our band played at a Slovakian wedding. The local priest performed the ceremony and then came the food, more drink, and dancing. We played everything, including some Jewish dances. After five hours the priest stood on the bride and groom's table—he was a bit drunk himself—and quieted everyone. Softly he began to sing a haunting melody. It had no words. As he sang he began to cry and then others began to cry. We didn't know what to do. It was a long melody. He sang maybe fifteen minutes. Then he stopped and began to speak in Slovakian about the bride and groom and the village, and then he said something I will never forget as long as I live:

"'We are all like branches of a tree and can only survive if we stay connected to that tree. Once a branch is separated, it will die. When all the branches are separated the tree is forever weakened. All of us—Slovak, Pole, and Jew—must fight to stay as friends. When the enemy of hate will come and invade our land we must fight them all with all of God's strength.'

"We Jews in the band were completely surprised at the priest's words. It was rather still for a moment and then my father yelled: 'We will play a *czardas* (Hungarian folk dance), polka, and *reydl* (Yiddish, circle dance) in honor of the priest and the newlyweds.'

"Everyone cheered and we began to play. The music lasted until sunrise, then everyone went home to sleep.

"When the Hlinka came to power, the priest was arrested and no one knows what happened to him. I'll never forget how he looked when he spoke. When the Germans marched on Stryj, I knew then he had been not just any ordinary priest, but a prophet."

Over the next three hours I continued to tape Arye playing and speaking. Marta was as fascinated as I was, if not more so. She'd grown up knowing Arye but never knew his story.

The next morning, I left for Brno.

BRNO

Brno did not seem promising from the start. Its *kehile* was quite small and there wasn't a kosher kitchen. When the small *kehile* got together, it was in the shul. But there were only services on Shabes and that wasn't for another five days.

I walked around what little remained of the former Jewish quarter. I met a couple of Jews at the synagogue office, of whom none knew anything about klezmer and frankly none wanted to talk to me, period. In truth, I was a bit dismayed, but I decided to make the best of Brno before I trekked off to Bratislava. So the next day I decided to play tourist and visit the tourist highlights of the city.

As I walked out of the city's fine art museum, I happened to glance over the shoulder of the elderly man sitting in a chair next to the exit. He was about seventy, with bifocals, a head of thick white hair, and a grayish-reddish beard. He was reading a paper that was clearly Jewish because its masthead logo was a graphic of a Mogen Dovid and menorah. He didn't seem to notice me, so I just blurted out, *"Sholom aleykhem."*

He immediately looked up, squinted for a moment (I was standing in front of a brightly sunlit window), and answered in perfect English:

"And peace be with you, Mr. Jew."

I was so stunned at his off-the-wall answer I just began laughing. Then I went into a ten-minute monologue about who I was and what I was doing in Brno. When I finally finished, he replied calmly and in a rather droll way:

"My name is Phillip. I'm a retired professor of botany, and to keep busy I write for the monthly Jewish newspaper *Vestnik.*"

He also had a terrible secret, which he confided to me over dinner that evening at a local Chinese restaurant.

After six months of the same flavors and smells, I was really looking forward to my Chinese dinner. My taste buds had begun to atrophy and I needed to stimulate them in a most overt way, with some spicy hot sauce.

When I arrived at the restaurant, called the Great Wall of China, Mr. Engelsmann was already sitting in a corner table, looking quite dapper. He had on black dress pants, a purple dress shirt with a red carnation in the lapel, a purple vest, and a black corduroy jacket with black leather elbow patches. His brown 1940s-style fedora was on the table. I, of course, was dressed in my usual casual threads, but at least I'd shaved.

I was so excited about eating the broccoli and bean curd with garlic I had ordered that I was hardly paying any attention to Mr. Engelsmann as he spoke to me. He realized this, so we both ate our meal in silence. I drenched my food with hot sauce. By the time I finished I was sweating and panting and my mouth was on fire, but I enjoyed every moment of discomfort. The endorphins had taken over and I was enjoying a considerable food high. I let out a satisfying belch, ordered another Czech pilsner beer, and was ready for some adroit conversation. I had no idea what was in store for me.

Mr. Engelsmann was born in Olomouc but came to Brno as a child with his parents. He grew up in a rather secular home where political Zionism was stressed over religion. For a brief period when he was seventeen years old, he belonged to the Hashomer Hatzair (Hebrew, the Young Watchmen; a socialist Zionist youth organization) and worked on a *khakhshara* (training farm).

He then entered the university to study botany. His specialty was the plant life of the desert and how and why these plants needed little water to survive in such harsh conditions. He had planned to immigrate to Palestine, where he wanted to do research in the Negev, but he was afraid to leave his parents after Hitler became chancellor in Germany in January 1933.

"I am sure you have heard many of these Holocaust stories from others you have met while traveling," he said, "but I will tell you a story about what happened to me when I returned from Terezin. Just my brother and I survived. My parents, grandparents, aunts, uncles, and cousins all perished. My brother Stefan left for Israel in 1946; he still lives there. I stayed because I met my wife Ilina, who was a classmate of mine at the university. Now I am all alone; she passed away three years ago.

"After I got back to full strength at the end of 1945—I was only forty-seven kilos when I was released from Grosswarden—I found work on a large farm. I did a little of everything on this farm. I worked with the animals, in the fields, but when I had some time off I worked with some vegetable plants in the green house. I was experimenting trying to create a natural pesticide for the tomato and pepper plants.

"Then one day in June 1947 this seemingly idyllic world was shattered. At the farm I became head of all the laborers who worked in the fields. One day I was walking back from the dairy barn when I saw a man, someone who was newly hired to work in the dairy. Something about him unsettled me, but I wasn't sure what it was. Then one very hot July day this same man had his shirt off when he was throwing some well water over his head to cool himself off. At first I didn't pay any attention to him. Then when I approached to get a drink of water myself I noticed that he had a scar on the left shoulder blade that looked like the shape of a small swastika.

"Then my memories began to erupt in my brain. This man who now called himself Otto Orlik had been a low-level guard in Terezin. I couldn't remember his name but I wouldn't forget that Slovak bastard's face ever. Once he had gotten into a fight with another guard and his shirt was torn and I remember seeing the tattoo. There were Jews from several countries in Terezin but he seemed to take special pleasure in tormenting the Czech Jewish prisoners. I saw him hit and beat helpless people. He even hit me a few times with a wooden club. Plus I would never forget that sadistic smile he had and his two chipped front teeth when he would stand six inches from your face spitting and screaming at you.

"I was positive this was the same man. I decided I was going to kill him by poisoning his food. But I didn't just want to kill him anonymously, I wanted him know it was I who killed him—a Jew. He lived in a small house just a few kilometers from the farm. I wanted to kill him in his home so no one could trace the murder back to me. I planned everything to the last detail. I was as methodical as the Germans were.

"When I knew the time was coming nearer to when I would kill him I told my wife I had to do some extra work in the greenhouse and had to come home late. During these evenings I experimented with mixing rat poison with fresh milk and seeing what amount was fatal to mice.

"My plan was to visit him on a Sunday morning and pretend I wanted to talk to him about expanding the dairy and putting him in charge of all of the activities.

"The day came, the last Sunday in August, just before Orlik was going to take his summer vacation in the Tatra Mountains. I walked the whole distance instead of bicycling—this way I could take a different route home, which would make it harder to trace my footsteps. I even brought a different pair of shoes that I would wear when I returned home. I was surprised how calm I felt, as if I was just going to work like any other day.

"While we ate breakfast together I asked him about the war and what had happened to him. He said the Germans took him to Germany where he worked as a slave laborer in a munitions factory near Stuttgart. I told him I had been in Terezin, which elicited no reaction from him. Maybe I was wrong and this wasn't the man? I pushed the thought immediately out of my head and brought out the fresh milk I had left in the kitchen. There I had squeezed some raspberry juice into the glass just to mask the possible taste of the poison. Then I took a small jar from my pocket and poured in two spoonfuls of rat poison and returned with his drink and mine.

"It took only fifteen minutes before I began to see some results. He dropped a dish and couldn't quite pick up all the pieces. Slowly, slowly, his nervous system was being attacked and he didn't know why. He sat down on his couch and took a drink of Slivovitz. I continued to clean up and talk to him. Then he got up to go to the toilet but before he could get to the outhouse he urinated in his pants. He was dying and I felt no remorse, no guilt.

"I stood over him as he lay sweating in his wet pants, in pain, and told him who I was and when we first had met. He asked me to get a doctor, which I ignored. God was my witness as I murdered him. I told him this was revenge for the death of my siblings, parents, and grandparents.

"When he heard me say all this he had such a look of despair and fear on his face. He began to mumble something about mercy and that I was killing an innocent man. Can you believe he had the gall to say I was killing an innocent man? As the poison began to seize his body I went back into the kitchen and finished eating my breakfast. Another hour went by until finally the execution was complete. I went into the bedroom and saw he had rolled onto the floor. I left and took a different path home. I only told my wife what I had done just before she died."

After this story, we paid for the meal and walked the streets of the former Jewish quarters. He was telling me some facts about certain buildings and asking me questions about my travels. I know I answered him, but afterward I couldn't remember a word he or I said during that walk. It was all babble. After we said good-bye I walked home, still in a daze from the shock of the story. I lay awake in bed for several hours and replayed the story over and over again in my head. I always came back to the same question: what would I have done? A part of me said I would have eagerly relished the chance for revenge on this Nazi sadist. I had by now heard so many stories from the survivors I had met and seen how pain still haunted and ravaged them that my knee-jerk reaction would have been "kill the bastard!"

But then other thoughts crept into my head, as if there was an opposing defense lawyer in my brain. What if he really had been innocent? If he was truly guilty, maybe he should have been shot and not tortured? Maybe he should have been brought to a court so his trial could have been made public? Maybe the process of the trial would have brought home the great tragedy of the Holocaust to the Czechoslovakians? Maybe this could have helped in some kind of healing, a rapprochement of sorts between the Jews and non-Jews?

I had had the *mazl* not to have suffered like most of the informants I'd met. No matter how many stories of murder and survival I heard, I would never know what it was like to walk in Phillip's shoes. For me, at that moment, as I lay awake in bed, the best answer I could think of was from a quote I had read in a biography of Primo Levi. A fellow Italian prisoner in Auschwitz, Antonio Paccagnella, had said: "Nobody has truth in their-pocket."

What I did know was I had no more interest in staying in Brno. I felt uneasy and lugubrious, so I left the next morning for Bratislava.

BRATISLAVA

Still disturbed by Phillip's story, I sought solace and reflection at the shul in Bratislava. Perhaps I would find some answers to the questions that troubled me from one of the leading rabbinical authorities of all of Europe, the Hatam

Sofer (Moses Sofer, 1762–1839), who established a famous yeshiva, the largest since Babylonian times, in Bratislava.

If I Had Golden Wings

I walked through the shul's front doors into a hallway that led to the main sanctuary. From the looks of the brown mosaic-tiled floor and the yellow-painted plastered walls, it seemed that the shul had been remodeled sometime in the early 1960s.

The sanctuary was a rather large room. There were *tallisim* of varying discoloration draped over the back of the wooden chairs, *sidurim* on the seats, and the bimah and some *tefiln* boxes strewn about over the lecterns. The scene had been frozen in time and covered in thick dust. It looked like the shul hadn't been occupied in years; the only evidence of any visitors was spider webs.

I could hear the murmurs of *davening* coming from another section of the building. I followed the sounds to the *besmedresh*. Typical of many I had been to, this one was small, without any windows. There were fifteen nondescript older men davening. They all wore *tefiln*. Some wore theirs over their shirts, others over sweaters, allowing the left sleeve of the sweater to dangle loosely by the side. Besides the *tefiln,* they all wore nappy black wool winter hats, which sat on their heads like pillboxes.

The men were all standing, shaking and swaying to their own internal rhythms. Only a couple of the men glanced my way as I walked in. A burly man in a corduroy work shirt, overalls with suspenders, and a 1930s-looking cap came over to me and asked in Yiddish if I wanted to put on *tefiln*. I agreed and soon my coat sleeve was dangling from my left arm like theirs.

It was quite cool inside except near the ceramic tile heater (many of the men were hovering near it), so I kept my jacket on like the rest of them. Everyone prayed at his own pace, coming together in unison only to say "*ameyn*" (it is true) and to say the Kaddish.

Afterward the burly guy came out with a tray of cloudy shot glasses and some honey cake. Each said his own blessing over the vodka and cake and then inhaled both items. I took two of the vodka shots and was soon quite warm and a little tipsy.

As everyone put their *tefiln* away and conversed with each other, the burly man came over to me and introduced himself as the *shames,* Naftuli Blau. He asked me what I was doing in Bratislava and this time I gave him the direct, truncated answer:

"I'm looking for klezmer music."

He gave me a brief, strange look, scratched the stubble on his face, adjusted his cap, exhaled strongly into my face (his breath smelled terrible), then in one swift motion stood up on a bench and yelled, "This man is looking for some stories about klezmer musicians and theirs songs; can we help him?" And to me he said, "Now Yitzkhok, do something for me. Tomorrow there will be a funeral and please come to help us."

That was one way of asking everyone all at once. Some of the men shrugged their shoulders and went back to doing whatever they had been doing; a few others began to sing "Mayn Yidishe Mama" (My Jewish Mother) and "Mayn Shtetle Belz" (My Town, Belz) at the same time. This was hilarious! I quickly grabbed my camera and took some photos as they continued to very seriously sing these classic Yiddish songs.

One man came up to me and insisted I take out my tape recorder so I could tape him while he sang. I tried to explain to him I wasn't interested in any of these well-known Yiddish songs, but he just kept on insisting, so out came the recorder and microphone. He loudly cleared his throat, told everyone to shut up, then began to sing a Hasidic Yiddish song. Gradually, one by one, the men in the *besmederesh* stopped whatever they were doing and began to sing: "Volt Ikh Hobn Gildene Fligen" (If I Had Golden Wings).

It was amazing, a chorus of old men singing this wonderful melody at the top of their lungs. I was suddenly invigorated by their strength and warmth. Naftuli joined in, adding his booming bass voice to the others. Not wanting to be left out, I joined in as well.

The spirit in which the men sang was so uplifting that then I realized why I had met Phillip in Brno and heard his tragic story. I could only begin to really appreciate these men and what they had all endured in the Holocaust if I too had felt just a little of their deep despair. These men were true survivors.

When I asked one of the men, Rudolf, about the song, he told me it was from his childhood. His teacher would take him and the other children out into the forest to celebrate Shavuos (Hebrew, weeks; a Jewish holiday celebrating the giving of the Torah). There they would sing, dance, play games, tell stories, and eat fresh cheese, apples, and apricot blintzes. It was Rudolf's favorite holiday. He said, "When I sing this song it takes me back to my childhood. It was a time when I really believed *Hashem* [Hebrew, the name of God; an expression used to avoid speaking God's name] would always protect me."

For some of these Jews, surviving the Holocaust had become a heavy burden they carried. They constantly had to bear witness and remember all the horrors that had happened to them and their loved ones on a daily basis. In contrast to those survivors who lived outside of Europe, for them forgetting, even for a brief time, was impossible because every step they took was in the very streets where the Holocaust was perpetrated, where their families' blood had flowed. Their conscience wouldn't let them forget and neither would the world.

The Burial

Despite the extreme cold, a large group of people crowded into the funeral chapel. The woman who had passed away had been a pillar of the community; she had left three children and seven grandchildren. None of the family members could read Hebrew so it was left to Naftuli to conduct the burial services and read the appropriate prayers. After twenty minutes it was time to take the body to the gravesite. I was cold and very happy to move.

Over the snow and ice the body of the deceased woman was carried on a wooden stretcher by close friends from the chapel. It was rather far to the gravesite, so only a few people accompanied the body. It was clad in a white cotton shroud and covered with a heavy velvet mantle with Hebrew writing on it. The stretcher was placed on a wagon and it took five older men, including Naftuli, to push the wagon. Every thirty yards or so the men stopped pushing and Naftuli read some psalms. After about ten minutes of this I saw one of the men who was pushing having a difficult time because they were going up an icy hill that led to the gravesite. I tapped him on the shoulder and took his place. I had taken my gloves off so I could feel the camera controls better, and now my hands were really hurting, as if burning, from the freezing air.

Who would have thought that pushing a little old ninety-year-old woman would be so strenuous? It was the stopping uphill to allow Naftuli to recite some psalms that was the most difficult. Any forward momentum we had gained was always lost. Finally, after another five minutes we got to the gravesite. We removed the velvet mantle, lifted the shrouded body off the stretcher (I had never touched a limp dead leg before), and lowered it into the grave.

The next few minutes were a comedy of errors that the Marx Brothers would have been proud of. First the body got stuck in the grave at a strange angle. The grave had not been dug long enough to accommodate it. One man took a shovel and tried knocking loose some of the dirt around the head to create a little more space. He had a difficult time because the earth was frozen solid. Then Naftuli jumped into the grave and tried to move some of the dirt with his bare hands, to no avail. Finally Naftuli motioned to me to grab the shovel and jump into the grave. Without a moment's thought, I grabbed the shovel, lowered myself into the seven-feet-deep grave, and began stabbing the dirt and stone around the woman's head. Finally I dislodged a huge stone that allowed us to lower the body to the floor of the grave.

Naftuli took off the shroud from the woman's head and placed shards on her eyelids. This was done so that her eyes would only open when the Messiah had appeared. Then he took out of his pocket a plastic bag containing dirt from Israel and sprinkled it around the grave. This was done because even though the woman died in the Diaspora she still was buried with earth from the Holy Land. Naftuli recited the Elmolerakhamim ("God is full of mercy," a prayer) and the Kaddish and then we both climbed out of the grave on our hands and knees. Naftuli shoveled some dirt into the grave, then laid the shovel down and quietly walked away. The cemetery worker finished the job.

By this time everyone who had come to the gravesite had left, but I stayed to take a few more photos of Naftuli walking in the distance. The fading afternoon light splayed through the clouds on the horizon created such a beautiful tableau that the cemetery had both an ominous and a sacred feel to it. No camera I could have had would have captured the scene as I remember it.

KOSICE

There is a Jewish legend that a minimum of thirty-six anonymous righteous men in the world in each generation——the Lamed Vovniks——are needed to help preserve the world, and these thirty-six are known only to God. One

Naftuli Blau,
Bratislava

thing became clear to me on my trip: if these Lamed Vovniks existed, then I met one in Kosice, Czechoslovakia, and his name was Eli Mermelshteyn.

I hadn't slept at all on the night train from Bratislava to Kosice, having been kept awake by five big, smelly, soiled, and drunken couchette-mates who barked and laughed as they smoked and passed around a bottle of bathtub gin.

From the time I checked into the hotel to the time I ventured out to find the shul (about two hours) it had snowed eight inches. Quite lovely, but not so lovely to realize your boot has sprung a leak in a driving snowstorm. It was a straight shot from my hotel to the shul and luckily not too far. With every step, I could feel the slushy, freezing water soak more and more of my sock.

The shul, at 5 Zvonarska Street, formed part of the wall that enclosed the courtyard. The shul was locked and there was no one in the *besmedresh,* so I walked around looking for the *kehile* office, figuring it would be located in the courtyard. I heard some typing upstairs and followed the sound to a corner office. I was anxious to get inside so I could take off my boot and dry my sock. My toes were starting to feel numb.

I knocked and knocked, but whoever was typing didn't hear me or was ignoring the knocking. So I slowly turned the doorknob and walked in. At the other end of the room sat a lean man with a worn green sweater and small gray fedora, hunched over this old fashioned typewriter. He looked to be in his mid-sixties, with a terrible overbite. He turned his head and said, "*Sholom aleykhem*. I will be finished in one minute."

I went over to a space heater, sat down, and took off both boots and socks. Then I draped the wet sock over the heater. The man kept typing, so I wandered the room looking at the photos, paintings, and books.

On one wall was a photo of the Munkatsher *rebe* Rabbi Hayim Eliezer (1868–1937). The Munkatsher Hasidim were known for singing some beautiful *nigunim*. And since Kosice wasn't far from Munkatsh (Ukraine), maybe I'd find some people who remembered some of their melodies.

I wandered through another two adjacent rooms, trying not to seem impatient, but now I was wondering if this guy would ever finish typing. Plus, my feet were aching and a chill was creeping through my body. Finally he stopped his work.

"Sorry for the delay. I had to fill out these forms and write an obituary. A member of our *kehile,* an eighty-one-year-old man, passed away last night and we will bury him today."

This is how I met Eli Mermelshteyn, who was born in Batfa on the Slovakian-Ukrainian border in 1920. He had lived in Kosice since the end of the war, working as a bookkeeper for a few small businesses before he retired, and then became the secretary and bookkeeper for the *kehile*.

Unfortunately Eli didn't have much time to chat because he had to help make all the preparations for the burial. He told me to come to shul the next day at 7 A.M. and then after the morning prayers we could talk. He had been an amateur fiddler and knew some klezmer tunes. He told me I could stay as long as I liked in the office so I could completely dry my sock and boot; then he left.

A Pious Man

When I left it was still snowing out and I considered staying inside to write and practice the rest of the day, but I thought of the funeral. Eli had invited me, but I had declined. But maybe I could be of some help? I really didn't want to go, but I started to feel a little guilty. How could I stay here in this warm room while the old buried the old? I asked the hotel clerk for a map and directions.

He asked, "You know Jews in Kosice?"

"I just was at the synagogue down the street."

"More dead Jews at cemetery than on the street."

"Well, thanks for your insight. I have to go meet some living Jews."

By the time I got to the cemetery the funeral procession was pushing a wagon with the body to the gravesite. None of the attendees looked wracked with grief; if anything, the pain on their faces was from the cold, biting wind. Looking out at the funeral while taking photographs, I had a pain in my heart. I was witnessing and recording the end of Yiddish culture as my grandparents knew it. With every death there was one less Jew whose mother tongue was Yiddish.

I saw Eli and he pointed out to me some of the key people in the *kehile*. There was Shimshon Grossman, who recited the prayers. He was the *shoykhet* for all of Slovakia and the de facto religious leader of the *kehile*. He was born in Michalovce. Then there was Binyomin Bernshteyn, who was the *kehile's shames.* He was born in Kralovsky Chlumec, a small town on the border of Hungary. And there were the Goldberger brothers, Yitskhok and Mordekhay. They were both born near Kosice and ran the kosher kitchen. Even though I hadn't really wanted to go to the funeral, it paid off. I got a quick overview of some of the key people in the *kehile* and they met me.

A couple of days later, as he was koshering chickens, Shimshon Grossman said something I never forgot:

"You probably think it is difficult to be a Jew here. Well, it is only difficult when you do not have faith in the Almighty. We are fortunate to have a shul, but even if we didn't have an actual physical building it wouldn't matter. Every Jew carries within himself his own spiritual place, the foundation of the Temple itself, in his soul. Tomorrow I will sing some songs from my own personal Temple during *shaloshudes*." (This is the third meal, which takes place on Shabes at midafternoon. Torah or Talmud is studied and there are singing and refreshments.)

Eli was a master storyteller. He recounted some enchanting stories about his life in the Carpathian Mountains before he and his entire family were transported to Auschwitz. Two stories in particular gave me a sense of Eli's character:

"In 1933, when I was thirteen years old, I met a girl named Moncy. She had beautiful black hair and I had feelings for her. She and her parents were visiting the mountains from Kosice for the summer months. She told me she loved the violin, so I thought I'd learn to play for her. By the end of the summer, I had taught myself how to play a few Hasidic *nigunim*. I then went to her window one evening to play for her, but, sadly, she had already gone back to Kosice with her parents. I never saw her again.

"We didn't have a shul in our village so I walked every Shabes about ten kilometers to Velki Kapusany with my father. My father was the *bal-tfile* and loved to sing. So while we walked to shul he practiced singing his prayers and made me repeat them, so I knew them too. He said it wouldn't look good if the *bal-tfile's* son couldn't *daven*. He also liked to sing Yiddish songs he had learned. 'Vu Zaynen Mayne Ziben Gite Yor?' [Where Are My Seven Good Years?] was one of his favorites, because, he said, although a Jew always should accept what God had given him, he still had the right to ask and even argue with Him for something better.

"When the war began we were all deported to Auschwitz: my parents, sister, and younger brother. Only my sister and I survived. The last time I saw my father was when he was led into the gas chambers."

After Eli said his last word he put his head down into his arms, which were folded across the table, and began to softly cry. This of course made me cry as well. I jumped up for the box of tissues I spotted on the bookshelf. It was then that I saw the scroll of the violin hanging over the edge of the shelf eight feet above me. I dragged the chair over to reach it. All of its strings were there, but it was badly out of tune, so I quickly began to tune it.

I played him the song I had just learned in Bratislava. This prompted him to tell me one more wonderful story.

"You know my mother loved to sing Yiddish songs. I learned prayers from my father but all the Yiddish songs I know today I learned from my mother. When she sang she forgot whatever she was doing, so if she was ironing or cooking our clothes and food were both burned. But she truly was a nightingale of Yiddish song."

Then Eli sang one of his favorite Yiddish folk songs—it happened to be one of mine as well. I had learned it as "Bulbes" (potatoes); he had learned it as "Beblekh" (beans).

I asked him if he remembered any of the tunes from the itinerant klezmers who'd come through his village. He played me one tune he remembered in particular because the klezmer was blind. When this klezmer came to town

"Bulbes/Beblekh" (Potatoes/Beans)

Traditional

Zintik bulbes, Montik bulbes,	Sunday potatoes, Monday potatoes,
Dinstik un Mitvokh bulbes,	Tuesday and Wednesday potatoes,
Donershtik un Fraytik bulbes,	Thursday and Friday potatoes,
Shabes in a novene, a bulbes-kigele,	Sabbath there is a surprise, a potato pudding,
Zintik vayter bulbes!	Sunday continue with potatoes!
Broyt mit bulbes, fleysh mit bulbes,	Bread with potatoes, meat with potatoes,
varemes un vetshere bulbes,	lunch and dinner potatoes,
ober un vider bulbes,	over and over potatoes,
eyn mol in a novene, a bulbes-kigele,	once, for a special treat, there is a potato pudding,
Zintik vayter bulbes!	Sunday continue with potatoes!
Ober bulbes, vider bulbes,	Still potatoes, ever potatoes,
nokh amol un ober amol bulbes,	always and again potatoes,
haynt un morgn bulbes,	today and tomorrow potatoes,
ober shabes nokhn tcholnt, a bulbes-kigele,	but after Sabbath pot roast, there is a potato pudding,
Zintik vayter bulbes!	Sunday continue with potatoes!
Zintik beblekh, Montik beblekh,	Sunday beans, Monday beans,
Dinstik un Mitvokh beblekh,	Tuesday and Wednesday beans,
Donershtik un Fraytik beblekh,	Thursday and Friday beans,
Shabes in a novene, a beblekh-kigele,	Sabbath there is a surprise, a bean pudding,
Zintik vayter beblekh!	Sunday continue with beans!
Shvemlekh mit beblekh, kapuste mit beblekh,	Mushrooms with beans, cabbage with beans,
gepregelt un tseribene beblekh,	fried and crushed beans,
nokh amol un ober amol beblekh,	again and again beans,
Shabes in a novene, beblekh mit smetene,	Sabbath there is a surprise, beans with sour cream,
Zintik vayter beblekh!	Sunday continue with beans!

with his band, he was always invited over to Eli's house for a meal. Then Eli would walk him to the town square, where he and the rest of the band would give a concert for donations before traveling to their next location.

Over the next few days I hung out with Eli and followed him wherever he went. I shopped for the food and medicine that the *kehile* would buy and distribute to poor, elderly housebound Jews. I visited his sister, who was ill and didn't get out much, and we visited the local city archives to look at some of the photos of Jewish life before the war.

Eli was such a selfless man, doing so much for others, that I wondered why he hadn't done something for himself—like move to Israel.

"When we returned to Kosice after the war, my sister was quite sick and couldn't travel. Then in December 1946 she married a gentile. We had still planned to immigrate to Israel but I waited for her and she waited for her husband. I didn't want to leave her all alone. She was my only family to have survived the gas chambers. I always I had my bags packed, but the years have taken their toll on both of us. Now she is a widow and too sick and too many others in the *kehile* depend on me. It's like that song my father used to sing, 'Where Are My Seven Good Years?'—if not seven, God, how about just a few?"

I was so awestruck by Eli's benevolence that I wanted to stay in Kosice longer than I had planned just to be with Eli and help him. Whether one of God's chosen Lamed Vovniks or simply an *ish ha-tsadek* (Hebrew, pious person), I could really learn a lot from my new friend.

Hidden Microphone

On the following Shabes, I went to shul. It was 3 P.M. and the sun was sitting low on the horizon. The rays poked through the speckled cloud cover and mixed with the light snowfall, bathing the streets and crumbling buildings in a luminescent glow.

The Shabes goy (a gentile who makes the fire and turns on the light for observant Jews) had stoked the heater with a lot of coal, so the room was quite toasty. At first I was a bit surprised to find twelve men sitting around the table either studying or talking. But then I realized that to these pensioners, *shaloshudes* was not just a religious custom but an important recreational event every Shabes afternoon, especially during winter. It gave them a forum where they could socialize with free food and drink on a wintry day. And who would turn down free food and drink?

I wasn't allowed to take any photos because Shimshon Grossman didn't allow it. This also meant no visible tape recorder either during *shaloshudes* later on. I had a plan, however. While they studied, I went to the bathroom to tape the tape recorder to my upper thigh. Then I plugged the microphone into the machine and ran its cord up my shirt sleeve and secured the mike to my wrist with tape. I could start, stop, and pause the tape recorder from the controls on the microphone. I put in fresh batteries and a one-hour tape. I was quite proud of the contraption. Now I just needed some good tunes— and to remember not to move my right arm very much so I wouldn't get any sleeve or mike sound.

I sat down in between the Goldberger brothers and helped myself to some chickpeas, pickled black radish, and *kikhlekh* (egg and wheat sugar cookies) and just watched and listened as Shimshon led a discussion on a passage from the Talmud. After another ten minutes he closed the Talmud and took out his prayer book. He said a few words in Yiddish and the Torah portion and then began to sing a *zmiros* (song sung especially on Shabes). I discreetly turned on the tape recorder with both my arms under the table. Then I gently placed my arm on the table and turned it toward Shimshon.

Unfortunately, I had a directional microphone: it had to be pointed exactly toward the source of the music for the best results and fidelity. After Shimshon finished singing, the man sitting next to him started another *zmiros* and then when he finished, the next man, and so forth. This custom forced everyone to be a leader as well as a participant. As each new *zmiros* was introduced the volume level grew. Then some of the men began to pound out the rhythm of the song on the table. I had to be careful because my arm was resting on the table. Soon some of the men even began to dance.

What a scene this was, with the last rays of the day's natural light coming through the windows onto the large chipped, wine-stained wooden table covered with *sidurim,* Talmuds, food crumbs, and shot glasses. Those not dancing sat around the table pounding their fists with their eyes closed and mouths agape.

Added to this were the darting shadows of the men cast upon the back wall by the light of the *yartzayt* candles (memorial candles lit for the anniversary of those who have died). Where was my camera when I needed it? This was a Roman Vishniac photograph come to life.

The room was beginning to get quite warm, with the fire in the heater and the heat being generated by the dancing. All of a sudden Eli grabbed my arm and pulled me up to dance. I joined him for half a minute, forgetting that I had the tape recorder taped to my thigh. When I remembered, it was too late—to my great embarrassment, it fell to the floor.

Luckily, in the din of the room no one noticed but Eli. I quickly dragged my foot toward the back door that led to the bathroom. Eli came over to shield me as I bent down to pick it up. I then stepped inside the bathroom, took off the contraption, put it away in my backpack, and returned to join the others in their *shaloshudes* revelry. Then Eli came over and whispered in my ear: "You got the good songs. They will finish soon."

Hanukkah Party

On the first night of Hanukkah a small party was held at the kosher kitchen. As I walked to the shul courtyard, I realized I had been on the road nearly six months. I felt good knowing I had collected more klezmer tunes

Eli Mermelshteyn,
Kosice

Latkes

POTATO PANCAKES

3½ dozen latkes

First, you cannot walk away from frying latkes. Second, be sure to squeeze the excess moisture out of each spoonful of batter before you place it in the oil—this will give you a nice latke that sticks together, but more important, it will prevent splattering. Third, never turn a latke more than once: using the tip of a metal spatula, gently lift one edge—if the whole latke moves, it's time to turn it over. The same is true for the other side—a perfectly fried latke will want to leave the pan. About the oil: canola is the healthiest you can go with no added taste, but peanut oil has a low smoke point—you choose.

These latkes freeze well: simply transfer the cooled latkes to a lidded container, using waxed paper in between the layers, and freeze. Before serving, heat the oven to 450°, transfer the frozen latkes to a baking sheet in a single layer, and bake for 12 minutes.

10 medium (not small!) russet potatoes, washed but not peeled	2 large onions
1 cup flour	4 whole eggs
2 Tbsp. salt	Canola or peanut oil for frying
54 grinds of fresh pepper	Sour cream
	Applesauce

and seen more of Jewish life than I ever anticipated. I hoped tonight's party would be the capper for the midway point of my trek.

The kosher kitchen was filled with all the usual suspects as well as Jews from the *kehile* whom I had not met. It was especially gratifying to see a number of young people and children. There was a tape player blaring out the traditional Hanukkah songs; it sounded like a cassette from Israel. Some played dreydl, gambling with chocolate gelt, while others stood around talking and eating the latkes and jelly-filled donuts. These were really tasty, crunchy latkes. The Goldberger brothers were busy cooking and serving,

1. Cut anything discolored from the potatoes but don't peel them. Cut the potatoes and onions into large chunks (to feed through the food processor).

2. In a large mixing bowl, combine the flour, salt, and pepper.

3. In a food processor fitted with a grating disc, feed the onions and potatoes together. If the processor fills, dump the contents in with the flour mixture and keep going until all the potatoes and onions are done.

4. Break one egg at a time into a small mixing bowl and stir. Add to the processed potato-onion mixture and stir until well combined.

5. Heat your frying pan, and add 1 inch of oil. With impeccably clean hands, mix the batter thoroughly. As you go, the batter will get wetter and wetter, but it doesn't matter! Working with a small spoonful at a time, squeeze the batter out in your fist and then *transfer back to the spoon* (you don't want your hands in hot oil, right?). One squeezed-out spoonful at a time, lay the batter gently in the oil and press gently to flatten. Place the latkes around the edge of the pan and put one final one in the center (about 6 latkes per panful) because the center one will cook the fastest. Cook about 3 minutes on a side, turning only once to cook both sides—they should be dark, as opposed to golden, brown. Transfer to a platter or baking sheet covered with paper towels. After draining a short while, flip each latke to blot the other side. Serve topped with sour cream or applesauce.

Shimshon was telling a Hanukkah story to some parents and children, and Eli and I sat at a table with a plate full of latkes smeared in thick sour cream, drinking delicious Czech beer.

I stayed a bit longer to talk with some of the people my age. I got a sense from our conversations that if given the opportunity, they would leave Kosice—a few for the United States but most for Israel. This was mainly due not to their just being weary of the political situation in Czechoslovakia, but to the severe economic predicament the country was in and their limited job opportunities.

I ate my fill of the latkes, and the Goldberger brothers, like good Jewish mothers, packed me a box full of latkes and jelly-filled donuts. They were delicious, but I wasn't sure how they would taste tomorrow night in their greasy day-old condition.

When I entered the shul courtyard I could hear Eli practicing his violin. He said I had inspired him to play once again. Then he told me he had a Hanukkah gift for me. He took his violin (holding it folk style against his breastbone) and began to play a beautiful Hanukkah melody he had learned from his mother. After he finished playing we hugged each other and said our good-byes. I honestly could say I was going to miss him.

Eli helped me take my bags to the street, then I leisurely walked to the station. How ironic and sorrowful it was that thirty-seven years ago the train I was about to board to Krakow had traveled the same rail line to Poland, only it carried Eli and his family to their nightmare in Auschwitz.

Chapter Four

POLAND

I ARRIVED IN KRAKOW with reservations about coming to Poland at all. At the height of Yiddish culture it had been the capital of "Yiddishland" in Eastern Europe. At the time of my visit, for most Jews in the world, it had become a gigantic graveyard.

As I walked, I noticed a kind of subdued pall over the city. Every few blocks, groups of police and armed soldiers stood on the street corners, warily eyeing the people and traffic as they passed. I then recalled that the premier, Wojciech Jaruzelski, had declared martial law only ten days earlier. No wonder the border crossing had been so easy—I had entered a country that was currently under siege by its own government! Leaving probably wouldn't be as simple.

KRAKOW

At the train station an old lady greeted me by grabbing my instruments and camera bag. I had followed her for half an hour when she turned down a street and pointed ahead to what I figured was her apartment building. We had passed some streets with Jewish names—Izaaka, Jozefa, and Estery. Perhaps I was going to be staying in Kazimiercz, the former Jewish quarter. (The Jews were expelled from Kroke by the Jews in 1495 and moved to Kazimiercz, which was next to Krakow. Many of Krakow's Jewish institutions were built in Kazimiercz.) Sure enough, we entered the dark corridor of 17 Szeroka Street. As we walked up the six flights of stairs, I noticed and smelled the debris littering the stairwell. I hoped the lady's place had hot water and a toilet.

After I unpacked, I went out to get some lunch and visit the *kehile* office. The weather was cold and overcast. As I walked through Kazimiercz I noticed the charm of the buildings. The older architecture dated from the fifteenth and sixteenth centuries, while the newer was from the nineteenth century. The Krakowians had the ironic luck to have had their city become the capital of the Polish General Government (October 12, 1939) during the Holocaust under Hans Frank, the governor general, who made his headquarters and home in the Wawel Castle. Consequently, the Germans did not systematically strafe and bomb the city as they had Warsaw.

Walking around Kazimiercz, I got a sense of how Jewish this area had been. In some ways it reminded me of the Jewish quarter in Prague, where all the Jewish buildings and Jewish-named streets were located in a small neighborhood; but unlike Prague, Kazimiercz hadn't been refurbished and maintained. Instead, the buildings were falling apart; some were abandoned, with homeless and alcoholic squatters; garbage overflowed from the bins strewn across the streets; and there were few commercial buildings. This once glorious Jewish quarter now looked like a slum. I discovered later that the *kehile* was too poor to maintain all of the approximately 130 formerly Jewish-owned buildings. Most were owned by the state and had been converted into factories, warehouses, and residences.

At a small grocery store, I bought some delicious blackberry kefir and what they called a bagel. It was round, small, hard, and not nearly as doughy as the bagels in America. It was like a cross between an unsalted pretzel and our bagel. It had just come from the bakery and was still warm. It tasted so good that it became my staple snack throughout my stay in Poland.

Leopold Kozlowski: The Last Klezmer

I first met Leopold through the *kehile* offices. An elderly woman whose lack of spark matched the drably furnished interior of the *kehile* building had given me his name. While I would never return to the *kehile* offices, I would be eternally grateful for this introduction to Leopold, because with him, I hit the mother lode of my klezmer research.

When I arrived at his apartment, Leopold had just come home from a rehearsal with two non-Jewish singers preparing to do a Yiddish cabaret concert. He lived in a modest two-bedroom apartment that had the usual nondescript décor: a couple of armchairs, a couch, a few paintings on the walls, some throw rugs, plus an upright piano in the living room. Leopold was short and stocky, with a bald pate with graying fringes, thick mutton-chop sideburns, and a mustache. He was quite animated in his speech and had a kind of cute elfin quality. He spoke fluent Yiddish occasionally mixed with some German. Leopold's wife was resting in the bedroom, but he invited

The Jewish History of Poland

By the sixteenth century, Poland was the undisputed leader in Ashkenazic religious scholarship. Polish yeshivas became so numerous that the majority of Jewish males knew both Hebrew and Aramaic and were well versed in the Talmud and the commentaries.

The Polish Jewry established a countrywide organization of the *kehiles* called the Va'ad Arbe Aratsot (Hebrew, Council of the Four Lands). This was constituted at a congress in Lublin in 1581. The Va'ad Arbe Aratsot represented all the Jews and governed all aspects of Jewish life. It lasted until 1764.

In 1648–49, the Cossack leader Bogdan Chmielnicki (1595–1657) led the Cossacks and the Tatars in a revolt against the Polish nobility, whom they regarded as exploiters of the Ukrainian peasants. Even though most Jews were just as exploited, Ukrainian and Polish peasants looked upon them as bitter enemies.

The Chmielnicki massacres were the worst tragedy to happen to the Jews prior to the Holocaust: some historians claim that more than two hundred thousand Jews were murdered and three hundred Jewish communities destroyed.

Just as the Jewish populace was beginning to fully recover from the Chmielnicki massacres, a peasant revolt was organized by the Haidamacks (paramilitary bands of Ukrainians) in 1768. Many tens of thousands of Jews were murdered. Subsequently the majority of the Jews were so downtrodden they were ripe for a new spiritual leader.

The philosophy known today as Hasidism saw its beginnings in the eighteenth century. The movement was founded in the village of Mezibozh in the Carpathian Mountains by Israel ben Eliezer (c. 1700–1760), better known as the Ba'al Shem Tov (Hebrew, master of the good name). The Ba'al Shem Tov was a healer, herbalist, and informal preacher who was able to have conversations with learned rabbis, simple Jews, and non-Jews alike. He taught that there were no divisions between sacred and secular. He rejected asceticism and emphasized joyfulness. By the end of the nineteenth century there were some two million Hasidim living in Poland and another two million outside of the country. This philosophy ultimately influenced the character of the shtetl more than any other.

The beginning of the end of Poland's independence occurred in 1772 when it was first partitioned by Austria, Prussia, and Russia. The third and last partition occurred in 1795, and independent Poland disappeared until 1919. However, Polish Jewry continued to grow and by the end of the nineteenth century there were about 1,250,000 Jews living in the territories of former Poland—about 70 percent of all the Jews in the world.

During the late nineteenth century, thousands of Polish Jews were killed in pogroms, spurring thousands more to escape to the United States, England, Canada, and Latin America. The same period also saw the development of Zionism, the Jewish labor movement, and socialism, as well as a revival of the Hebrew language.

More pogroms contributed to the general horror of World War I. The Treaty of Versailles attempted to protect Jewish rights in the Polish state reborn after the war. But the new government limited Jewish participation in commercial life and in many ways continued to encourage Polish anti-Semitism. Many Jews chose to leave Poland, thus draining the *kehiles* of their vitality.

During the interwar years, despite economic and social hardships, the *kehiles* throughout Poland were culturally still vibrant, making Poland the capital of Yiddish culture in the world. There were Jewish cafés, literary salons, Yiddish and Hebrew newspapers, magazines, books, Yiddish theater, films, and plenty of klezmer. By 1938, nearly 37 percent of the total population of the city of Warsaw was Jewish.

The destruction of this bastion of Jewish culture began on September 1, 1939, when 1.7 million German soldiers invaded Poland. On September 17, 1939, the Soviet Union invaded and by the end of the month the country capitulated. Germany and the Soviet Union partitioned Poland along the Bug River. Those Jews who could escaped to Soviet-occupied Poland, where they lived relatively normal lives unless they were deported to gulags or to the Central Asian republics. Then Germany attacked the Soviet Union on June 22, 1941, the final death knell for Polish Jewry.

The Holocaust quickly revealed its most horrible face to Polish Jewry. The ghettos, concentration camps, and labor camps, and the gas chambers of Auschwitz-Birkenau, Belzec, Treblinka, Maidanek, Sobibor, and elsewhere saw the willful murder of three million Polish Jews.

At the end of the war there were about 250,000 Jews throughout Poland. Some returned home from the camps, others from the forests and other hiding places, but the majority came from the Soviet Union. After several pogroms throughout Poland in 1946, many Jews left for good. By 1960 most had immigrated to Israel, and the Jewish population of Poland was 35,000. Then in 1968 the Polish Communist government launched a major anti-Semitic campaign, blaming those "rootless cosmopolitans" (code for Jews) for not being patriotic and trustworthy. This led to the last of the large-scale emigrations of Jews from Poland.

Officially, there were around seven thousand Jews in Poland in 1981 and are ten to twelve thousand today, although the actual figure is probably closer to twenty thousand.

me into the kitchen and offered to cook me lunch. When I told him I was a vegetarian he replied:

"A klezmer without meat is worse than a boy without his *bris.*"

I was taken aback for just a moment, but then joined Leopold in his hearty laughter. This was the first of many such Yiddish sayings and jokes with which Leopold would regale me over the course of our meetings.

While he cooked, he hummed a klezmer tune written by his father. I was so excited about meeting him—I wanted to just record every moment—that I asked if I could begin tape recording him while he cooked. But he

Kasha with Mushrooms and Onions

Makes 6 to 8 servings

This recipe turned me into a kasha fan. And now that I make it regularly, I have become a successful "kasha missionary"—even first-timers love it! It's one of the healthiest vegetable proteins. Add a package of cooked bowtie noodles for kasha *varnishkes.*

2 to 3 Tbsp. vegetable oil	Salt and pepper to taste
2 large onions, chopped into 1-inch pieces	1 cup whole kasha (uncooked buckwheat groats)
2 cups sliced mixed mushrooms (button, portobello, shiitake, cremini)	1 large egg
1 clove garlic, minced	2 cups hot chicken or vegetable stock
	Fresh chopped parsley for garnish

1. In a large skillet with a fitted lid, heat the oil and brown the onions, mushrooms, and garlic. Transfer to a bowl and wipe out the skillet with a paper towel. Season the mushroom/onion mixture with salt and pepper.

2. Beat the egg in a small bowl and add the kasha to thoroughly coat. Return the skillet to the heat. Add the kasha in a thin layer and stir for 2 to 3 minutes to toast. Reduce the heat and add the stock. Stir, cover, and simmer until the stock is absorbed, about 7 to 8 minutes.

3. Stir in the onions and mushrooms. Garnish with parsley and serve.

wanted to eat lunch first and get to know me a little better before we began to "work together," as he put it. He said if I was patient I would leave home with some of the finest klezmer tunes ever heard in Krakow (he also was not one to shy away from hyperbole), so I sat down to a lunch that held me until breakfast the next day. I had kasha and mushrooms, homemade cabbage with apples, black bread and butter, and for dessert, poppy seed cookies and prune tarts baked by his wife.

After lunch, Leopold said, "I have one small favor to ask you. I need you to help shlep something from the basement to the street."

All I had to do, Leopold explained, was get a hot-water tank up twenty-five stairs with an old dolly and leather straps. At first, I thought he was joking; but when I saw the hot-water tank I knew he was serious. After a great deal of shlepping, straining, and sweating, I got it up the stairs and across the street. Finally ready to get down to business, I began to get out my recording gear. But just then, Leopold remembered he had to go to the Krakow radio

Kapusta z Jablkamy
POLISH CABBAGE WITH APPLES
Makes 6 servings

1 medium head green cabbage, shredded

2 medium onions, sliced into thin rounds

1 16-oz. can sauerkraut, drained

1 Tbsp. butter or margarine

4 medium-sized tart green apples, peeled, cored, and sliced

1 tsp. sugar

Salt to taste

1. Put the cabbage and onions in a large bowl and cover with boiling water. Let stand for 10 minutes. Drain.

2. Melt the butter in a large saucepan with a fitted lid. Add the cabbage and onions, the apples, and the sauerkraut.

3. Add the sugar and simmer until tender, about 20 minutes. Salt to taste while cooking.

station to give a twenty-minute live Hanukkah concert that would be broadcast across the whole country.

I asked if I could come and watch, but he told me he couldn't bring any guests without advance notice. I accepted this answer. But as I would get to know Leopold over the years, I would realize that he never felt 100 percent at ease about broadcasting his Jewishness (or my working with him) to non-Jewish strangers. I am sure that this suppression began during the Holocaust.

The next day, Leopold met me at his door in his suspenders and undershirt, with greasy hands, in the middle of making lunch. I walked to the sofa in the

Polish Poppy Seed Cookies

Makes approximately 6 dozen

These cookies are traditionally mild in flavor; they are also quick and easy to make.

2 sticks unsalted butter, room temperature	1 large egg yolk
1 cup superfine sugar	Juice from half a large navel orange
Pinch of salt	Grated zest from a large navel orange
1 large egg	2½ cups all-purpose flour
	3 Tbsp. poppy seeds

1. In a large bowl, place the butter, sugar, salt, egg and egg yolk, orange juice, and zest. With an electric mixer on medium or by hand, beat until fluffy and well blended.

2. Reduce the speed to low and add the flour and poppy seeds. Beat just to combine; do not overmix. Divide the dough into four pieces and shape into flattened balls. Wrap in plastic wrap and refrigerate for one hour.

3. Preheat the oven to 375°. Line baking sheets with baking parchment.

4. Working with one ball of dough at a time (keep the others refrigerated), pinch off a teaspoonful of dough and roll between your palms to smooth. Place balls of dough on the parchment ½ inch apart. Refrigerate any leftover dough for the next batch.

5. Bake until the cookies are golden, about 12 minutes. Transfer immediately to racks to cool.

other room and sat down while Leopold talked to me from the kitchen. As I browsed through his Yiddish music books, Leopold told me he had just finished arranging the music for the next production at the Yiddish State Theater. They were going to be presenting Sholom Aleichem's play *Di Yerushe* (Yiddish, The Inheritance). (Sholom Aleichem, 1859–1916, was a Yiddish writer and playwright who took his name from the traditional Yiddish greeting.) I asked him who went to the theater and he explained there were still Jews, as well as many Poles, who loved to see stories about Jewish life before the Holocaust.

"Yitskhok, the gentiles are nostalgic about Jewish culture because it was so much an important part of their own."

Then he told me how good the actors were and that he was most proud about the fact that the non-Jewish actors sang the Yiddish songs as if Yiddish were their mother tongue. For me this sounded a little strange, but as I was finding out, in the Eastern bloc Jewish life had taken on many different permutations.

Finally, lunch was ready: scrambled eggs with garlic and onions, cheese and sauerkraut pierogi, and black currant–raspberry pie. I complimented Leopold on his cooking prowess and he replied, "All my friends tell me I am the best klezmer among the cooks and the best cook among the klezmers."

While we ate, Leopold asked me if I had ever heard of the virtuoso klezmer clarinetist Naftule Brandwein, who played and recorded klezmer in the United States after he immigrated after World War I. In fact, I knew who he was and loved to play his soulful "Firn Di Mekhutonim Aheym" (Yiddish, Leading the In-Laws Home). To my astonishment, Leopold told me that Brandwein had been his uncle. I couldn't believe it. I was sitting with the great Naftule Brandwein's nephew!

I asked him what he could tell me about him. He replied, "Yitskhok, I was hoping *you* could tell *me* more about my uncle. He left for America before I was born. But before we continue, let me hear you play a klezmer tune on your fiddle."

I washed my hands, opened the violin case, rosined the bow, adjusted the shoulder rest, tuned the strings, and then nervously began to play Brandwein's "Firn Di Mekhutonim Aheym." I was more nervous now than I had ever been during the whole journey up to this point. I got to the sixth measure when Leopold stopped me and began correcting my fingering, bowing, and ornamentation. We continued with the lesson for the next hour, only stopping because Leopold ran out of things to correct.

Pierogi

Makes about 3½ dozen

The sauerkraut pierogi are a bit labor-intensive but really worth the effort. If you want to cut down on a step, you can try substituting frozen empanada wrappers, if your market has them; if you do, thaw them thoroughly. It's not an exact match, but for me, these are all about the filling. As with all stuffed dough, from ravioli to samosas, be careful to not over-stuff, or your pierogi will spring a leak during cooking. One teaspoon of filling is all that's re-quired for each pierogi. Another note: if you use egg white to seal the pierogi, use it on only one side—it will stick to the dough but not to itself. Finally, note that the sauerkraut filling must be refrigerated overnight before proceeding.

For the sauerkraut filling:

1 small head green cabbage
2 10-oz. cans sauerkraut, rinsed, drained,
    liquid pressed out
1 small onion, chopped fine
1 clove garlic, minced
1 stick plus 2 Tbsp. butter or margarine
Salt and pepper to taste

For the dough:

4 cups flour (approximately)
3 medium potatoes, boiled and mashed
2 to 3 Tbsp. potato flour or corn flour
1 egg
¼ cup water
½ teaspoon salt
1 egg white (optional)

For the cheese filling:

1 cup farmer's cheese
2 tsp. butter, melted
1 egg, beaten
2 Tbsp. sugar
1 Tbsp. lemon juice

1. *For the sauerkraut filling:* Shred the cabbage and place in a pot. Cover with boiling water to scald. Cover the pot, bring back up to a boil, and cook for 15 minutes. Rinse, drain, cool, and thoroughly wring out all the moisture. Place in a bowl and add the sauerkraut.

2. In a separate large skillet, simmer the onion and garlic in 3 tablespoons of the butter until translucent. Add the sauerkraut mixture and the remaining butter, stir to combine, and add salt and pepper to taste. Simmer, covered, until tender. Uncover and simmer, stirring constantly, until all the liquid evaporates. Transfer to a colander in the sink and press out any remaining moisture. Allow to cool. Process in a food processor until fine. Transfer to a bowl, cover, and refrigerate overnight prior to making the pierogi.

3. *For the cheese filling:* Combine all the ingredients and refrigerate 1 hour.

4. *For the dough:* Combine the flour, potatoes, potato flour, egg, and salt and knead thoroughly. The dough should have a smooth, elastic consistency. Add the water in small amounts if needed.

5. To assemble the pierogi, sprinkle your rolling surface and rolling pin with plenty of flour. Roll out the dough to about ¼ inch thick and use a 4-inch round biscuit or cookie cutter to cut out circles.

6. Place about 1 teaspoonful of filling on each round, fold in half and seal the edges. If the dough is too dry, brush a bit of egg white on one side to seal.

7. Bring a large pot of water to a boil and season liberally with salt. Place about 8 pierogi at a time in the water. Lower the heat and simmer gently for 6 to 7 minutes, turning them over once halfway through. Use a slotted spoon to transfer to a colander in the sink. Rinse with hot water and drain. Serve with sour cream.

Eventually, over the course of my stay in Krakow, Leopold told me more about himself.

"I was born in Przemyslany, which is near Lemberg [Lviv, Ukraine]. My grandfather, Peysekh Brandwein, who played the violin, had ten sons and four daughters from four different wives, all of whom played in his band. They performed throughout the county of Volyn in Galicia and were hired to play not only for the Jews but for the rich Polish landowners. My grandfather even played for Kaiser Franz Joseph when he got married, and for the Premishlaner *rebe* Rabbi Mayer ben Aron Leyb [c. 1780–1850] during the intermediary days of *Sukes* and *Peysekh*. Just before World War I all the sons immigrated to America, except for three, including my father. My father formed his own large band. They performed in Galicia as well as Lemberg, Tarnopol, Stanislawow [L'viv, Ternopil, Ivano Frankivs'k, all in Ukraine today], and other towns in eastern Poland.

"When the Depression came, my father's band disbanded and he formed a band with me on accordion, my brother Dulko on violin, Shia Tsimbler on *tsimbl,* Dugi Brandwein on *sekund,* and Hirshele Dudlezack on drums. Then in 1933 my father went to Tres Arroyos, Argentina, where he was concertmaster in the philharmonic. He returned in 1937. Four years later, on November 5, 1941, he was led into a forest with 360 other Jews from the Przemyslany ghetto and shot by the SS. A little later on, my mother was shot when she was found hiding in a barn. Eventually Dulko and I escaped to the forests, where we joined a partisan unit. There we fought and I played music on my accordion until two weeks before we were liberated by the Soviets. While I was out getting food, some Ukrainian bastards found Dulko in a bunker—he'd stayed behind because he had terrible boils on his feet and couldn't walk. When I returned, I found him stabbed like an animal."

Leopold was the last klezmer to grow up in the tradition—in the Yiddish world of pre–World War II—who still taught and performed klezmer in Poland. Thirteen years later, I would direct a documentary about him called *The Last Klezmer: Leopold Kozlowski, His Life and Music*, which was released in 1994.

Jewish Music in the Strangest Places

After having visited the "Alte" synagogue, which was now a large Jewish museum, I left the square and wandered through the side streets, where I saw many dilapidated buildings, all once occupied by Jews. Suddenly, off to my left, I saw what seemed to be a young woman staring at me from down the street. She waved at me, then disappeared around a corner and out of sight. Curious, I quickly began to follow after her. I got to the corner to find only two dogs standing and shivering, looking pathetic and hungry. I threw them each a piece of a bagel from my pocket and walked a little farther down the street.

No sign of the woman, but there was a beautiful stone archway stretching across what had probably been two Jewish apartment buildings. Inside was what was once an old Jewish courtyard shared by the residences of both buildings. I walked into the empty courtyard to take a better look. This scene in front of me, the courtyard and the archway, seemed familiar, as if I had seen it somewhere before. I couldn't place it.

Maybe I'd seen a photograph? Whatever it was, I decided take some photos myself.

Just as I was focusing the camera, I was struck by a stone on my left shoulder blade. As a sharp pain stabbed me, I yelled and turned around to see who had thrown the damn thing. There above me was the same woman, now standing on a balcony. She had long brown hair and too much makeup and was wearing an overcoat.

I didn't quite know how to ask the question in Polish, but I did know the word for *why*: "*Dlaczego? Dlaczego?*"

The woman just laughed and laughed hysterically. She went inside and closed the door.

I was too angry to think straight. I ran up the two flights of stairs and knocked sharply on her door. There was no answer. Without thinking, I just turned the knob and walked in. There she was in a dimly lit living room, sitting on an old brown leather sofa, surrounded by ashtrays filled with cigarette butts and empty vodka bottles. Pillows and clothes of all kinds were strewn across the floor. Along one wall were a fireplace and a bookcase filled with books. Unframed photos were tacked on the other three walls.

She pointed to a rocking chair in a corner. I asked her if she spoke any German. She said no, but then told me in broken German to take off my coat and sit down. I asked her why she had thrown that rock at me. She didn't answer but just lit a cigarette and offered me one. As my eyes adjusted to the dim light, I realized that she was in her late forties or early fifties.

She asked me if I wanted any tea, but before I could even answer she got up and disappeared into what looked like the kitchen. Feeling both nervous and still curious, I went to take a better look at the photographs on the walls. I heard meowing, looked up, and saw a large gray and brown cat sitting on top of the bookshelf. Just then the cat startled me as it leaped the six feet from the bookshelf to the floor and scampered into the kitchen.

I looked at the various photos. To my amazement, they were of life in Kazimeircz and Krakow before World War II. Two were of Hasidim walking in the snow; another was of the archway of the very courtyard downstairs. Now I remembered where I had seen them before: I had seen a photo with the archway, and the two photos of the Hasidim, in *The Vanished World,* a book by Roman Vishniac. Vishniac (1897–1990) was a photographer who traveled throughout Central and Eastern Europe from 1934 to 1939, photographing Jewish life before its destruction. He was an inspiration to me— now here I was looking at his photographs in an apartment in Kazimierz, where Vishniac had been in 1937. But who was this woman? I didn't even know her name.

After ten minutes she brought out tea and cookies and put them on a small chipped table, sat down on the couch, and introduced herself as Anka. I asked her where she had gotten the photographs. She said she had cut them from a book she stole from the library. You'd think I would have bolted right then and there, but I was still curious. She told me her apartment had belonged to a Jewish woman who had left Poland in 1968 for Sweden during the time when the Polish government fostered a lot of anti-Semitic rhetoric in the newspapers and on the radio and television. When the woman left abruptly one night, Anka moved in.

I told her why I was in Poland; she left the room for a minute and returned with a record, which she put on a record player that had been hidden by all of the mess on the floor. She explained that she had been a cabaret singer and had learned this song from her mother. The song was called "Rebeka" but the non-Jews referred to it by its Yiddish name, "Rivke." (This song was among the most well-known Polish popular songs of the mid-1930s. Both the composer Zygmunt Bialostocki and the lyricist Andrzej Wlast were Jewish. Non-Jews considered it a Jewish song.) The female vocalist on this record was Ewa Demarczyk.

I asked Anka if she was Jewish. She very adamantly said no—but said she believed there were Jewish ghosts living in her apartment and she was able to communicate with them on *erev* Yom Kippur.

This scene was getting weirder by the minute. Anka again left the room and I just sat there listening to the hiss of the needle. It had been the last song on the record and she hadn't bothered to remove it. Anka came back in, wearing only her white underwear and a black bra, and asked me if I wanted to dance. She had a great body and for one split second I was tempted to stay. Then my common sense kicked back in. I thanked her for the tea, cookies, and music, and I left.

The Old Jewish Cemetery

It was overcast and cold as I stood in front of the grave and gazed out over the wide expanse of the cemetery. Unlike the one in Prague, this cemetery only had trees bordering the edges of the wall surrounding the cemetery. I blurred my vision and turned in a complete circle as all of the graves melted into each other, becoming one giant rock, a kind of mass burial for Krakow's Jewry.

The old Jewish cemetery behind the Rema shul was the original cemetery for the *kehile,* but it was now closed for burials. The cornerstone of this *kehile* was the Rema shul, built first in wood in 1553, then rebuilt in stone and brick in 1557. Its name is a contraction of Rabbi Moses ben Israel Isserles (c. 1520–1572). Rabbi Isserles was a scholar of the Talmud, philosophy, astronomy, and history. He wrote on many Jewish subjects but is best known for his interpretations of the Sephardic Rabbi Joseph Caro's Shulkhn-Orekh (Hebrew, Set Table, the collection of laws and prescriptions for leading a life as an Orthodox Jew), which he codified for the Ashkenazim. His Talmudic learning spread throughout Europe.

Rabbi Moses Isserles was buried in the Rema. I went looking for his gravesite. It wasn't hard to find, since his was the most-visited grave in the entire cemetery, especially by Hasidim who revered him. His epitaph read: "From Moses to Moses, there was none like Moses." The stone was covered with melted wax from all of the *yartzayt* candles and *kvitlekh* (Yiddish, notes from people to the rabbi) that had been placed on and around the tombstone.

Mikhl the Translator

I met Mikhl at the old cemetery. He was walking through row after row with a notebook, writing down information about specific headstones. Mikhl was thirty; he had a scruffy soft brown beard, wore thick brown-rimmed glasses, and had a gray tweed cap covering his wavy brown hair. With his baggy cord trousers and his dark blue coat, Mikhl looked like a Jewish professor out of a Woody Allen film. He spoke excellent English and turned out to be one of the main pillars of Jewish life in Krakow for everyone, young and old. To earn a living, Mikhl was a translator of Polish history texts into English, but his love and specialty was writing about Krakow Jewish history. He was a walking encyclopedia of Polish Jewish trivia and often gave an ironic or satirical twist to his commentary. He didn't make much money, but he was able to make ends meet by living with his elderly mother, a survivor from Vienna.

Mikhl offered to take me to a famous literary café, over one hundred years old, that was built into a cave. I met him at the Rema shul and waited inside while he finished his research there. It was only slightly warmer inside the shul, but that was enough to take the chill out of my bones. It was completely quiet as I sat on a bench, the silence only occasionally interrupted by the caw of a raven and the wind hitting the windows. This venerated shul could barely gather a minyan on Shabes—what would happen in the years to come?

A Party Turned Sour

One evening my landlady was having some kind of party. The living room was packed with men, women, and children all sitting around two long tables laden with food and liquor. The old woman invited me to sit and eat with her

Music of Change

With the winds of perestroika blowing in from the east, political change began to take hold in Poland in the late 1980s. Seven years after my first trek to Poland I would return to Krakow to codirect my first documentary film: *At the Crossroads: Jewish Life in Eastern Europe Today* (1990). The Rema shul would be packed with Jews and non-Jews listening to Rabbi Shlomo Carlebach, a rabbi in America famous for the spiritual songs he wrote and composed, who had come to concertize in Poland. Right then and there, as he stood on the bimah, he spotted me with my violin and yelled for me to take it out as he composed a *nign* on the spot. That tune, "Krakow Nign," is sung all over the world today.

family and relatives. I was hungry, but when they brought out the big roasted suckling pig with a baked onion in its mouth, I quickly lost my appetite. The oldest son took the carving knife and began to cut into the flesh. It was bronze on the outside but seemed hardly cooked on the inside. It was so rare that there was blood dripping from the knife. Any rarer and this pig would have leaped off the table and run out the front door.

Still, I decided to stay and hang out for a while; these were all non-Jewish Poles, with whom I hadn't yet had much interaction, and I was enjoying a delicious bowl of mashed turnips with butter and garlic. The old woman explained to her guests who she understood I was and that she especially liked hearing me practice my violin. Now, I never told any of the gentiles I stayed with during my entire visit exactly what I was doing in their fair city. During the Communist era, it was best to keep your personal business to yourself—especially if you were from the West and most assuredly if you were Jewish or doing anything that involved the local *kehile.* My Polish landlady knew only that I was a folklorist researching Polish and Rom folk music.

The din of the conversation, eating, constant clinking of glasses with lots of toasts being made, and the children's game-playing all allowed me to zone out and really look at each person carefully. The landlady, her twin brother, and their younger sister were in their seventies, so they would all have been in their thirties during World War II. I wondered whether they were collaborators or righteous gentiles during the war.

The turnips hadn't taken the edge off my hunger; I really wanted to eat the food I'd bought earlier that evening and was about to excuse myself from the table when one of the old lady's sons whistled loudly to get everyone's attention. Immediately it was quiet. This tall, handsome, dark-haired, mustachioed man in his forties began to speak. From the expressions on everyone's faces, it seemed to be some kind of story or joke. Then I heard the words "*Pan Zyd,*" "*Chasyd,*" and "*stare Zyd*" (Mr. Jew, Hasid, old Jew) several times, his voice rising each time for more emphasis. His punch line was met with a great burst of laughter from everyone. (The word for Jew in Polish is *Zyd,* unlike the Russian *Evrei,* borrowed from the Hebrew. When a gentile Pole uses the word *Zyd,* it can sometimes carry a negative connotation.)

Everything seemed to go into slow motion as I got up from the table to walk to my room. All I could see were their mouths agape, distorted and sinister as the laughter seemed to grow in volume. And even though I didn't fully understand the joke, the fact that they didn't even suspect me of being Jewish somehow made it worse. I wanted to shout "*Ja jestem Zyd!*" (I am a Jew!). Instead, I walked resolutely to my room, finally understanding why many of the Polish survivors I had met back home (and even some of their children) had vowed to never set foot on Polish soil again.

Vevel and the Long-Forgotten Nign

One day, at the kosher kitchen, a man I had seen several times came over to me and asked if I wanted to have a bowl of hot borscht with garlic. He had observed that I was eating only bread and jam with an occasional piece of potato kugel, and he thought I might be hungry. His name was Vevel Mayles; he was a retired teacher. He insisted on feeding me, so I walked with Vevel back to his apartment. He was stooped over and walked very slowly. Every few meters he stopped and gave me a history lesson about a particular street or building. He spoke good Yiddish and told me that some young Jews came to his home once a week to learn Yiddish from him. Vevel said it was harder these days under martial law, because the government was so suspicious of any group of people getting together in a private home—some students had been intimidated by the police not to attend his class.

Then he said, "They can go to hell and lick my *tukhes!*"

I just cracked up. There was something about many of these older men and women survivors I had met. They all had true grit. Whatever the hassles their communist governments heaped on them, it didn't come close to what they had endured under the Nazis.

Vevel wore a light blue, deceptively light-looking cotton jacket that was actually quite thick to the touch, and matching pants. I had seen a lot of men who worked outside, especially on the railroads, with the same outfit. I thought they looked cool and asked Vevel where I could buy a pair. He laughed and told me these were the same kind of clothes he wore in the Soviet gulag during the war. I said I didn't care. He replied, "It just so happens I have an extra pair at home. Maybe you can start a line of chic communist clothing? You'll import them from me, and like a true communist you'll send all of the profit except 10 percent back for distribution among the elderly Jews of Krakow."

I looked at him to see if he was at all serious. He slapped me hard on the back and laughed so hard he doubled over with a terrible coughing attack.

Luckily we had just entered his apartment building. We walked up the seven flights of stairs and were met at the front door by his wife Basia. She was not Jewish and she was probably fifteen years younger than Vevel. They had one daughter who was studying medicine at Jageillonian University. Basia scolded Vevel for being out so late in the cold weather. He just turned to me with a grin and said, "She's like a Yidishe mama. Always worrying about me even when I misbehave."

Basia showed us the table in a room that served as both dining and living room. There were a few paintings on the wall, a large blue sofa, a television in one corner, a fireplace in another, and bookshelves filled with books, many of them in Yiddish. Basia brought out the hot borscht and some rye bread she had baked that day. All the food, especially the big chunks of fresh garlic and dried mushrooms in my soup, was extremely savory. I ate nearly the whole loaf of bread myself. As we ate, I got around to asking Vevel if he knew anything about klezmer. He left the room and returned with a violin. Not only did he play the violin, he'd played in a family band in Walbrom—a shtetl near Warsaw—before the war.

Was I just lucky? I had met a former klezmer and he sought me out at a kosher kitchen. I should have known that wherever there was Jewish food, a klezmer would be not too far away.

After lunch, Vevel began to tell me his klezmer story.

"In my shtetl of Walbrom, there was the Shpruvatch family band led by Borekh on first violin; his brother, Yosef-Leyb, on *sekund;* a cousin Nison who played trombone; and his brother Yekl, who played contrabass; and there was a *marshalik* [Yiddish, wedding jester or master of ceremonies] named Avromchik who sang rhyming songs. They were hired to play at my older sister's wedding.

"The groom came from Olkusz, so when he arrived by horse the klezmorim greeted him with a march. Then came the *bazingen* of the bride [Yiddish, literally, the singing of the bride—the *marshalik* sings sad and happy songs to bring about a full range of emotions from the bride and her female attendants] from Avromchik, then the wedding blessings, and finally the klezmorim led everyone to our home for the celebration with a special march.

"While this happened, all the children threw snowballs at the bride and groom as they walked behind the klezmorim. I even threw some myself.

"The party was your typical wedding party with lots of food, drinking, and dancing. Then came the moment when Borekh went up to play for the bride, groom, and their parents a special *zogekhts* [Yiddish, a plaintive display piece]. The klezmorim had just taken a break when Borekh took his bow and came down hard on his A string and nothing happened. I mean there was no sound. He drew his bow again and still nothing. Then he looked at his bow and realized that someone in the band had put goose fat on his bow hairs for a joke. Well, everyone in the room started laughing, even Borekh—what could he do? Then he told the rest of the band to play some *freylekhs* while he ran home to get another bow.

"Now Borekh wasn't a young man; he was eighty-five years old. But he ran all the way home and returned in about twenty minutes. He then stood up on the bride and groom's table and began once again to play this beautiful *zogekhts,* while sweat dripped down his face."

Then Vevel remembered another tune. But before he played it, he yelled to Basia to come and bring out the pear-flavored vodka with two glasses. I sipped mine while he knocked his back, wiped his mouth with his sleeve, and said, "Ah, this helps clear my mind so I could focus on this Alter Gerer *nign* [Yiddish, Old Ger song; Ger was the name of a sect of Hasidim from the town of Gora Kalawaria]. My sister's wedding happened to be on the fifth day of Hanukkah. The Gerer always sang this *nign* in their *shtibl* in my town. The *shtibl* would be overflowing with so many people, that even though it was wintertime and cold outside the band would end up going outside, playing this *nign* while everyone danced in the snow. Never let it be said, Yitskhok, that liquor dulls the mind."

He then launched into the melody and others as if he had played them just yesterday. As he played, he softly sang some words, which brought tears to his and Basia's eyes. This was probably a song Basia might never have heard if I hadn't helped to jog Vevel's memory. I invited Vevel to come to the Hanukkah concert at the Jewish club in Krakow.

Lessons from the Master

The club in Krakow was packed when I walked in. I had been in Krakow for two weeks, so I recognized some of the people from the kosher kitchen, the Rema shul, and the *kehile* office, and from the streets. It was mostly an older to elderly crowd, with a few youth. Mikhl was there, of course, frenetically

"Ropshitser Nign"

Collected by Yale Strom

helping some of the elderly to their seats, setting up more chairs, and stoking the brick wall heater with more coal.

The Jewish club was part of a network of Jewish social and cultural clubs established in the late 1940s by the Polish government. Since most of the Jewish infrastructure had been destroyed during the Holocaust, buildings had to be built or rebuilt and institutions reestablished. The Polish government allowed some of the shuls to be reopened but really wanted to encourage secular, rather than religious, Judaism. Anything to do with religious Judaism was played down in Poland. If the elderly survivors went to shul, that was OK; however, they much preferred that the youth and middle-aged Jews go to the Jewish clubs. These Jewish clubs were usually one or two large rooms where performances, classes, and recreation took place.

Leopold was in a small back room, drinking some tea and going over his music. He was dressed in dark dress pants, white shirt, and suspenders. Here I was in blue jeans, my boots (one held together by tape), and red flannel shirt, and unshaven.

Since it was the last night of Hanukkah, the lighting and the blessing over the candles was performed. Mr. Weiner, who was a sort of elder statesman and a much venerated man in the *kehile,* lit the candles and recited the blessings. Not surprisingly, most of the young people mouthed the words because they didn't know the prayers. Everyone then sat down (I sat in the back, my violin next to me) and waited for Leopold. It had just turned 7 P.M.—the time the concert was set to begin—but Leopold hadn't appeared. Then it became 7:10 and 7:15. Finally, at 7:17, Leopold came out in a most dignified manner, bowed to the clapping audience, ran his thumbs under and down his suspenders, and let them snap against his chest. He adjusted the piano stool and struck the first chord at 7:20—typical for JST, namely Jewish Standard Time.

Leopold had a wonderful potpourri of melodies. Before each tune he stood up and explained its origin, who'd composed it, and the occasion for which it was played. What a performer he was. His body language mirrored exactly the temperament of each tune. During an upbeat *freylekhs* he literally stood up from the stool and bounced up and down. When it was a slow and pensive melody he crouched down, hovering only inches above the ivories, sometimes singing Hasidic style along with the melody. He sped up the tempos, he slowed them down; at times he played loudly, often suspending the chords with the pedal; at others he barely touched the keys with his right hand, sometimes only with his stiffened index finger.

He played for eighty minutes nonstop. His energy level seemed to grow stronger with each new tune he played. For his last number he played the popular Yiddish song "Mayn Shtetle Belz" (My Town Belz), composed in America by Alexander Olshanetsky (1892–1946).

Originally, when Olshanetsky composed the song, it concerned the shtetl Belz in Bessarabia, and it became so popular among Jews throughout Eastern Europe that some substituted their town's name for Belz so they could sing about their idyllic lives when they were children in the shtetl. The non-Jewish Poles knew and loved this Yiddish song as well and called it "Mia Steczko Belz." Some in the audience sang it in Yiddish and others sang it in Polish. As soon as he finished, everyone stood up and gave him a much deserved ovation.

Then, as the audience kept clapping, Leopold waved for me to come up. He introduced me as a special guest all the way from California; he said he was proud to know that the music of so many klezmers who had lost their lives during the Holocaust would be kept alive through my research. As I got my violin out I knew this was going to be a hard act to follow.

Before each tune I briefly said a few words about it and then Mikhl translated them into Polish. I was a bit nervous, so I decided to launch into a Stoliner *nign* I had learned from my father—something I knew I could really play well. They seemed to like the tune, but I wasn't getting the same response as Leopold, so I decided to sing a few Yiddish tunes like "Bulbes/ Beblekh," "Dire Gelt" (Yiddish, Rent Money), and Vevel's Gerer *nign*. As I felt more relaxed I began to engage with the audience in Yiddish and a little Polish, which made them all laugh. I began to move up and down through the aisles, stopping to play for certain individuals (especially the women), and finished up with "Heyveynu Sholom Aleykhem" (Hebrew, We Brought Peace to You), which everyone, including me, sang at the top of their lungs. When I finished, the audience went wild with enthusiastic clapping. They wanted more, so I turned to Leopold to see what he thought.

He said, "Yitskhok, great concert. Let them leave not completely full. They'll come back next time even hungrier."

Auschwitz

I was among fifteen tourists from abroad, except for one Polish woman who sat silently while being jostled from left to right and up and down as the bus traversed the pitted dirt road that led through the town of Oswiecim (Auschwitz in German) and eventually to the entrance of Auschwitz. I stared out the window at the gray slate sky, the barren fields, the leafless trees, and the occasional farmer in his horse-drawn wagon. The railroad tracks pretty much followed the dirt road. I was transfixed by the scenery going by and couldn't help but wonder what the trees, fields, and farms had witnessed as the trains with their human cargo relentlessly passed this way in the years from 1940 through 1944. (The first deportations began on June 4, 1940, with Jews from Krakow; the camp was liberated by the Soviet soldiers on January 27, 1945.)

As I stared out the window, I recalled an old lady who had come up to me after the Hanukkah concert. She had tapped me on the chest and said, in Yiddish, "For me, you were a Chagall with your music, a painting of movement and sound. Thank you for this memorable Hanukkah gift."

Her outstretched arm had revealed her tattooed Auschwitz numbers. I hugged her and went on my way without really thinking about her words. But later that night, as I was lying in bed, her words struck a deep chord in me. I realized it was fate that had brought me that chance meeting with a Holocaust survivor.

The bus dropped us off in front of the visitor center, where you could decide whether to join a group led by a museum guide speaking your native language. In the visitor center was a café and bookstore. I understood why these businesses were here, but I couldn't see myself taking time to relax in either place. For me, Auschwitz was not about understanding how one human could be so inhuman to another, but rather about trying to understand and feel some small measure of the pain and suffering of all of the survivors I had listened to and cried with.

From the warm confines of the visitor center I took my first steps on the actual grounds where the prisoners had walked. The cold wind stung my face as I put my hands deep into my pockets, searching for a little warmth. Down the crushed rock path, with the eerie cawing of the ravens above, I walked, when suddenly I came to the main entrance gate with the infamous Nazi slogan: *Arbeit Macht Frei* (German, Work Sets You Free). As I crossed the threshold of the sign I walked more slowly than I had walked so far on my journey. Each building had a different exhibit with historical facts, archival photos, drawings by the prisoners, and glass-enclosed exhibits (mounds of hair, shoes, luggage, prosthetics, and eye glasses) depicting how the Nazis had systematically dehumanized each prisoner.

One photo that really spooked me was of a camp orchestra playing music as the Jewish prisoners jumped and fell out of the cattle cars that brought them to Auschwitz. The photo had an arrow that identified a man in civilian clothes at one end of the train platform. Next to the explanation was the same photo of the man, enlarged many times. He was the "Angel of Death"— Dr. Joseph Mengele—who had chosen the fate of each prisoner: who would work and who would go immediately to their death in the gas chambers. I stood transfixed by the photo, looking at the scared expressions of the newly arrived prisoners and the stoical, empty faces of the musicians. The only smiles were on the faces of the Nazis who stood by, watching the macabre scene. I recalled the story Leopold had told me about when he played music in the Jaktorow (near Lemberg) labor camp:

"In Jaktorow I played either the piano or accordion. It was much harder for my brother Dulko because he didn't have a violin and it wasn't easy to find one. Finally I got a violin from a guard. I bribed him with one of my gold teeth I pulled out of my mouth. With this violin, Dulko and I could occasionally see each other when we played for an event together.

"But once there was this big ball for all the SS in the camp, and they only brought me to play. In this room was this table set with all this food and drink. It was excruciating to be in this room, smelling all this food, while playing and feeling such starvation. Halfway through the party they ordered me to take off all my clothes, get up on the table, and play the accordion. I had done this for a few minutes when they ordered me to bend over. As I bent over they took a lit candle and stuck it deep into my anus. Everyone then took turns lighting their cigarettes and cigars as I continued to play while they laughed."

After another hour in Auschwitz and its two subcamps I took the walk to Birkenau. In Auschwitz only 10 percent of the arrivals—those who looked the fittest—were selected for work. The remainder (except for those few who worked in the crematoria) were sent to Birkenau, which meant certain death by the Zyklon B gas administered in the showers, into which hundreds of prisoners were crammed on the pretext of being disinfected. As the Soviets advanced in December 1944 and January 1945, the Nazis began to retreat back to Germany. They didn't want to leave any clear evidence of their barbarity, so they blew up all of the crematoria and gas chambers they could in Birkenau.

I remembered Mikhl saying that in Warsaw, once a week, there was a huge outdoor flea market where one could buy all kinds of Jewish memorabilia (ritual objects, books, records, photos, even ghetto money), most of which had been stolen from Jews' homes after they were deported. I thought of those Jews who'd survived the war and returned to live in Poland, who might later discover something of theirs at a flea market and have to buy back their own personal belongings.

There were only a few hints from the stone foundations of the former crematoria, with their tall red brick chimney stacks reaching toward the sky. The wide-open sparseness against the background of the denuded trees lining the outskirts of the camp was odder than anything I had seen in the Auschwitz exhibit. The emptiness, the void as I stood in the middle of Birkenau, made me feel insignificant. For the first time in my life I felt the weight of each survivor, of every drop of loneliness and sorrow I had ever experienced.

I set down the *yartzayt* candle I had gotten at the *kehile* offices. As I quietly recited Kaddish to myself, the wind licked the wick violently, making the candle burn quickly and unevenly. I set it down onto the ground, braced by some loose stones. Then I walked back to where I would catch the bus, never once turning around to look at the candle for fear I would start crying.

WROCLAW

Mikhl had given me the name of Sane Robak, the head of Wroclaw's Jewish club. I went directly there from the bus station. I was tired, so I took a taxi instead of my usual walking or public transportation. As I rode, I noticed that this city's architecture was similar to Krakow's. In both cities, the pre–World War I facades had interesting, almost whimsical masonry (gargoyles and human faces worked into the brickwork), and some of the taller buildings had the copper verdigris roofs common throughout much of Central Europe, but the more modern buildings had a drab, impersonal functionality. Luckily, there were parks throughout the city that counteracted some of this drabness.

Wroclaw is in the province of Silesia in western Poland. It had only become a part of Poland after the war. Poland had lost much of its eastern territory, such as the provinces of Galicia and Volynia, to the Soviet Union. To compensate for these territorial losses, Poland was given the German state Silesia. Before I'd left Krakow, Mikhl told me one interesting fact about the Wroclaw *kehile:* all of the survivors were transplants from former eastern Poland, so their klezmer memories would be about those regions and not about Wroclaw.

When we arrived I noticed that the taxi driver hadn't turned on his meter. He took out all my bags for me and then whispered "Two dollars," which I knew was more than it would have cost in zlotys (fifty cents).

I asked him, did he want to change some money? Was he willing to give me a higher rate than the official bank rate? He motioned for me to get back in the car and from underneath his seat he brought out a leather briefcase. He snapped opened the lock and revealed several neat rows of Deutsche-marks, U.S. dollars, French francs, Dutch guilders, and zlotys. At the bank, the exchange rate was two hundred zlotys for every dollar; he offered me one thousand zlotys for every dollar. I showed him two twenty-dollar bills and I watched him count out forty thousand zlotys.

I had heard of illegal moneychangers ripping off unsuspecting tourists by giving them a wad of bills that looked legitimate when they counted them corner by corner (but only the top and bottom bills were real); all the subsequent bills would turn out to be pieces of paper that had their corners glued to look as if they were real. He counted out the money and then I counted out each individual bill. It was all there to the last groschen (Poland's smallest coin)——forty thousand zlotys.

I gave him the two twenty-dollar bills. He looked at them in the light, shook my hand, and gave me his card so that when I needed a taxi (or bank) again in Wroclaw I could call his house. A bank on wheels——now that was something we didn't have back home. He left and I climbed——with all my gear——the three flights of stairs to the Jewish club.

The Jewish Club

The club was quite a lively place. There were men and women reading newspapers and books, others playing chess and cards, and still others drinking, eating, and talking. When I entered, everything stopped and all eyes focused on me as I dropped all my gear to the floor. A man in his early sixties, wearing a tweed suit jacket and gray dress pants came over, eyed my violin, and asked me in Yiddish if I was Jewish. I said I was and he looked at me askance. "Can you prove it?"

I replied, "I am a simple Jew with a circumcision to prove it."

The place exploded with laughter. The man who came up to me turned around and said, "You see a real klezmer, a simple, friendly Jew who had a circumcision. What more could we ask for?"

This was how I met Duvid, a former musician and retired choral leader. Duvid then introduced me to Sane Robak, a man in his early seventies, bald and with a smile you couldn't be sure was sincere or not. We shook hands and he said he knew all about my klezmer research from Mikhl in Krakow—how could he be of help?

I asked him if there was a Jewish family from whom I could rent a room for a couple of weeks. He asked what I was willing to pay. If I paid in dollars it would be cheaper because they could turn those dollars into a hell of a lot of zlotys on the black market. And I happened to know a moneychanger, so I blurted out: "Three dollars a day." Sane replied that would be fine and began to make some calls on my behalf. Duvid just grinned and said, "The communists make the best capitalists. You could have offered two dollars and that would have been sufficient. I know him"—here he looked askance at Sane as he spoke on the telephone—"he'll take a dollar off the top for every night you stay and call it his finder's fee."

Duvid's comment somewhat confirmed my uneasy feelings about Robak, but still, he was helping me find a place to stay, and what did I care if he made something on the side?

The Chess Match

After eating a lunch of sauerkraut with pickled apples (which really made my mouth pucker, but I still ate three of them), regular dill pickles, challah, and plum compote, Duvid and I began a chess match. Now, I'm really an amateur chess player; I usually played maybe a dozen times in a year. But my competitive juices were flowing and I really wanted to put up a good fight. After about half an hour I realized that some of the men in the club had stopped what they were doing and were either sitting or standing around us. I guessed Duvid was the best player in the club and I had played him pretty evenly (only by luck) until I captured his queen.

A man with thick horn-rimmed glasses to Duvid's left said in a beautiful, loud baritone voice, "Duvid, this simple klezmer from who-knows-where seems to have you by the throat!"

Everyone laughed. Now all the men and women in the club were watching us, all the while whispering just loud enough so we could hear them. I never knew that chess was such a spectator sport. A few more moves went by as we exchanged pawns. Then I captured his second bishop. Instantly, it got quiet in the room, so quiet I could hear the traffic from outside. Duvid's determination glared out in his tightly furrowed brow, while his hand hovered above the board, ready to make the next decisive move. I actually began to sweat; my hands became clammy. A minute went by, then another and another. No one dared whisper. Then Robak abruptly let out this ferocious sneeze that made us both jump. But when Duvid flinched, his knee caught the edge of the chessboard and scattered the pieces all over the floor.

It was as if time had stopped. Everyone froze. There was an interminable silence. Then Duvid said, "Oy, I was just about to capture your queen. For a simple klezmer, you played well. Let's have some tea."

And that was that, as if nothing had happened. Everyone dispersed and I sat there a little dumbfounded while Duvid picked up the pieces.

Recording Some Tunes

One afternoon, I had an appointment to record some klezmer 78 LPs at the Jewish club. Mr. Robak had laid out all of the records that were klezmer on the table, ready to be put onto the record player. Before I began to record, Mr. Robak once again had a political question for me, as he'd had every time I saw him the previous week. So I humored him once again.

"Yitskhok, do you think that having the United States in Central America is any different from the Soviet Union being in Afghanistan?"

"No, Sane, I don't. I think both countries need to leave immediately. And let me ask you a question: when is the Soviet Union going to leave Poland?"

"Doyne/Freylekhs"

Collected by Yale Strom

Robak just laughed, slapped me on the back, and said, "Who knows? Only the Holy One above knows when that time will come."

I laughed as well and thought that was a rather clever answer, coming from a secular Jewish communist.

I recorded ten tunes: two Yiddish vocal pieces sung by Sidy Thal (a famous Yiddish actress from Romania) and eight actual klezmer instrumentals. Most of the tunes I recognized, but there was a *freylekhs* and *doyne* for accordion and *tsimbl* I had never heard. I walked out of his office into the main room and saw Duvid playing chess with another man. Duvid called to me:

"So, Yitskhok, you want to play after this one?"

I declined, saying that I had an appointment.

Genia and Mikhl

I was staying at Genia Tabashnik's apartment (thanks to Robak) in the heart of the city. Genia was short and wore wire-rimmed glasses; her dark brown hair was secured in a tight bun. She spoke fluent Yiddish. Her apartment was a rather large pre—World War I abode with four bedrooms. Recently all of the plumbing and wiring in the whole apartment complex had been renovated. I didn't know how productive my two weeks in Wroclaw would be, but at least my accommodations were quite comfortable.

Genia was born in Vladimerets (Wlodzimierzec, Ukraine). When the Germans attacked the Soviet Union on June 21, 1941, she and her family (father, mother, three brothers, and one sister) went to Alma-Alta in Kazakhstan. There she went to school with Russians, Kazakhs, Uzbeks, Persians, and Tatars, and she never felt any anti-Semitism. After the war her family returned to Vladimerets, but this part of former Poland was now part of the Ukraine and the local Ukrainians were some of the worst anti-Semites before, during, and after the war. Because of the anti-Semitism, Genia and her family bribed their way into Poland. With just the clothes on their backs, they crossed the border and settled in Wroclaw.

Genia offered to make me dinner. And what a surprise—none other than sauerkraut with pickled apples, pickles, and some delicious pickled cucumber soup as well.

I had taken the bus from the Jewish club to Genia's home, where I met her friend Mikhl Lepert. Mikhl wore glasses and had thinning salt-and-pepper hair and a pencil-thin mustache. Mikhl was born in Drohobitsh (Drogobic,

Zuppa Ogorkowa
POLISH SOUR CUCUMBER SOUP
Makes 6 to 8 servings

This soup is surprisingly soothing, with a pleasant sour taste. Serve warm with a thick chunk of warm, crusty black bread.

10 cups vegetable stock

5 medium potatoes, peeled and diced

½ stick butter or margarine

1 medium onion, finely chopped

6 kosher dill pickles, diced

2 carrots, peeled and diced

½ tsp. minced garlic

1 bay leaf

Salt and freshly ground pepper to taste

½ cup dill pickle juice

1 pint sour cream

2 Tbsp. flour

1. Put the stock in a stockpot and bring to quick boil. Add the potatoes and boil until soft.

2. In a frying pan, melt the butter and add the onion, pickles, carrots, and garlic and let them cook until onions are soft and clear.

3. Add the mixture to the stockpot, and add the bay leaf, salt, pepper, and pickle juice. Taste and add a little more pickle juice if necessary—the soup should have a pleasantly sour taste.

4. Mix the sour cream and flour until thoroughly combined. Slowly stir into the soup. Allow to simmer until the soup is lightly thickened—do not boil. Season with salt and pepper to taste. Serve warm.

Ukraine); he and Genia had gone to the Yiddish shul in Wroclaw together as children and had remained close friends ever since. I could see that Genia and Mikhl really enjoyed each other's company.

After a refreshing shower I dressed and headed to the living room. Before I entered, I saw that Mikhl had moved next to Genia on the sofa and was holding her hand. It was nice to see romance between two survivors. I stood there voyeuristically watching them as I recalled various quotes from the survivors I had recorded. I realized that one emotion that stood out, as it was so rarely discussed or exhibited among them, was passion for the opposite sex. Too often it was buried deep under the scar tissue.

I waited a few more minutes, then walked in. Mikhl said:

"Ah, Yitskhok, you took so long I was afraid you would rub off all your skin."

We all laughed. While Genia brought out some tea, I took out my violin and played them the waltz that I had learned from Rut in Zagreb. As I played, Mikhl and Genia gracefully danced about the room. I relished this moment more than the concert I had played in Krakow. To be able, with my music, to make people move and lose themselves to this world for even just a brief moment was truly magical.

Making Kutia and Meeting Raphael

I went to explore the former shul, known as the White Stork shul, that had been built in 1829 and closed in 1960. It had been part of the Breslau Jewish Theological Seminary established by Rabbi Zachariah Frankel (1801–1875) in 1854. His philosophy of Judaism became the cornerstone for Conservative Judaism in the United States. The seminary became the model for rabbinical seminaries throughout the western world.

The building stood across from the kosher kitchen and had been quite obviously vandalized since its closure in 1960. It was three stories high, with large, fluted, stone beams separating the Palladian windows. Inside the dark, cavernous hulk I carefully climbed the aged stairs, which moved and creaked under my weight. Pigeons and bats had made the upper rafters their roost; below lay mounds of their dried guano. The place looked like it was used by the homeless—I saw broken glass bottles, newspapers, discarded shoes and clothing, and even human waste.

Ester (in background) preparing food in the kosher kitchen in Wroclaw

After trying to find any semblance of a former Jewish presence, I walked out into a room on the top floor that had a broken wall; this allowed me to survey the whole bottom floor, which looked like it had been the shul's main sanctuary. Written in white paint on the curved brick arches below me were the words *ostania godzina rabiego* (Polish, the last hour of the rabbi), with a Mogen Dovid above it. I took out my camera and took several shots of this poignant epitaph. Those three words said it all about this shul and seminary.

Across the courtyard from the shul was the kosher kitchen. Here I met Ester, the caretaker and chief cook for the kosher kitchen. She wore an apron over her striped sweater and green shirt. Her face and the way she combed her thick black wavy hair reminded me of photographs of Alice B. Toklas.

She invited me for some lunch: boiled potatoes and parsley, pickled tomatoes, black bread with butter, and a special dessert I hadn't yet had, called *kutia,* consisting of poppy seeds, lots of honey, and crushed walnuts. One could eat it just with a spoon or spread it on bread. It was the perfect dish to cut the saltiness of the pickled tomatoes. Ester was making another batch of the *kutia* and asked if I would help her crack open the walnuts and separate and crush them. Man, my hands were sore after that and I had a small blister from where the nutcracker had hit the palm of my right hand.

While I was crushing the walnuts, I notice a bespectacled, bearded man in his mid-seventies, eating chicken soup and reading a French magazine. His pants were held up by suspenders and he wore hiking boots. From the looks of his threadbare clothes he was rather poor. I asked if I could move my operation of crushing the walnuts and sit down with him.

With a twinkle in his eye, he stretched out his hand, and shook mine, introducing himself as Raphael ben Itskhok Zielinski. He was born in Drohobitsh, into a poor Hasidic family. His father, Itskhok-Yosl, worked as a wheelwright and played violin in the local klezmer band. His father was also a violinist. In 1926, Raphael went to Lille, France, to study dentistry. When the war broke out he joined the French resistance. After the war he stayed in France until 1950, married a French woman, and even became a French citizen. While he practiced dentistry he became interested in sports medicine. Divorced, he moved to Wroclaw and was eventually sent to Moscow by the Polish government, where he became a gymnastics coach. When he returned to Wroclaw after three years, he worked in a military hospital until he became blind in one eye and was forced to retire. These days he spent most of his time reading and writing in Polish, Russian, Yiddish, English, French, and Hebrew.

After he finished talking I asked him about his father's experiences as a klezmer in Drohobitsh. In response, he shared the song his father had sung to his mother, a picturesque song about Drohobitsh.

Afterward, we walked down the street together. We said good-bye and I watched Raphael turn around and slowly walk away. He had several patches on the back of his pants and his jacket was really worn. I ran after him and

Kutia

POPPY SEED AND WALNUT SPREAD

Makes 1½ to 2 cups

This is fast and simple to make, and sweet—a little definitely goes a long way. Try spreading a spoonful on bread in place of jam, or on challah at the Shabes table. *Kutia* also makes a nice filling for cookies, even hamantaschen (as a variation on the usual poppy seed filling). One word of warning when working with poppy seeds: be prepared for a few to scatter to the far corners of your kitchen. It's a small price to pay for the experience of making and eating authentic *kutia*!

1 cup poppy seeds

¼ cup honey

¼ cup hot water

⅓ cup sugar

½ cup walnuts, chopped fine

1. Put the poppy seeds in a saucepan and cover with boiling water. Simmer for 3 to 5 minutes. Drain in a fine-mesh strainer (so the water goes out but the seeds remain).

2. Grind the poppy seeds in a mortar and pestle or in a food processor fitted with a steel blade. Set aside.

3. Combine the honey and hot water in a bowl and set aside to cool.

4. Combine the poppy seeds with the cooled honey water, the sugar, and the walnuts. Keep refrigerated and serve cold.

impulsively gave him ten dollars. At first he didn't want to take it, but I convinced him it was just a little token of my appreciation for his stories and beautiful song. He stuffed the bill into an inner pocket in the jacket, hugged me, and silently continued down the street.

Tomasz

One day I was meandering to the kosher kitchen when I saw a young bearded man with glasses, about my age, walking rather briskly toward me. He was repeating some Hebrew words over and over, rather loudly. He paid no attention to me. I tried to get out of his way but he bumped into me, hard, knocking me to the ground. He was quite apologetic and helped me to my feet. This was how I met Tomasz.

Tomasz was twenty-four and had two sisters and a brother. His father was Jewish, his mother Polish. Tomasz was born in Drohobitsh, moved as a young child to Lancut in eastern Poland, then grew up in Zielona Gora in western Poland, in a Catholic home. Both his parents had died in an automobile accident when he was fourteen. The only semblance of *Yidishkayt* he received as a child was from his father's father. He moved to Wroclaw to study interior design and had been living with Dr. Abraham Greenzweig (age eighty-nine), a retired physician. They had met at shul and now Dr. Greenzweig had become like a father figure for Tomasz. Tomasz was learning everything he could about Judaism from Dr. Greenzweig. Eventually Tomasz planned to immigrate to France, for many reasons. The two he gave me were that (1) he wanted to meet a nice French Jewish girl, and (2) art supplies were scarce and expensive in Poland.

Tomasz and I sat for several hours at a café next to the Rathaus (German, city hall), one of Wroclaw's architecture pearls and typical of nineteenth-century German architecture. Tomasz was extremely interested in my research; he told me that Mr. Greenzweig had some old sheet music that he believed were Jewish melodies.

Tomasz and I met again a couple of days later at the Rathaus café, and we walked along the Odra River toward his home. I told him of my melancholy experience in Wroclaw's Jewish cemetery the day before. The cemetery really was in disrepair. There were stones that had fallen over, others had sunk into the ground, and still others were broken. There was also refuse all over, especially broken vodka bottles and cigarette butts.

"Drohobitsh"

Traditional

Tsvishn grine berg,
oyf Voliner erd,
dortn iz mayn shtetele gezesn
dortn——geborn,
dos beste ongevoyrin,
dos vel ikh shoyn keyn mol nisht fergesn.
Di grine berg, bakroynen dikh,
di velder vos bashaynen dikh
di kvalekhlekh krishtolene tsufusns
dayn sheyn panorame.
Oy Drohobitsh——mayn mama
der sone hot mir blut geton bagisn.
Di shuln un fareynen,
un tate-mames heymen,
alts azoy blutik ongevoyrin,
eyn mol im nisht sheken——
dem natsi-daytsh——gedenken
dos hob ikh oyf eybik shoyn geshvorn.

Between green mountains,
On Volyner earth,
there sat my town,
there I was born,
the best I lost,
this I will never forget.
The green mountains crown you,
the forest that lends beauty to you,
the springs and cut grass are at the foot
of this beautiful panorama
Oy Drohobitsh——my mother
the enemy spilt my blood.
The schools and fraternal clubs
and my parents' homes,
all are bloody, lost,
the German Nazi——remembered
we will never forgive him.
This I have already sworn——forever.

CHORUS

Oy Drohobitsh,
oi mama shtot
hartsik ful mit kheyn.
Oy Drohobitsh,
eybik libe alte heym,
oometoom vu ikh bin vestu mit mir zayn.

Oy Drohobitsh,
oy my hometown,
full of sincere charm.
Oy Drohobitsh,
forever my dear old home,
everywhere I am you are with me.

He agreed with me that there had to be a major renovation of the cemetery (which had opened in 1760 and closed in 1940). Along with some other young Jews and non-Jews, Tomasz was formulating a plan to formally submit to the local city government and cultural department in Warsaw. He explained that the biggest problem was not getting permission to clean and fix up the cemetery, but finding the funding. The Polish government was too poor to worry about dead Jews and hardly seemed to concern itself with those still living in the country.

Dr. Greenzweig and the Incredible Vegetarian Meal

When we arrived, Dr. Greenzweig was sitting in his library in a purple bathrobe and slippers. He was small and distinguished looking, with silvery white hair, a small goatee like Freud's, and a pair of bifocals that hung down from his neck on an ornate gold chain.

With a deep mellifluous baritone voice, in impeccable English, he said, "Yale, Tomasz told me you are a student of Jewish culture and eager to learn more about Jewish music, specifically klezmer." (It took me by surprise to be called Yale—over the last nine months I had grown accustomed to being called Yitskhok.) "You have come to the right place. I have a few pages of music from a man who was a friend of my father's in Loshits [Losice, Poland]. When my father died in 1960 I found them among his personal papers. I believed his friend played the trombone in the town's band.

"But before I go and get this music, tell me more about yourself and what you have found during your travels in Eastern Europe. Take your time; Tomasz will prepare some supper, and for dessert you will play for us."

After several hours of conversation, we sat down to an incredible vegetarian meal in honor of Tu B'Shvat (the fifteenth of Shvat, celebration of trees). Tomasz said his initial interest in Judaism came from the Jewish foods he ate at his grandfather's in Lancut. Then he had asked Ester—of the kosher kitchen—to teach him some more recipes. Dr. Greenzweig said that he was lucky he hadn't met Tomasz ten years earlier or he would be weighing over three hundred pounds now.

First we had *krupnik* (mushroom-barley soup), which he served with warm poppy seed flat bread (*cebulak* in Polish) with butter. I could have stopped there and been completely satisfied, but then Tomasz brought out

Krupnik

MUSHROOM AND BARLEY SOUP

Makes 6 servings

There is nothing more satisfying than a good, thick bowl of mushroom-barley soup, and I have yet to meet anyone (kids included) who doesn't like it. This is a staple in European Jewish cuisine and is relatively easy to make. Note: when you add the water or stock to the soup, one cup is reserved—you can always use it if the soup needs thinning toward the end of cooking. The barley and potatoes will thicken the soup considerably. You can omit the sour cream if you choose, but mmmm, life is good, enjoy yourself!

1½ oz. dried mushrooms

2 small onions

2 medium potatoes

2 small carrots

2 small turnips

2 large stalks celery, washed and deveined

¼ cup pearl barley

9 to 10 cups water or vegetable stock

Salt and pepper to taste

1 cup sour cream (optional)

1. Soak the mushrooms in enough hot water to cover for 15 minutes, until softened. Rub the mushrooms with your fingers to make sure any sand is removed. Drain, reserving the liquid. Chop the mushrooms. Strain the liquid to remove any grit.

2. Chop the onions, potatoes, carrots, turnips, and celery. Place in a stockpot with the mushrooms, barley, and mushroom liquid. Add all but 1 cup of the water.

3. Bring to a boil, season with salt and pepper, and turn the heat down low enough to just simmer for ½ hour. Check the liquid and add more if needed. Continue simmering for another ½ hour. The soup is done when the potatoes are soft and the barley is plump.

4. Stir in the sour cream and serve.

raisin- and almond-filled knishes along with cheese and onion knishes. Then we had some boiled potatoes with parsley and grated garlic and finally apple cake for dessert. I was so full when it came time for dessert that I got up from the table and walked around for ten minutes so I could make room for it. Mr. Greenzweig seemed to have no problem having seconds of every dish, plus finishing off two bottles of beer.

After dinner we all went back into the library, where I just wanted to lie down on the couch and fall asleep. I tried to summon the energy and interest to play the violin. When I saw the old notated sheet music with finger stains from the musicians handling the music and realized these were some klezmer tunes never before played in the United States, I immediately got up to play them. I played each one several times before I left that night.

The day before I took the bus to Warsaw, Tomasz gave me generous provisions for the trip. I had had such a wonderful time in Wroclaw and my living accommodations had been so comfortable, I didn't want to leave. But Warsaw was calling.

A Stopover in Lodz

The express bus left at 9 A.M. and was supposed to arrive in Warsaw at 5 P.M. The bus was rather comfortable and clean compared to many of the trains and other buses I had taken. And unlike in Hungary and Yugoslavia, it wasn't crowded and only one person was smoking. The bus went through Katowice, then through Czestochowa before we finally made a stop in Lodz, where I had thirty minutes to get some fresh air and stretch my legs. Before World War II, Lodz had the second largest *kehile* in Poland, with some 233,000 Jews, and was known as the Manchester of the East (the heart of the textile industry was in Lodz).

After strolling a few blocks through the downtown area, I returned to find some kind of yelling commotion in front of the bus. Apparently, a Rom mother with her four children only had enough money to buy three tickets to Warsaw. They were obviously poor and she seemed to be offering tourist postcards that they normally sold to the bus driver in exchange for two tickets. The other people just looked on, some with obvious disdain for the Rom family (prejudice against the Rom in Eastern Europe was—and still is—a virulent problem). I walked over to the ticket counter, bought the tickets for her, and gave them to the bus driver. It wasn't a hard decision to make; the tickets were cheap, I felt bad for the Rom family, and I was anxious to get to Warsaw.

When I handed the tickets to the bus driver he looked at me as if I was nuts. I grabbed the Rom woman's bags and climbed aboard. She was very grateful and gave me some postcards depicting the famous Black Madonna of Czestochowa (Tchenstokhov in Yiddish). She also gave me a meat pie, but I explained to her I didn't eat meat, which made all her kids laugh.

WARSAW

I stepped out of the bus station and onto one of the main boulevards in Warsaw. It was loud, cacophonous, and urban. The traffic was stop and go. Car horns were honking and pedestrians were walking here and there. Giant billboards advertised both products and communism.

I already knew which bus I had to catch to the place where I would be staying with the mother-in-law of Dan, my best friend back home. I knew she would be anxious to see me. But I decided to walk a bit, taking in the sights and sounds of the city that once had been home to the largest Jewish population in all of Europe.

One building in particular stood out in height, girth, and ugliness. The cultural center had been a gift from Stalin to the Poles in the early 1950s. It was the typical boring, staid, ascetic Stalinist construction. It looked to me like the *Daily Planet* offices from the *Superman* comics; and from that moment to this day I've referred to it as the *Daily Planet*.

My walk took me to the huge square in front of the posh Intercontinental Hotel. The square looked like it was used for public rallies. Some soldiers were standing in front of a memorial on the other end of the square. As I crossed, I could begin to make out the memorial—the soldiers stood stoically in front of some kind of eternal flame. Then I saw the plaque with the names of the concentration camps and words to the effect that this was a memorial to all the martyred Poles murdered during World War II. Conspicuously missing was any specific mention of the three million Polish Jewish victims.

The Nozyk Shul

The Nozyk shul wasn't hard to find, because its location was marked on the city map with a Mogen Dovid. As I walked toward the shul I realized I was walking through the infamous former Warsaw Ghetto—before the war a neighborhood of forty thousand Jews. Gazing up at the apartment buildings, I saw pockmarks of various diameters haphazardly scattered across the walls. At first I thought it was the typical wear and tear common to many old buildings in the Eastern bloc. Then I stopped to look more carefully and realized these pockmarks were some of the last vestiges of the Warsaw Ghetto uprising. This bullet-ridden façade was a kind of memorial. I was glad it hadn't been cemented over.

As I continued my walk to the last edifice of religious Judaism left in Warsaw, I remembered reading how rich and diverse Warsaw Jewish life had been before World War II, with the Hasidim on the right, the Yiddish-speaking socialists and communists on the left, and everyone else in the middle. I left the apartments, crossed a wide street to a park, and turned a corner to find an incongruously modern-looking building that did not seem to fit in with all of others. This was the Jewish Culture House. Inside the building were the *kehile* offices; editorial offices for the Yiddish/Polish monthly newspaper, the *Folkshtimme* (People's Voice); and the Yiddish State Theater of Poland.

Behind this building was a grass lot; in one corner stood the Nozyk shul, built in 1902. Its architecture wasn't spectacular: two stories of large faded yellow stone blocks, with the typical Ten Commandments inset in stone just underneath the peak of the roof. I climbed the stairs and tried the doors but they were locked. I went to a window and peered inside. It looked like it hadn't been touched by humans since the end of the war. Benches were overturned, dirt and dust caked everything, prayer books were strewn across the floor, and a huge brass menorah was upended and leaned awkwardly against the bimah. It was as if the Polish government had left the place in its plundered state as an exhibit of what the Nazis did to the Jews. Actually, during the war the only reason the Germans didn't blow the shul up as they had done to the others in the city was because they used it as horse stables.

Kosher Kitchen

I sat in a corner of the kitchen with my back to the window, just to observe and take photos. Like clockwork, the first person—a clean-shaven, square-jawed little man—walked in carrying an empty satchel. By noon there were about twenty men and women there eating vegetable soup, roast, potato kugel, and some kind of cherry loaf cake.

While I was writing some notes in my notebook, a tall, mostly bald man with prominent thick lips (which made him look like he was pouting) came over and started interrogating me in Yiddish. Who was I? What was I writing? Why was I here? Did I have permission be here? I tried to explain, but he just kept saying I had to see the *roshekool*. Finally I told him it was none of his business and ignored him. He yelled something in Polish, spraying me with spittle, and stormed off. Everyone in the room turned to see what all the commotion was about. Then after only a few seconds they went back to what they were doing. Obviously they had seen this kind of behavior from this shmuck before.

After a few more moments, a middle-aged, dark-haired woman with olive skin came over and introduced herself in English:

"Hello, I'm Roza. I'm sorry for Olek's rude behavior. He was in the Judenrat in Lodz and I think he will always feel guilty about this." (The Judenrat—German for Jewish Council—was a body heading the Jewish community in ghettos throughout Poland, appointed by the Germans during World War II; they were responsible for enforcing the Nazi orders that affected Jewish communal and administrative affairs.) "I'd like to talk with you some more, but I have an appointment. But go over and visit with Menashe. He'll happily answer all your questions."

Just like that, Roza left, carrying her leftover lunch in a canvas bag, while Olek yelled "*Kurva!*" (Polish, whore) at her and then glared at me. Everyone continued to ignore him while I went over to introduce myself to Menashe.

Menashe

Menashe looked like an archetype of a religious Jew who might have lived in Warsaw before World War II. Sitting there loudly sipping his soup, dipping pieces of bread to soak up the broth, Menashe was a man in his late seventies with a long gray beard. He wore a yarmulke and a long black suit coat and pants. I asked if I could sit down and he motioned to the empty seat across from him. When he was served the roast he offered me a slice, but I told him I was a vegetarian, which prompted this reply in his gravelly voice:

"Did you know that the Rambam was a vegetarian? So you are in good company." (Rambam is an acronym of the name Rabbi Moses ben Maimon [1135–1204]. He was one of the most outstanding rabbinical authorities of Jewish history as well as a codifier, philosopher, and physician. His most famous book was *The Guide to the Perplexed,* a synthesis of rabbinical Judaism and Aristotelian philosophy, which was then prevalent in the Islamic world.)

Menashe yelled something in Polish to one of the women in the kitchen and she promptly brought me some mashed potatoes mixed with fried onions and garlic. We both ate without saying a word to each other.

I noticed that Menashe ate slowly and methodically and before starting each new dish he said a blessing to himself in Hebrew. The room gradually emptied until it was only Menashe and me.

He began to tell me his story:

"I was born in Rokitno near Dombrovitsa [Dubrivicja, Ukraine]. My father was a carpenter and we were like most Jews—observant and poor. I left school, learned carpentry from my father, married, and tried to be a God-fearing Jew.

"Then the war started and I joined the Russian army. In the beginning it was hard because the Germans had more weapons than us and caught us by surprise. We lost many men and my whole family was shot after they were taken first to the ghetto. I was extremely depressed and was losing the will to live. Then one night, after we had retreated over thirty kilometers, I fell into a deep sleep and had a very special dream that was like a vision. In it I saw my parents with my two younger brothers walking on a bright sunny day to shul. We were talking and laughing the whole way there. But when we approached the shul entrance my parents and brothers seemed to have vanished. I opened the door to the shul and climbed a staircase that seemed to go up forever. The higher I climbed the brighter the light. Then when the light became impossible to bear, even with my eyes closed, I suddenly saw my family standing in front of the opened Holy Ark, singing this song 'Min Hamaytser' [Hebrew, From the Depths]. It was a prayer my father recited on Rosh Hashana.

"After they finished the song I was awoken by a hail of bullets from the fascists flying over my head. But instead of being frightened or depressed I felt elated, because I knew then there was a reason to fight on and survive. I also made a vow to *Hashem* that if I survived the war I would dedicate my life to doing his work on earth. I survived, as you can see, became religious, and learned the trade of being a *shoykhet*. But because I lived in Erets [Israel]— where my daughter lives today—for a couple of years and then returned to Poland, the government took away my job. They said I was too old to travel in Poland doing my work, but it really was that they didn't trust Jews who were Zionists. So they have to bring a *shoykhet* from Budapest twice a month to Warsaw. Today I serve Hashem by studying, reading from the Torah, leading the prayers, and being a *shtekh* in the government's *tukhes* [Yiddish, a stick in the government's behind]. They don't like to be reminded that many Jews looked and acted like me before the war."

With that, Menashe let out a loud laugh and prepared to leave. He asked me if I would come to shul to help make a minyan. During the winter it was more difficult to get a daily minyan. Of course, I agreed; I told him I would come every day if they needed me. Menashe put his coat on, walked halfway to the door, and turned to say one more thing, which haunts me to this day:

"Yitskhok, remember it was only *beshert* [predestined, inevitable] that you sat on that side of the table interviewing me, and not where I sat being interviewed by my son."

He left and I had to think about it for a minute before I grasped what he said. It was only kismet that allowed my grandparents to leave their shtetl before World War I to come to the United States, for if they hadn't, my parents either would have become victims of the Holocaust (and I would have never been born) or would have been among those who survived and remained in Poland all these years later, irreparably wounded.

The Ghetto Monument and Jewish Historical Institute

As I walked to the Warsaw Ghetto monument I thought about Menashe's words and realized that fate, luck, and ironic choices—sometimes made unconsciously—seemed to be propelling me on my journey in the Eastern bloc. It was hard to believe that in 1931, 33 percent of Warsaw's population had been Jewish.

Where Anielewicz and Zamenhof streets meet, on the site of the Jewish central command where the first Jewish fusillade was fired on April 19, 1943 (the first day of Passover), stood a huge thirty-foot bronze statue mounted in front of a towering granite wall. The granite had been imported by Hitler from Sweden for a projected victory monument. The wall represented the burning side of an underground bunker; the central portion of the bronze depicted the ghetto in flames, and the fighters, surrounding Mordecai Anielewicz—leader of the uprising—were men, women, and children in tattered clothes, facing death fearlessly, armed only with stones, sticks, and naked fists. On the back of the monument was a bas-relief depicting the contrasting visages of fear and despair worn by those herded off to the gas chambers. Two huge menorahs flanked the main part of the monument. On the base, in Yiddish, Hebrew, and Polish, were the words: "To the Jewish People, Its Heroes and Its Martyrs."

The monument was erected on the fifth anniversary of the uprising. It was designed by Nathan Rapaport, an Israeli sculptor. The square was surrounded by blocks of apartment buildings. I looked up and saw a woman on her balcony beating her carpet, another standing in the window with a cigarette in her mouth, and another talking on the phone and staring blankly at me. As I slowly walked away, I wondered: did any of these women in their apartments ever think about the bones and ashes of the tens of thousands of Jews who had died in the Warsaw ghetto, those Jews buried in their park, their little oasis of serene contentment in this tumultuous city?

The Jewish Historical Institute housed a magnificent Judaica collection, assembled from remnants of the Jewish libraries and museums looted by the Nazis throughout Europe, then abandoned in a long line of freight cars on a railroad siding in Silesia. The upper floors were devoted to the story of the Warsaw ghetto and other Polish ghettos.

The most remarkable exhibit consisted of only two tin milk cans and ten tin boxes. These milk cans and tin boxes were unearthed from 1946 to 1950 when engineers and surveyors were helping to rebuild the former Warsaw ghetto. They contained thousands of pages that had been written and collected by Emanuel Ringelblum (1900–1943), the appointed historian and archivist for the Warsaw ghetto, who had formed the Oneg Shabbat (Yiddish, Friday evening gathering in honor of the Shabes) archives. He was determined to help the Jews document all their activities through writing and collecting. He hoped this material would help build a new Jewish identity.

During one of my visits to the Institute, I met Dr. Marion Fuks, a musicologist with a specialty in Jewish music. He played me a tune he had recorded from a Jewish violinist he met in 1965 in Shedlets (Siedlce), Poland. It was a beautiful melody, a Ger *nign*. As I listened, I realized that despite my initial misgivings about Poland I had found a few significant pockets of Jewish life (and music) that had survived the Holocaust. (And sure enough, in 1990, the Krakow Jewish festival was born, using klezmer music as its artistic cornerstone. Today it is the largest such festival in all of Europe.)

Monika and the New Kehile

Monika was a breath of fresh air for me after having spent several weeks among the elderly and among Jews whose lives had been disrupted by the Holocaust. I met her downstairs in the archives of the Jewish Historical Institute (which miraculously survived the war), while I was looking at several books. Next to her was a pile of black-and-white photographs that depicted Jewish cemeteries. Monika was a striking, fairly tall woman with jet-black straight hair and high cheekbones. She was involved in a project she had started the previous year, documenting all of the Jewish cemeteries in Poland from a historical perspective as well as examining the tombstones' carvings and inscriptions as an art form.

She and her husband Staczek had traveled extensively throughout Poland, visiting cities, small towns, and villages for these forgotten (often disappeared) Jewish cemeteries. Many of those that had nearly completely vanished had become part of a farmer's field or yard. She was very enthusiastic about her work and interested in mine, and she invited me to her apartment that evening.

There I met a whole different stratum of the *kehile* (outside of those who went to the kosher kitchen and shul). Its members were clandestinely involved not only in preserving Jewish culture, but in learning and creating it as well.

In the shul and kosher kitchen, many of the survivors had obviously been psychologically affected by their Holocaust experiences and were still paying the price for having survived. For many their motto during the war was "by any means necessary." I never wanted to mythologize any of the survivors I had met during my journey, but I still felt sorry for them, and this included Olek and his buddies I'd met in the kosher kitchen.

The main difference between the survivors and their children and their gentile friends' children was that they were born after the war and only knew of the Holocaust through the painful memories of their parents. Many of them had grown up in homes where their Jewishness was rarely spoken of and Judaism was a void in the home. Now, when they got together there was music, food, discussions—they were hungry to know more about this culture that had been nearly completely obliterated from Poland. Now, as democracy was gradually cracking the chains of the fascist government, they were no longer as afraid as their parents had been in the 1950s through the 1970s.

Because this was during the time of martial law, the government was suspicious of any nongovernmental organization, especially if its membership was primarily Jewish. And they were doubly suspicious of groups whose membership was made up of many former members and sympathizers of the outlawed labor union Solidarnosc (Solidarity). I was invited over the next three weeks to participate in meetings, speak about my field research, and play some of the tunes I had discovered. Each time we met in a different location and often we didn't know it until that very day. My reputation as a pied piper was growing, and these clandestine gatherings turned into lively, raucous music parties that often lasted into the wee hours of the morning— or until they were broken up by the police.

Parting Words

As I packed my bags and got ready for my arduous sixteen-hour journey to the Carpathian Ukraine, in the Soviet Union, the parting words of Dr. Fuks resonated in my head:

"Yitskhok, klezmer did not die in Auschwitz. We Polish Jews who live here today will not let the culture vanish. If we do, we have completed Hitler's work."

Chapter Five

SOVIET UNION:
UKRAINE

T FIRST I HADN'T PLANNED on traveling to the Soviet Union; I was going to focus my research solely on the Eastern bloc countries. But one evening, while visiting over at Monika's home in Warsaw, I met this wonderful and engaging Jewish woman named Ludmilla, who had spent her childhood in the Soviet Union. She told me that when she traveled to the Carpathian Ukraine she didn't meet any Jews, but she met Rom who played klezmer. This casual statement sowed some of my initial interest in the Carpathian region, which continues to this day. I decided then to get a little flavor of the Soviet Union while looking for klezmer—in the very mountains where the Ba'al Shem Tov was born.

Ludmilla had mentioned the town of Vinogradov (Vynohradiv, Ukraine, called Seylish by the Jews, from the Hungarian name for the town, Nagyszollos), near the Romanian border. Since Romania was to be my last stop on my trek, visiting Seylish would work out just fine. From Warsaw, I got a second-class ticket, since all of the sleeper wagons were sold out. The train arrived at the Polish-Soviet border at 3 A.M. This time not only did we have to go through the same passport control rigmarole (with the guards, dogs, flashlights, searching through baggage, and incessant asinine questions), but we all had to get off the train with our bags, cross over several train tracks, and board the Soviet train that would take me to Lemberg (Lviv, Ukraine). I would catch a train to Munkatsh (Mukacevo, Soviet Union; Mukaceve,

176

Ukraine) and change there to a small commuter train to Seylish.

The Soviet Union had purposely scaled their entire railroad system to a smaller gauge track from the rest of Europe. It was just another way for them to protect themselves from the West.

Once we boarded the train in Brisk (Brest-Litovsk, Ukraine—the border city one crosses into after leaving Terespol, Poland), I saw the conductor only once more. The train trip was rather relaxing. One of the charming customs the Soviet trains had was to make piping hot tea available free for all passengers. In each wagon there was a (presumably) Russian woman who had a samovar in her couchette. She would brew the tea and carry it with sugar on ornately decorated trays. The tea was served as it had always been served in the shtetl, in a *gleyzele* (Yiddish, a small glass) with a shiny tin holder. I watched carefully as my fellow passengers each took a cube of sugar, held it between their teeth, and sipped the tea through their pursed lips, straining the hot liquid through the sweet, sticky cube.

I tried it, only to burn my lips and then immediately spill the tea on my pants, scalding my crotch. I put down the tea and ran to the bathroom. I doused my crotch with cold water while I held my nose and tried not to step in the waste matter on the floor. Luckily, it was only a slight burn.

I was welcomed back to my couchette with hearty laughter from everyone, including a rather attractive Russian woman. How embarrassing—but it could have been worse.

I decided to sleep in Munkatsh and take the train to Seylish the next morning, figuring it would be harder to find a hotel late at night in Seylish. There was an inexpensive hotel near the train station. I unloaded all my gear there, then took a stroll through Munkatsh, known to Orthodox Jews for its once-great Hasidic dynasty.

The first Munkatsher *rebe* was Rabbi Solomon Spira. He was born in Lancut in 1832 and was the chief rabbi of Strzyzow, Poland, before he came to Munkatsh in 1880. From 1880 to 1883 he was the leader for all Hungarian Hasidim. His son Rabbi Khayim Eliezar, born in 1868, took over the dynasty, and through his great intellectual prowess and magnetic personality he attracted many more thousands of followers. Rabbi Khayim was a virulent opponent of Zionism and socialism and politically campaigned against all the Jewish candidates who espoused either. He believed that settling the land of Israel before the Messiah came was heretical and that all secular Jews— "free thinkers" like socialists who believed in man's will over God's will—

were heretical traitors to the Torah. He died in 1937, but not before he had convinced too many Jews not to seek refuge in America as the Nazi noose slowly tightened around Europe.

Before the tragic deportation of the Jews in May of 1944, their numbers in Munkatsh had reached nearly fifteen thousand. Sad to say, there are now more Munkatsher Hasidim in Brooklyn than there are Jews in the Carpathian Ukraine.

MUNKATSH

The older architecture in Munkatsh reminded me of some of the older neighborhoods in Budapest. The narrow side streets that led from the main boulevards were paved with cobblestones. None of the apartment buildings

The Jewish History of the Carpathian Ukraine

The history of the Jews in the eastern Carpathian Mountains is connected with Hungary through the end of World War I. Though there are documents stating that Jews were living in the counties of Ugocsa (Seylish) and Maramaros (Khust) as early as the late fourteenth century, the first major migration of Jews to the eastern Carpathian Mountains was from Galicia during the Chmielnicki pogroms of 1648 to 1649. The Hungarian landlords wanted to repopulate the region, so in 1730 they offered incentives to business owners and skilled workers if they would become permanent residents; this attracted many Jews.

The next wave of Galicianer Jews to reach this region came after the first partition of Poland in 1772. At this time the region became a part of the Austro-Hungarian Empire. When the Jews moved from Galicia south across the Carpathians into northeastern Hungary, they found similar living conditions: Ruthenian peasants, small mountain villages, and dire poverty.

The Jews adopted many of the customs of their Ruthenian neighbors. They wore fur hats and woolen clothing in the winter; in the summer their children were covered with long white skirts. Along with farming, peddling, and working in small handcrafts (shoes, clothes, leather), the other big industry for many Jews was timber.

Hasidism began to take

hold in this region at the beginning of the nineteenth century, with Munkatsh (Mukaceve, Ukraine) becoming the center for Carpathian Hasidism. There were also Hasidic dynasties in Ungar (Uzhhorod), Seylish (Vynohradiv), and Sziget (today, Sighetu-Marmatiei, Romania).

On the eve of World War I there were approximately 130,000 Jews living in the eastern Carpathian Mountain region. Most were poor, while many eked out a living farming. In fact, this region had the largest percentage of Jewish farmers (17 percent) in all of Eastern Europe.

After World War I, there were intense political negotiations as to which state should take over the Carpathian region. Eventually it was decided that the liberal approach of the new Czechoslovakian leaders, promising to grant autonomy to Subcarpathian Ruthenia (the new name for the region), was the correct approach. After the borders were finalized with Poland, Romania, and the Soviet Union, the Jewish population was only ninety thousand.

During the interwar period (1919 to 1939), the history of the Jews in Subcarpathian Ruthenia became part of the history of Czechoslovakia. The regions of Bohemia, Moravia, part of Silesia, Slovakia, and Subcarpathian Ruthenia that now constituted Czechoslovakia had been parts of the prewar Habsburg (Austro-Hungarian) Empire; the Czech lands had been in the Austrian portion, and the poorer and less developed Slovakia and Ruthenia had been in the Hungarian portion. During the interwar period, Subcarpathian Ruthenia had the largest percentage of Jews of all the provinces of Czechoslovakia: more than 14 percent of the total population was Jewish, and 80 percent of these Jews lived in *shtetlekh* and villages.

On September 30, 1938, the day of the Munich agreement, the Czechoslovakian government realized that its twenty-year period of independence was soon to end. Taking advantage of the instability in the Czech government, in November 1938 the Ukrainians established an independent state called Carpatho-Ukraine. On March 15, 1939, German troops marched into Bohemia and Moravia, and Carpatho-Ukraine was annexed by Hungary. Now the fate of its approximately ninety thousand Jews again became intertwined with the fate of all Hungary's Jewry.

Germany occupied the entire region on March 19, 1944, and by May had deported to Auschwitz the approximately fifty thousand Jews who had not already been taken prisoner and impressed into the labor battalions that served the Hungarian army. By the winter of 1944 some forty-two thousand of these Jews had perished in Auschwitz. After the war, only some sixteen thousand Jews returned to Subcarpathian-Ruthenia, which had become part of the Soviet Union. In 1981 there were some five thousand Jews in the region. Currently there are fewer than two thousand.

were more than six stories tall and some were built around a communal courtyard. Many of the storefronts bore the name of the person who had built the building or a sign of what it was used for prior to World War I in Hungarian. As I passed people on the streets, I soon realized how diverse the local population was. I heard Ukrainian, Russian, Hungarian, Ruthenian, and Romani. I was sure I was the only American in town and when I spoke to someone I used only my limited Hungarian, Russian, and Yiddish to make myself understood. I tried never to stand out, especially with my wardrobe. I loved this feeling of anonymity.

I had had so many incredible experiences up to this point that even if I didn't form a klezmer band when I returned to San Diego, I was keenly aware I was lucky to be where I was at that very moment. Even on days when I felt drained physically and mentally, I knew that the next adrenaline rush was just around the corner.

The next morning I took all my gear and went to breakfast at a restaurant I had noticed the night before. From the posters of fruits, vegetables, and sports figures on the wall, it looked like some kind of natural foods eatery. The place was called Latorica, named after the river that runs through Munkatsh. The place was clean and had an extensive menu, but there was just one catch: they didn't have half the items listed. Why? Because this was the Soviet Union, and nothing was ever really as it appeared.

In his broken English, German, and some Hungarian, the proprietor told me, "This is what we would like to serve here one day, but because of money, low supplies, the long winter, and Soviet bureaucracy, we still are waiting for that day. But let me serve you a hot bowl of kasha with some dried apricots sprinkled on top and black bread with peach preserves."

And that's exactly what I had—two bowls of the stuff, since I was quite hungry. The proprietor was ethnic Hungarian and interested in my violin. He looked at it, seemed rather impressed, and made a telephone call to someone. Ten minutes later, a Rom man, about fifty-five years old with a round cherubic face and gray hair, walked in and asked to look at my violin.

A Fateful Meeting with a Rom

He took the bow and began to play a Hungarian Rom melody. He was good, and I asked if he knew any Jewish melodies. Instantly he began to play a tune his father had played for the Munkatsher *rebe* in the 1930s, but when I took out my tape recorder he stopped. He wouldn't play as long as it was out. He explained through his friend that he was afraid his muse would be trapped inside the machine forever. He only wanted his music to be heard live, because once it was recorded it was no longer fresh. Music, he said, was meant to be heard live, not to be archaically preserved. He likened it to canned fruit versus freshly picked. If he had to, he ate canned fruit, but it was always best eaten fresh from the tree. The first bite was indescribable, and he wanted live music to be experienced that way.

He took a more careful look at my violin, then he asked if I wanted to sell it. At first I thought he was joking, but I knew he was serious when he pulled out a wad of rubles from his pocket and counted out one hundred dollars worth of rubles. By this time, another couple had come in and were watching us as they ate breakfast.

I tried to explain that the violin wasn't for sale and that it was worth quite a bit more than what he'd offered. Even if he did have the money, the violin meant too much to me. It had been given to me by my uncle after his son, my cousin Arnold, passed away. And what would I do without a violin during the rest of my trek?

The Rom violinist laughed, as if it had all been a joke, then put the violin away. He then tugged on my sleeve to follow him. The proprietor explained that he wanted to invite me to his home, where I would meet some other musicians. I told him I needed to catch the train to Seylish, but he said not to worry, since we were headed in the same direction, and that where we were going was not far from Seylish.

As we walked outside, he turned around and formally introduced himself to me. His name was Geza. I picked up my gear at the hotel and we walked through downtown, then to the outskirts—I thought he had said he lived nearby—and continued for another half hour.

In Tiszaujlok

As we walked on and on down a dirt road, I was starting to get just a little suspicious, but I pushed any negative thoughts out of my head and slogged along. A truck slowed down. The driver seemed to know Geza. They spoke briefly, then Geza motioned me to jump into the back of the open bed. I was glad to get off my feet and stop shlepping all my baggage. Yet I was beginning to wonder how far we were going that we needed to get a ride there. As it

The History of the Rom

The Rom were originally a nomadic low-caste tribal group from India. They earned their living as musicians, entertainers, and metal smiths. They were the only tribe to work with iron in ancient India because, according to the Hindu religion, iron was considered dangerous and impure to handle. The largest group of them settled in the northwestern region of Rajasthan.

The disintegration of the Indian empire in the seventh century brought wave upon wave of conquering armies, which swept through India and eventually Europe. Many Rom were captured and enslaved by the invading armies and taken to new lands. By the late fourteenth century, the Ottoman armies had conquered all of the Balkans, capturing the Rom and scattering them throughout the region. At the beginning of the fifteenth century the Rom were spread throughout Central Europe, and by the end of the sixteenth century they could be found in all of Europe.

The Rom were called different names by the indigenous peoples of each country through which they traveled. Some of these names have intriguing origins. For example, the Persians called the Rom *Karaki,* and the French in lower Provence, *Caraque.* The root word for both of these names is *kara* (common to all languages in the Near East), which means "black" in Tatar. The Rom were originally dark-skinned people and were thought to have originated from many different places. The Yiddish word for them, *Tsigayner,* came from the Greek word *athigganein* ("not to touch"). And then there were those Europeans who thought the Rom originated from Egypt and thus called them *Gypsies* in English.

The prejudices against the Rom were as varied as their names through the centuries. In the fourteenth century in Romania and parts of Serbia they became slaves of the landowners, knights, and the Church and were not emancipated until 1864.

However, the darkest times for the Rom were during the rule of the Third Reich. The first of many anti-Rom laws began with the Nuremberg Race Laws of 1935, declaring Rom and Jews to be second-class citizens, having "alien" blood. Considered asocial and parasitic people, the Rom and the Jews were the only ethnic groups throughout Europe to be singled out by the Nazis for annihilation. From August 1 to 3, 1944, the Germans liquidated the "Gypsy" camp in Auschwitz. The few able-bodied men and women were transported to slave labor camps; the rest, some twenty-five thousand, were gassed. By the end of World War II, more than five hundred thousand Rom had been systematically murdered.

turned out, we passed Beregszasz (Berehovo, Ukraine) and kept going for about eighteen miles before the truck pulled over to the side of the road and we jumped out.

There were other people, carrying various bags of food, drink, and other sundries, walking along the road toward a small town about half a mile ahead. I was grateful for the ride and couldn't imagine Geza walking this distance too often. Geza turned around and said we were just about there, another fifteen minutes through the town and we would be at his home. I laughed and pointed to my feet, indicating that they were tired and sore. Geza smiled, turned around, and kept walking. We turned from the highway onto the road into town. The sign said Vylok (the Ukrainian name), and underneath, in smaller letters, Tiszaujlok (the Hungarian name). It was late morning when we arrived in the town.

The town was rather nondescript. There were very few trees on the main street. The buildings were made either from wood or brick and were mostly two or three stories high, some only one. Most of the display windows were dirty and any items in them were in disarray. There were no street lamps—I'd later find it eerily dark at night, the only illumination coming from the dim headlights of an occasional car, light in the window of a house, or the burning end of a cigarette. There was very little automobile traffic; most people walked through town on the wide dusty street. A few people stared at me because I was carrying so much, but most were involved in their own private conversations, or merely said hello to Geza as we passed.

We crossed a little bridge, went down a dirt hill, and came to the narrow street of a poor Rom neighborhood. We passed little homes with chickens, ducks, or goats in the front yard. Other front yards were filled with detritus and mud, waiting for the spring gardening. An increasingly large entourage of Rom children was following us. They wore mismatched winter clothing—some new, most of it old, soiled, and worn—boots with holes in them, and boots four sizes too big. None of their faces exhibited anything but bliss.

Geza's small house was made from a combination of mud, bricks, and wood. As soon as we entered I gratefully unloaded my backpack on the floor and sat down next to it. My shirt was drenched with sweat.

The place was sparsely furnished, clean, and warm. The dirt floors were covered with rugs. The walls were painted white and green and decorated with photos of people and a painting of the Virgin Mary. There was a roaring fire in the kitchen fireplace. While I rested and got my bearings, Geza made me coffee and then went out to get his wife and kids.

I had to go the bathroom. I could tell from the looks of the neighborhood there was no indoor plumbing, so I went out to look for the outhouse. It was relatively clean and had toilet paper. When I went back into the house, I decided to take out my violin and play "Drohobitsh," the song I had learned from Raphael in Wroclaw.

When I was halfway through, Geza walked back in with a violin. He had also brought two other Rom: Pityu Bacsi, with a cello, and Laci, with an accordion. Pitchoo, a man in his fifties, wore pants much too baggy for his slender frame, and Laci, who seemed to be in his thirties, sported a soft fedora that balanced his wild black beard. None of them had cases for their instruments; they just carried them, regardless of the cold.

My violin was a hundred years old. I bet it wouldn't reach a hundred and one here.

Geza started to play a Rom tune. Then Pitchoo and Laci kicked in with rhythm and harmony. After ten minutes an old Rom woman, maybe in her eighties, wearing a red and yellow scarf around her head, walked in carrying a chair and sat down right in the middle of the room. I had the sense that she was either the mother of one of the musicians or some respected matriarchal figure in the neighborhood. Whoever she was, she scrutinized me carefully, which made me a bit uncomfortable.

Then another woman came in. Before long, the room was packed with children of all ages and their parents. They sat on the sofa and on the floor in the bedroom, in the kitchen—wherever there was some floor space, it was occupied by someone. It was so crowded Geza hardly had enough room to move his bow up and down. When they finished their tune, I started one I had learned from Arye Kolman back in Kolin, Czechoslovakia. They listened for a few bars, then joined me. Damn, these guys had incredible ears! Their playing and the spirit from the audience made me play even better. I didn't want to be shown up by these guys.

The room became so hot, with all of the combined body heat and perspiration, that I took off my sweatshirt. This elicited giggles from the teenage girls.

As I played, I noticed that many of the faces seemed to radiate pure joy. Then one young woman, wearing a long red and purple dress, got up and danced. She was joined by a man with knee-length boots, mustache, and black fedora. Everyone squeezed and pushed back to make room for them to dance. The man did the Hungarian folk steps I had seen done by some Rom in Miskolc. He slapped his boots, thighs, and chest with his open palms, jumped frenetically up and down, snapped his fingers, and occasionally turned in a circle, all in rhythm with the music. The woman held the hem of her dress outstretched from her sides and took fast, furious little up-and-down steps, basically in the same spot. Some people clapped; others made percussive sounds with their mouths.

Then I began to sing the Yiddish song "Ale Brider" (Yiddish, All Brothers), which took everyone by surprise. When I began to sing the chorus—"*oi, yoi, yoi*"—everyone joined me. It was a picture of kinetic frenzy and musical chaos all wrapped together. No one left the room and we played for three hours nonstop. The fingers on my left hand were black from my strings and my right hand ached from holding the violin bow for so long in one position.

Finally the old woman with the pretty red and yellow scarf got up and grabbed her chair. Everyone stepped aside and made way for her to walk out the door. It was like Miriam crossing the Red Sea. After she left the room everyone followed her, but the music kept on until the room was completely empty except for us musicians and one young man named Zoli.

Zoli, Geza's nephew, was in his early twenties, tall, dark, and handsome, and a guitarist. He was clean-shaven, with a baby-soft complexion and jet-black collar-length hair. Unfortunately he didn't have any strings for his instrument because they were too expensive and couldn't be found in the entire town. He spoke fairly good English, and he asked me all sorts of questions, then translated the answers to Geza and the others. Then I had one question for them: Could I stay with someone that night? I figured Seylish could wait until the morning—if I still was going to go there at all.

Geza said I could stay with his brother Valentin (Zoli's father). He had a larger home and I would be more comfortable there. Then Geza spoke to Zoli in Romani for a moment and Zoli asked me if I wanted to go to the wedding of Geza's daughter, Maria. Are you kidding? A Rom wedding? When and where? I asked. It was in a nearby village called Salang (Salanka, Ukraine) and we would leave the next morning to get there by evening, when the wedding was to begin.

I was so excited about seeing a Rom wedding, I got up and did a little dance while I sang a Stoliner *nign*. They all laughed and then accompanied me as I tried to do some of the folk dance steps. Nothing like embarrassing yourself in front of strangers. They laughed and laughed and then for my encore I tripped over a chair and fell hard on my ass (it was sore for a few days). This brought down the house. Zoli suggested we get something to eat at his home, where I would be staying. I readily agreed—I was starving.

As I packed my violin, I asked if they thought it was worth going to Seylish to meet some Rom who played klezmer. Pityu Bacsi said that tomorrow I would meet his brother, a bass player who used to play in a band until all of the Jews in the band emigrated in the early 1970s. There was no need for me to travel to Seylish. His brother would play some Jewish tunes with the other musicians tomorrow.

Just as I was leaving Geza's, he told me that while I was in Tiszaujlok I should only walk around with Zoli. The local police might get suspicious of my presence. Strangers from the West didn't visit their town too often. Zoli said there were only three Jews left in the town. In the early 1970s there had been twelve or so, but they had moved to either Budapest or Israel.

It was five o'clock when Zoli and I walked to his home, which was indeed larger and more furnished than Geza's. He showed me my room, which had a bed piled high with eiderdown quilts. There was a mirror on the wall next to a statue of Jesus. Zoli apologized about having no running water and said if I wanted to wash myself he would boil some water from the well. There was an iron bathtub in the backyard. I had sweated so much from the journey getting to the town and then from all the playing, plus I hadn't showered in over thirty-six hours, and even I could smell that I needed to bathe. It was relatively mild (mid-forties), so I thought taking a bath outdoors wouldn't be too excruciating—boy was I wrong.

STREAKING IN THE CARPATHIANS

The bathtub was near the outhouse and behind some canvas partitions for privacy. I undressed and jumped right in. Zoli had boiled enough water so I was able to sit down in the bathtub and have the water up to my navel. It might have been mild out, but standing naked in forty-degree weather was rather bracing. The water felt good and I was happy to wash, especially my hair. While I washed I thought about my grandparents. I wondered how often they had been able to wash themselves in a week, considering the great effort it took to prepare a bath, especially in wintertime. Taking a bath in a small town, in the Rom neighborhood, outdoors in the wintertime was indeed shtetl life. It was fascinating, and my firsthand experience made for good storytelling, but one should never romanticize it. Forget about threats from the non-Rom population (and the non-Jewish population during shtetl times)—just getting through everyday life would be difficult, tedious, and tiring. There was nothing sentimental about going to the bathroom in an outhouse, where the toilet seat was wooden boards placed over a deep hole.

Needless to say, I didn't linger too long in the tub. The water was beginning to cool and I was cold from my chest up. Just as I was stepping out of the tub, two kids—a boy and girl probably eight and ten—stepped around the canvas partition and grabbed my clothes. I yelled for them to come back; then I yelled for Zoli. There was no answer. Then I yelled that I would give them some candy. Finally I told them I would pay them each a dollar if they returned my clothes. The wind began to blow and I was beginning to really feel the cold draft, so I had no choice. I climbed out of the tub (the stinkers had even taken my towel) and went looking for them. There I was, stark naked in the dirt among the chickens and ducks (ducks can be ornery and will peck you if provoked), with everything flapping in the breeze.

At last the kids came from behind a shed, laughing and running with my clothes. I yelled and ran after them around the outhouse and bathtub and finally out into the street where there were a number of people. I never did catch them, but they dropped my clothes on a bicycle that was parked against the fence. I jumped into my underwear and pants so fast I almost tore them. Those on the street were thoroughly amused at my expense, clapping and laughing while I bowed and curtsied, yelling out in Romani "*nice-tuke*" (thank you).

I walked back to the well to wash off my mud-splattered feet and legs. Just then Zoli came out from his neighbor's house, laughing, and told me he had heard what happened. He apologized and hoped I wasn't too angry. Instead of being angry, I laughed too and told Zoli that now I could brag to my friends back home that I had streaked in a Carpathian village.

That night at dinner I met Zoli's two younger sisters (twins) and his father and mother. I asked where his sisters were going to sleep tonight and he said at another uncle's home. I was quite surprised that they had given up their

Galushke

STUFFED CABBAGE

Makes 12 servings

My mother always worked when we were kids, and because she was short for time, her meals tended to be simple and nutritious. But my brother and I have distinct memories of her occasionally springing into action and preparing this recipe. Hands down, this is the best thing my mother ever cooked, and my brother and I still salivate thinking about Mom's stuffed cabbage. She learned this recipe from her mother, Sylvia Frackman, and her grandmother, Bella Schwartz. The sweet-and-sour flavoring is classic Ukrainian and Russian cuisine.

For best results, the cabbage should sit, so the flavors can become saturated. The last time I made this, I refrigerated the leftovers, and when I reheated the stuffed cabbage two days later, it was actually better. But it's also great right out of the oven. My mother puts the raisins in the filling, but I prefer to layer them over the cabbages as they cook; if someone doesn't like them, they can just push them to the side.

One last note: While this recipe may seem a bit labor-intensive, the microwave reduces a lot of effort. I've also provided a method for those without a microwave.

2 large heads green cabbage

2 medium onions, peeled and sliced

2 lb. ground meat (or vegetarian ground meat substitute)

1 cup cooked brown rice, cooled

2 large eggs

1 cup seasoned breadcrumbs

¼ cup ketchup

2 medium onions, finely chopped

Salt and pepper to taste

¼ cup water (if needed)

1 large can sauerkraut, drained

1 cup white raisins

1 cup firmly packed brown sugar

Juice of 2 lemons

1 28-oz. can chopped tomatoes

1. Rinse the cabbage heads and wrap them in plastic wrap. Microwave on high for 5 to 7 minutes, until the outside leaves are soft and wilted. Cool slightly by running under cold water. (If you don't have a microwave, bring a pot of water to a boil, reduce the heat, and simmer the cabbages—without the wrap!—until softened, about 10 minutes.) Remove the outer leaves and return the heads to the microwave (or water) to soften and remove more outer leaves. Repeat until all the large leaves are softened—each head should yield 12 to 14 leaves. Each remaining cabbage head should be about the size of a large softball.

2. Using a sharp knife, trim away any remaining core or thick ribs from each leaf (don't go overboard—you need enough pliable leaf to wrap around the filling). Set these leaves aside. Halve the remaining cabbage heads, cut out the core, slice the cabbage, and layer it on the bottom of a lasagna pan or roasting pan along with the sliced onions.

3. In a large bowl, combine the rice, meat, eggs, breadcrumbs, ketchup, and chopped onion with salt and pepper to taste; *season well.* If mixture seems dry, add the water. (My mother goes by sound; if you mix it together and it sounds "gloopy," it's the right consistency!)

4. Preheat the oven to 375°. To assemble, lay a leaf down with the stem end toward you, hollow side up. Place 2 to 3 tablespoons of the filling in the middle of the leaf; gauge the amount by the size of the leaf. Roll up the bottom to cover, then the sides, and finally, fold over the top. As you work, place each cabbage roll, seamed side down, on the onions and cabbage in the pan. Pack them tightly together; they should form a single layer. Cover with the sauerkraut and raisins.

5. Combine the brown sugar, lemon juice, and chopped tomatoes and pour it all over the dish, allowing the juices to run to the bottom of the pot. Cover tightly with foil and bake. After 2 hours, check for doneness—the cabbage rolls should be brown from the sauce. Serve warm, or allow to cool and refrigerate for 24 hours; to serve, preheat the oven to 350° and cook, covered, until thoroughly heated, about 30 minutes.

bedroom to me. Zoli explained, "You are our friend. Your music has touched our hearts and as a Jew you understand how we have suffered in the past."

I was so touched by his words it brought tears to my eyes. They hardly knew me, but they treated me like family.

The dinner table stood in the middle of the living room. It was a sturdy table made by Tibi, Zoli's father. He was a carpenter and earned more than most of the other Rom in the neighborhood. Zoli's mother worked in a box factory, while Zoli's twin sisters watched after their younger cousins—the same kids who had stolen my clothes.

During dinner everyone had questions for me. What was California like? Had I ever been to Hollywood? Did I ever meet Michael Jackson or Sylvester Stallone? I answered all their questions as I kept an eye on what was being served: sarmi (stuffed cabbage), soup with some kind of meat, a corn and barley dish with a lot of oil in it, and roasted potatoes. When I told them I was a vegetarian, everyone just looked at me as if I were crazy. Then Zoli told me the barley dish was cooked with lard, so the only thing I could eat was the potatoes. Zoli brought out a little cheese for me as well and I dined on three roasted potatoes, bread, cheese, and some homemade apricot vodka.

After dinner, Tibi asked me if I would sing a Yiddish song, because he liked hearing the language. While growing up in the town, Tibi used to go over to the home of the Vanshils, his Jewish neighbors, to play with their son Asher. He remembered some of the Yiddish words he heard them speak the many times he visited, like *khazer* (pig), *tcholnt* (traditional stew made from beans, potatoes, meat, and spices, eaten on Shabes afternoon), Shabes, *taykl* (river), and *sazshekle* (pond)—a word I had never heard until Tibi had said it. To show my appreciation for dinner, I sang "Bulbes/Beblekh." It seemed rather appropriate.

The next day, I was awoken by Zoli's mischievous little cousins. They jumped up and down on the bed and had a pillow fight. I wanted to get a little even for the stunt they'd pulled on me. I figured a few good wallops over the head with the goose-down pillows wouldn't really do too much damage. Then Zoli stepped into the room, shooed them away, and told me we were leaving in half an hour.

It was another mild day, and in a week it would be March. I was so looking forward to spring.

By Horse-Drawn Wagon

We all (Zoli's dad, mother, twin sisters, aunt, uncle, and I) got into a horse-drawn wagon. The wagon was pulled by two strong-looking, rather short, dark brown horses; Tibi was at the reins. I wasn't sure how far we were going, but as it turned out, we didn't get to Salang until late afternoon.

We traveled down dirt roads, passed by only a few vehicles. For most Rom, transportation was either by horse-drawn wagon or bicycle, or on foot. It was sunny and the wide expanse of the countryside was beautiful. We passed forests where the first spring leaves were beginning to bud, fields that were being planted, wooden and cinder-block homes, a few roadside businesses (food stands, tire fixing, homemade liquor and wine), and herds of sheep and goats, all at the foot of the snowcapped Carpathian Mountains. We stopped a few times to go to the bathroom (in the woods), to eat, and to rest and water the horses at a stream. I felt so alive, sitting in the wagon with Zoli and his family. This was an experience I never would have dreamed of having before I left San Diego.

In fact, sitting with these Rom and watching the passing landscape made me feel far removed from everyday life in San Diego. I didn't have a care in my head and didn't feel compelled to even think about time. I thought to myself, probably some klezmer band sixty years before rode down the same path going to play at a wedding. And from what I had observed so far in Tiszaujlok and its environs, not much had changed since.

During the trip, Zoli and his sisters sang different Rom folk songs. There was definitely a kinship between the Jews and the Rom. I couldn't quite put it into words, but when I listened to them singing, it unequivocally touched my *neshome* (Yiddish, soul). After they sang for an hour, they asked me to play a melody. I was so inspired by these people and the scenery, I decided to compose something right then and there.

My fingers danced about the violin neck with no predetermined impulse from my conscious brain. I'd linger on a note, then immediately slide to another and play a passage that repeated itself over and over until that thought was done. My fingers were working in accordance with my lungs and heart, all operating from some innate, primordial, natural impulse to live. After a few minutes, Zoli began to softly sing counterpoint to my *nign*. It was if his

"On the Road to Salang"

Yale Strom

melody and mine were long-lost siblings meeting for the first time. It all began to make sense as we continued our musical conversation.

The literal meaning of klezmer came from the combination of two Hebrew words: *kley* (tool, utensil) and *zmer* (melody). Zoli and I were only the vessels for these melodies, the tools for the songs.

Zoli's father and mother began to sing along with us. As I rode along the bumpy dirt road and looked out at the passing scenery, I felt a sense of spirituality I had never felt before, a sense of *dveykes* to Mother Nature.

We arrived in Salang at 5 P.M., having been on the road for nearly seven hours. The village square was packed with Rom, all dressed in various finery. The wedding ceremony was going to take place outdoors; afterward, the celebration would be in the largest building in the village, the town hall.

Geza and his family, who had taken a bus, saw us as we rode into town. He came over to his brother Tibi and sister-in-law, Maria, and kissed them on their cheeks, then pulled me down from the wagon and began to speak. As he spoke, a crowd of people formed a circle around us. Zoli stood behind me and translated. Basically he thanked everyone for coming to celebrate his daughter's wedding and he thanked Devla (Romani for God) for sending me to him, a Jew with a violin—and now a friend for life.

THE WEDDING

Everyone clapped, and then the band began to play an upbeat tune; everyone joined in with the lyrics. While the minister prepared to marry the couple, people came up to me, shook my hand, slapped my back, and offered me a drink from their bottles of cherry-flavored vodka. After five swigs of that firewater, I politely tried to decline—when that didn't work, I'd take a small gulp and then hold it in my mouth until the person turned away from me, at which point I could spit it onto the ground.

Geza's daughter Gabriella and the groom were both eighteen. She had a round chubby face and a big smile. She wore a crown of sorts connected to her white lace embroidered veil. The groom wore a black suit with a red flower in his lapel. His hair was slicked back and he too had a look of happiness—mixed with fear and anxiety. All of the other men wore suits and ties and many wore black fedoras; many of the women wore colorful long skirts with their long hair either braided or under a scarf. Some of the older women had braided a necklace made of old silver and gold coins into their hair. In Romani this was called a *bisaria*. Some of the younger women wore clothing that had been fashionable in the 1970s. (After nearly a year in the Eastern bloc I was able to ascertain that the countries were at least ten years behind the West in almost every aspect of modern-day society.)

The religious ceremony, held in the middle of the street, took only ten minutes. By this time the sun had gone down completely and the only light came from the flickering candles most people were holding in their hands. After the wedding vows, the music resumed while they embraced and kissed. Then they walked to the hall for the wedding reception, followed by the band and everyone else.

Zoli grabbed my arm and said, "You'll sit with us . . . and don't plan on sleeping until the sun comes up tomorrow."

The rest of the night I celebrated along with everyone else. I'm not much of a dancer, but during the course of the evening several attractive Rom women just grabbed my arm and dragged me to the dance floor. The music was a combination of Hungarian Rom folk music as well as Hungarian and Russian pop.

There was a lot of food, most of which wasn't (or at least didn't look) vegetarian. I managed to find some bread, vegetables (including a mushroom dish), and fruit to satiate myself until the dessert was served. The dessert was a combination of Hungarian and Ukrainian delicacies, including honey cake and cheesecake. Interestingly enough, the wedding cake was served only to the immediate family members, probably because it was small and wouldn't feed everyone.

By 3 A.M. I was so tired I went to a corner of the hall, pulled two chairs together, leaned my head against the wall, and closed my eyes. I wasn't really going to fall asleep with all of the noise and commotion, but it was relaxing to shut my eyes and only see through my ears. Soon all of the extraneous sounds and music became white noise.

The next thing I knew, Zoli was waking me up. I thought I had only dozed off for a few minutes, but it was 9:30 A.M. I couldn't believe it. I had slept through all of the noise for six hours and still felt groggy. It probably was all of that vodka.

Most of the people had left for home; some were sleeping with their heads down on the tables, while others were helping to clean up the enormous

Russian-Style Baked Mushrooms in Sour Cream

Makes 4 to 6 servings

This dish is so satisfying, it can be served as a main course, accompanied by a chunk of black bread and a tossed salad.

8 Tbsp. (1 stick) butter, in all

4 Tbsp. flour

2 cups sour cream

¼ to ½ cup milk (if needed)

1 lb. button mushrooms

1 medium onion, minced

2 Tbsp. grated hard cheese, such as Parmigiano-Reggiano

Salt and freshly ground black pepper to taste

Fennel leaves for garnish

1. In a medium saucepan, melt 4 tablespoons of the butter, then add the flour. Stirring constantly, cook the roux over low heat until it starts to turn golden, about 5 minutes.

2. In a separate pan, bring the sour cream to a boil, then reduce the heat and add the roux. Blend thoroughly until the sauce is a nice, smooth, creamy consistency. If necessary, add some milk, a tablespoon at a time, to thin it. Add salt and pepper to taste.

3. Preheat the oven to 350°. Slice the mushrooms. Place an oven-safe sauté pan or cast-iron skillet on the stove and melt 2 more tablespoons of the butter. Add the onion and sauté until translucent. Add the mushrooms and sauté for about 10 minutes, or until the mushrooms are soft. Add the sour cream sauce and bring to a boil. Reduce the heat, add the cheese, and dot with the remaining butter. Transfer the pan to the oven and bake for 10 to 15 minutes, until golden on top. Garnish with fennel leaves and serve.

Ukrainian Honey Cake

Makes 10 to 12 servings

½ cup butter

1 cup granulated sugar

4 large eggs, separated

1 cup honey

1 cup sour cream

3 cups cake flour

2 tsp. baking soda

2 tsp. baking powder

1 tsp. cinnamon

1 tsp. ground allspice

¼ tsp. salt

1½ cups chopped walnuts

1 cup golden raisins

1. Preheat oven to 300°. Generously butter and lightly flour a Bundt pan.

2. In a large bowl, cream the butter and sugar until light and creamy. Add the egg yolks one at a time, beating to incorporate each one. Add the honey and sour cream and stir to combine.

3. In a separate bowl, beat the egg whites until they form stiff peaks.

4. Sift together the flour, baking soda, baking powder, cinnamon, nutmeg, and salt. Alternating between the dry ingredients and the egg whites, gently fold into the batter. Fold in the nuts and raisins.

5. Pour gently into the prepared cake pan. Bake for 1 hour to 1¼ hours, until a cake tester or toothpick inserted in the center comes out clean. Immediately turn out of the pan onto a wire rack to cool. Serve warm.

mess. Zoli told me that Geza had wanted me to play a klezmer tune for the newlyweds some time in the night but I hadn't responded to their poking and prodding and couldn't be woken up.

I slowly hobbled to my feet, gathered my belongings, found the water pump, and stuck my head underneath it as Zoli moved the handle up and down. Wow! The water temperature was barely above freezing, but it felt so refreshing.

We walked back to the wagon to join the rest of the family who were all waiting for us (waiting for me, that is; everyone else had been ready to leave at 6:30 A.M.). We jumped into the wagon and started our trek home.

Back in Tiszaujlok

The next day I decided to take another hot bath, only this time I brought my clothes with me and told Zoli to keep a watch out for his cousins. After that Zoli had errands to do, but before he left, I asked him the best way to get to Iasi, Romania, my next destination. Unfortunately, even though I was just a few miles from the Romanian border it was not an international border crossing for tourists. Only truckers and local people who lived on either side of the border were allowed to cross near Tiszaujlok, so I would have to take the train to Czernowitz (Cernovcy, Ukraine). There I would change for another train across the Soviet border into Siret, Romania. From Siret I would take the train to Suceava and change there for the train to Iasi. I didn't know any of the train schedules, and there was no way of finding out in Tiszaujlok. But it sounded like it was going to take me a full day to get to Iasi, so I decided to leave the next morning.

After my bath, the house was empty. I did some writing for about half an hour before Pityu Bacsi came over looking for Tibi. They had to rehearse some music for a fancy wedding they were hired to play for the following week in Beregszasz (Berehovo, Ukraine). I asked him if he had a moment to play me a Jewish tune. He sat down, tightened his bow and began to play "Hava Nagila." I let him finish and asked him if he knew any others. Then he played a famous Israeli tune, "Yerushalyim Shel Zahav" (Hebrew, Jerusalem of Gold), which surprised me. I asked him where he had learned it. He said that back in the days when he was playing in a restaurant in Kiev, the bandleader had had them play a number of Israeli tunes when Jewish American tourists would come in and dine.

I tried to explain that I was interested in hearing some Hasidic melodies. I pantomimed the typical beard and side locks that helped define Hasidic men. He closed his eyes and leaned his chin on the cello for a minute. Then he opened his eyes, said something to me I didn't understand, and began to play something that sounded strangely familiar. I couldn't figure it out at first, then it hit me: he was playing "Hatikvah," Israel's national anthem. After he finished he got up, shook my hand, and carried his cello out into the cool damp weather.

I chuckled to myself. I had thought I was going to hear some incredible unknown klezmer tunes; instead, I'd heard music I'd learned as a child in Hebrew school.

I practiced for the rest of the day and then went for a walk through the town. I found a restaurant and went in. There were about ten round tables. The paneled walls were decorated with photos of the flora and fauna of the Carpathian Mountains. And in one corner there was an old-style jukebox

Geza and Pityu Bacsi in the railroad station in Vynohradiv

Pokhlyobka

VEGETABLE SOUP

Makes 4 to 6 servings

4 oz. dried mushrooms

2 Tbsp. butter or oil

2 onions, chopped

2 leeks, white part only, sliced

2 carrots, sliced

2 large potatoes, diced

2 bay leaves

4 peppercorns

2 Tbsp. pearl barley

Salt to taste

2 Tbsp. sour cream

½ Tbsp. flour

2 sprigs fresh dill, chopped

1. Soak the mushrooms in a pint of warm water for at least 2 hours. Rub with your fingers to remove any grit. Drain, reserving the water, slice, and set aside. Strain the water and set aside.

2. Heat the butter or oil in a sauté pan and fry the onions lightly until translucent. Add the leeks and carrots and fry together for a few minutes.

3. Transfer to a large stockpot. Add the reserved mushroom water and about 6 cups additional water. Add the mushrooms, potatoes, bay leaves, peppercorns, barley, and salt. Bring to a simmer, cover, and cook, stirring occasionally, until the mushrooms, potatoes, and barley are tender, about 20 minutes.

4. Combine the sour cream and flour, mixing well. Stir into the soup about 5 minutes before removing from the stove. Serve sprinkled with chopped dill.

where one could listen to Russian, Ukrainian, and Hungarian pop and even a few American tunes from the 1960s. I put some money in and picked the ska tune "My Girl Lollipop." The menu offered Hungarian and Ukrainian dishes like borscht, red beans with beef, cold fruit soup, pork with millet, beef goulash, chicken paprikash, baked carp, and noodles with cheese, bacon, and grapes.

I met a young Ruthenian woman who spoke English. The restaurant was managed by her parents. I asked her what it would cost to have ten people for a full-course dinner with some wine. She said, "Twenty-five dollars." I gave her the money and went back to tell Zoli. I had decided to take his family, as well as Geza's, out for dinner since they had been so hospitable to me.

They were quite surprised and enjoyed the dinner, which was fit for a *treyf*-eating carnivore (*treyf* is Yiddish for nonkosher). Fortunately, the soup was vegetarian; I dined on soup, baked potatoes, cooked peas, turnips, and ice cream.

The next day Zoli took me by bus to Seylish, my original destination. Just as I was purchasing the train ticket, in walked Geza and Pityu Bacsi with their instruments. They wanted to say goodbye with an old Jewish tune Geza's father used to play for the Spinke *rebe,* Rabbi Isaac Yitskhok Weiss (1875–1944). (The Spinke *rebe,* through his financial generosity, Hasidic storytelling, and genuine love, had helped to comfort his thousands of Hungarian followers who were mostly poor. After World War I, he had moved to Seylish from Munkatsh. In 1944 he was deported along with his whole family to Auschwitz.)

Apparently Pityu Bacsi had told Geza about my disappointment in the Jewish tunes he played for me yesterday. Geza was sure I hadn't ever heard this tune, and together they performed it in the train station while I waited for my train to Czernowitz. And sure enough, they played a *nign* I had never heard, a stirring one. Though I was all packed up, I couldn't resist turning on the tape recorder that was hidden in my backpack. Even if the fidelity wasn't great, I would still have enough of a recording that I could learn from.

I had been in the Carparthian Mountains for only a few days, but I knew I would return someday. There was something magical about this economically poor, but spiritually rich and beautiful region of the Ukraine. It was no wonder that such a region had nurtured the writer and philosopher Elie Wiesel during his youth.

Chapter Six

ROMANIA

THE TRAIN HUGGED the Romanian border as it chugged endlessly down the tracks. I was feeling melancholy, knowing that my journey was slowly coming to an end. I had made many friends, I had accomplished a lot of klezmer research, and I had thoroughly relished the carefree, wandering vicissitudes of my life over the last year. I hadn't had to worry much about money, schedules, time commitments, or being responsible for anybody but myself. And I had felt wanted and appreciated—fussed over, even—by those who took me into their homes; in this regard, my Eastern bloc adventure had become a personal opiate. Every day brought something new and challenging, whereas back home life was all too predictable, mundane, and infected with uncontrollable consumerism.

LAYOVER IN SUCEAVA

The train station was packed. Every seat was taken. People were lying or sitting on the floor with all of their baggage. I quickly surveyed the room and knew that except for me everybody there was Romanian—and judging by their clothes, most were peasants. Not only did they have their normal baggage, they were carrying sacks and sacks of potatoes, turnips, beets, cabbage, and onions, and live animals. I finally found a seat on a bench and realized that the man's satchel leaning against me was full of live ducks. A woman across from me had some chickens, and next to her was a goat. In fact, there were several goats just aimlessly walking about the train depot, their rope leashes dragging behind them as they devoured every crumb in sight. They even tried some of the produce in the satchels.

And to add to this already surreal scene, policemen walked around, hopping over bags, going up to certain individuals and asking them for their identification. These were simple farming folk. What could the police be looking for or monitoring? I wouldn't have been surprised if the police suddenly decided to round up the goats for questioning.

I kept a low profile, figuring that an American sitting in the midst of this barnyard (which was starting to remind me of *Animal Farm*) would draw some suspicions from the paranoid police.

After forty minutes, the stench of the animals and people mixed with the heat was starting to overwhelm me. I began to feel nauseous, so I left my instruments under the bench and my backpack on the floor by the woman who had the goat. She had shared some bread and brinze cheese with me and seemed to take a liking to me. I went out to get a bit of fresh air.

Outside, a number of soldiers were waiting for the trains to take them home or to their bases. I stood among them on the gravel that separated the tracks, aimlessly throwing stones while trying to eavesdrop on their conversations. I really didn't know more than a few words of Romanian but it gave me something to do. The cold, fresh air was invigorating but when that wind picked up it was excruciatingly, bitterly cold (five degrees Fahrenheit). It didn't seem like spring had sprung yet in Romania. My gloves were not at all adequate to keep my hands warm, so I tucked my hands inside my pants to warm them up against my body. How these young soldiers were able to stand around, some not even wearing gloves, smoking and bantering in such cold weather was beyond me.

After about twenty minutes of walking around and trying to keep my blood from freezing, I just couldn't take the severe cold anymore. I could barely feel my toes and fingers, so I went back inside the train depot. I got all my gear and brought it closer to the door so if the stench and heat got to me again I could just get a quick whiff of the frigid air to set me straight again.

Another hour went by. The train finally pulled into the station. You'd have thought this train was taking all of us on a trip to the beaches of Greece—before the train had even come to a full stop, everyone (goats included) ran out of the depot and rushed the doors. People opened the doors and crammed themselves and all of their belongings into the compartments and narrow hallways. Judging by the rush of people, it was definitely open seating. Whichever couchette someone could push themselves into, they went to the window, opened it, and had other people hand them the rest of the luggage, produce, and livestock as well. One couple had two goats; the man was handing them to his wife, who was leaning out of the window. She pulled in the flummoxed animals despite their loud bleating and kicking legs.

The conductor blew his whistle repeatedly, trying to get everyone in, as the train was about to leave. I knew I had to somehow get all of my gear onto this train. From the way the hallways were overflowing there was no way I could get it all through the door without breaking one of my instruments, so I yelled at the woman who had given me the food earlier. She was already in a couchette. I got her attention and without even trying to ask her, I just began handing her my stuff through the window. At least my bags were safely on the train—now I just had to squeeze into the wagon.

The whistle blew and the train lurched forward, slowly pulling out of the station. I ran to the door, grabbed the railing, and pulled myself up onto the stairs. A man with huge callused hands grabbed me by the shoulders and literally lifted me into the train. It turned out he was the woman's husband. They even saved a seat for me. Then they took out the *tzuica* (Romanian brandy, usually made from plums or pears), bread, and homemade pork sausage and prepared a picnic.

In two hours I would be in Iasi, the birthplace of Yiddish theater, with a headache . . . and a stomachache.

IASI

My first impressions of Iasi were, quite frankly, disheartening. There were people in long lines waiting to buy bread. They were queuing up in front of a farmer's wagon filled with carrots, cabbage, and potatoes. There were potholes and garbage strewn about in most of the streets. The electric trams and buses were all in a terrible state of disrepair, with doors hanging off the hinges and broken windows, and the few private cars and taxis were trucks that belched black smoke from their broken exhaust pipes. I also noticed a large number of Rom in the city, wearing their distinctive colorful clothes, scarves, and hats. Many had a horse and a wagon filled with bedding, children, and food. They all looked quite impoverished. At my hotel, there was no hot water and no heat in the rooms.

The city seemed to be a haven for all of the country's stray dogs. Most looked pitifully hungry, had mange, and were scared of most human contact. I threw pieces of bread to several of them, which of course made me their friend. As I walked they followed me at a distance.

The produce stores had very little that looked fresh, and the canned goods, judging by the layers of dust on them, had all been there for months. I didn't want to wait in any line and I wasn't about to eat some lead-filled can of food, so I satisfied my hunger with *langos*—greasy fried sour cheese donuts that were sold at kiosks on the street corners.

The Jewish History of Romania

Jews first settled in Romania in pre-Christian times, probably as part of the same migration from Persia and Palestine that created Jewish colonies along the coasts of the Black and Caspian seas and in the Caucasus in the sixth century B.C.E.

In the fourteenth century the principalities of Moldavia in the north and Wallachia formed the nucleus of what was to become Romania. Well-established Jewish communities already existed in both regions. Subjugated by the Turks in the sixteenth century, the two Ottoman Empire vassal states continued to be ruled by Christian princes whose Jewish subjects were under constant harassment.

Jews expelled from Hungary in 1349 and 1360 found a haven in Wallachia. Refugees from the Ukrainian pogroms of 1648 and 1649 poured across the border into Moldavia, and Ladino-speaking Jews from Turkey settled in both principalities between 1500 and 1700. Late in the eighteenth century, Jewish merchants and artisans from Poland, the German lands, and Hungary were invited by the Romanian nobles to create towns in Moldavia and to transform the feudal system into a modern economy. Jews who fled tsarist oppression in Poland and the Ukraine in the nineteenth century found greater freedom in Moldavia.

When the Kingdom of Romania came about in 1861—with the unification of Moldavia and Wallachia—there was a brief interlude of tolerance for the Jews. How-

It was hard to imagine what Romania the Yiddish singer-composer Aaron Lebedeff (1873–1960) was writing about when he wrote his hit Yiddish song "Romania, Romania" in 1925. It was an anthem to the delights and beauty of Romania and had one verse that went: "Oi Romania, Romania, it was a land, so beautiful, so fine." Alas, no longer.

To top it off, Romania, more than the other countries on my trek, was pervaded with a distinct paranoia, a fear and suspicion. I soon realized I was being closely watched by the notorious Securitate (secret police). They even questioned me when I checked into my hotel. Although I'm not an especially paranoid person, in Romania I started to look over my shoulder a little more and become more conscious of my movements. I still had six weeks to go of this precarious existence. Little did I know how much I would grow to love Iasi and the rest of Romania.

ever, this soon ended and the government began its official policy of anti-Semitism.

Romania was granted full independence by the Treaty of Berlin in 1878 on the condition that all inhabitants be accorded equal political and civil rights. Romania deliberately evaded and violated these provisions through discriminatory legislation and regulations aimed only at Jews. Romanian Jewry were a tyrannized minority from 1878 to World War I. Thus tens of thousands of Jews left Romania for America, England, and Palestine.

In the late nineteenth century most of Romania's Jews lived in villages and small towns, subsisted as artisans and petty traders, and supported several different Hasidic rabbis. However, there were some Jews who contributed to the development and growth of industry and commerce. They brought in French, German, and Austrian capital, developed mines, and built railroads.

In November 1940 Romania joined the Axis. The Iron Guard fascist party under the leadership of General Ion Antonescu terrorized the

Jewish population. During the Holocaust, the Jews of Moldavia, Bessarabia, northern Bukovina, and northern Transylvania suffered more than their brethren in Old Romania, in southern Bukovina and southern Transylvania. Some 385,000 Romanian Jews were murdered in the Holocaust. Nearly 400,000 survived the war, with half emigrating to Israel. In 1970 there were 100,000 Jews and by 1981 this had diminished to some 34,000. Today there are approximately twelve thousand.

The Kosher Cantina

I soon found out that in the midst of all the privation and paranoia, the kosher kitchen—and really, the entire *kehile*—was an oasis of calm and reason.

While in Iasi I would eat almost all of my lunches in the kosher kitchen. The food was delicious, fresh, and hot. Unlike much of the rest of the city, this building looked new and well kept up, and the grounds were immaculate. It was inside the courtyard that also housed the *kehile* offices and some storage garages in the back. Surrounding this entire compound was a wrought-iron fence and tall hedges and trees that helped seclude the place from the noisy street.

Inside, it was clean and well lit, decorated with posters from Israel and the Yiddish State Theater in Bucharest; there were a number of Jewish youth eating there as well. In fact, there were more Jews in this kosher kitchen than I had met in all of the other kosher kitchens combined. Iasi's decrepit infrastructure made it a dreary place, but its Jewish *neshome* was alive and well.

Several of the students who ate at the kosher kitchen were Israelis. Unlike the rest of the Eastern bloc countries, Romania maintained its diplomatic relationship with Israel after all of the other countries, including the Soviet Union, cut their diplomatic ties following the Six-Day War. Thus Romanian Jews could legally immigrate to Israel, but to do so, the Israeli government had to pay some large sum of money for each Jew who wanted to make *aliye* (Hebrew, to go up). This relationship also meant Israelis could visit Romania. At this time, before the 1990s flood of Soviet Jewish immigration to Israel, Romanians made up the largest ethnic group of Jews in Israel and many still had relatives in Romania. Many Romanian-Israeli youth who wanted to go to dental school went to either the university in Iasi or the one in Bucharest. They already knew the language, it was a lot cheaper, and the scholastic requirements weren't as stringent.

The day I arrived at the kosher kitchen there was quite a bit of activity going on among the youth as they hung pictures and decorations for the following week's Purim festivities. The Purim celebration was going to consist of the reading of the *megile* (Yiddish, scroll, Book of Esther) at the shul, then everyone would congregate at the kosher kitchen where there would be food, drink, and dancing to live music—specifically, Yiddish and Hebrew folk songs led by Izu Gott, who came from a well known family band.

Mamaliga

Makes 5 to 6 servings

This is probably the most famous Romanian dish—at least, according to Aaron Lebedeff! It's fast and easy, as you'll see. A note on the grated cheese: a sharp Romano (like Locatelli) would be fine, but for authenticity, look for brinze at a specialty cheese store—it's like feta, only drier and sharper.

2 cups water

1 tsp. freshly ground pepper

½ cup corn grits (polenta)

Sour cream, for garnish

Grated hard cheese, for garnish

1. In a saucepan, bring the water to a boil. Add the pepper and gradually stir in the grits. Reduce the heat and simmer gently, stirring constantly to prevent lumps, until the mixture is thick and smooth, about 4 minutes. Serve hot with sour cream and grated cheese.

After giving my usual explanation about being a vegetarian the waitress came out fifteen minutes later with mamaliga; tomato-rice-onion soup; *lokshn* kugel; a salad with diced tomatoes, green onions, fresh garlic, and cabbage; and for dessert, poppy seed hamantaschen in honor of the festival of Purim.

A Klezmer at the Shul

The Mare shul, located down the street from the kosher cantina, was built in 1671. It had an impressive round, shiny metal (maybe tin) roof that looked rather new. This shul was where the Apter *rebe* used to *daven*. The Apter *rebe,* Rabbi Abraham Joshua Heschel, was originally from Apta (Opatow, Poland). He was born in 1748 in Poland. In 1808 he moved to Iasi and became the chief *rebe* of the *kehile*. He presided at the Mare (Romanian, great) shul for five years until he could no longer take the hostility and antagonism that had erupted between the various factions of the *kehile*. He died in 1825.

A minyan was held twice a day, every day. The night I attended shul, there were fifteen men, including Rabbi Shlomo-Menakhem Dober from the *kehile,* and three Israeli students *davening.* Rabbi Dober also was the *shoykhet* for the *kehile* and the other *kehiles* in Moldavia. He was in his eighties and I wondered what would happen when he was gone. Although Jewish culture has grown in the former Eastern bloc countries, this did not necessarily mean religious Judaism had grown at the same rate. In Hungary there are still *shoykhetim,* but in Romania a *shoykhet* must come from Israel once a month to kosher the meat.

The *davening* took place in the *besmedresh,* since it was too cold in the main sanctuary and too expensive to heat the large room. The main sanctuary was

Sweet Noodle Kugel with Apples and Walnuts

Makes 8 to 10 servings

This is almost a dessert kugel, or as we Romanian Jews would say, *kigl.* Indulge!

2 cups cottage cheese

3 eggs

⅓ cup sugar

Dash salt

Zest from one whole lemon

Juice of one half lemon

½ cup peeled, chopped apple

1 cup chopped walnuts

1 10-oz. package egg noodles, cooked

¼ cup melted butter

1. Preheat the oven to 325°. Combine the cheese, eggs, sugar, salt, and lemon zest and juice in a large bowl. Add the apple and nuts. Add the noodles and toss thoroughly to combine.

2. Use roughly half the butter to coat the bottom and sides of a casserole pan. Pour any excess butter back into the remaining butter.

3. Place the kugel mixture in the pan and pour all the leftover butter over the top. Bake for 1 hour. Serve hot, warm, or cold.

like a giant cave. There were three great arches that supported the roof and the bimah was flanked by two triple-tiered candelabra. Over the Ark was a majestic double-headed gold eagle and crown. It was a beautiful sanctuary—silent but for the muffled *davening* that came from the *besmedresh*.

Each person *davening* stood in front of his own wooden lectern, which had either a shelf or a drawer in which they kept their *tefiln, tallisim,* and prayer book. All the walls were covered with various memorial plaques, some illustrations of the Apter *rebe,* and photos of the Stefaneshter *rebe,* some with names of those who gave money to help the Jewish families that lost sons during World War II. The Stefaneshter *rebe,* Rabbi Abraham Matathias Friedman (1848–1933), lived in Stefanesht (Stefanesti, Romania) fifty miles to the north. He was known as a modest, sincere, and wise *rebe* who was active in the last years of his life in helping the Jews who sought refuge from Poland's anti-Semitism. There were also memorial lights on to commemorate some person's *yartzayt* that week. The walls of the *besmedresh* were covered with so many articles, the place felt more like a little museum than a place of prayer.

Another interesting feature that made this *besmedresh* different from all of the others I'd seen were the light fixtures. These were round eight-inch-diameter globes, each bearing inscriptions in Romanian—some, also in Hebrew—with a person's Hebrew name and what day, month, and year of the Hebrew calendar the person had passed away. They were like *yartzayt* candles that, when illuminated, reminded people of the deceased members of the *kehile*.

As a few men began to gather their coats and satchels, the *gabe* (Yiddish, trustee or warden of the synagogue), Alter-Itsik, turned to one man standing in a corner and said, "And let us not forget the great Bughici family band."

The man—in his sixties, of medium build, with carefully coiffed salt-and-pepper gray hair—began to sing in a nice baritone voice "Mayn Shtetle Yas." This was the same song as "Mayn Shtetle Belz" that the Poles were so fond of singing, but instead of Belz they inserted Yas (Iasi).

I learned that the singer, Dumitru Bughici, was a composer, and he would be taking a late train to Bucharest that evening. He had a rehearsal with the Bucharest Symphony Orchestra, which was performing his trumpet concerto. He was very happy to meet and speak with me. Little did I know how famous the Bughici family band was in Iasi and its environs.

"My whole family were musicians," he told me. "My great-grandfather was a contrabassist, my grandfather was a cellist, and my father was a violinist. I used to be a violinist and now my son Pavel is the fourth-generation violinist.

"Unfortunately I don't remember my great-grandfather, since he died before I was born, but I remember my grandfather. He had four sons who all played in the band.

"The oldest was Fayvl; he played the violin and was the best. Then came my father Avram, who played violin and flute. Then it was Moyshe, who played violin, and the youngest, Yosl, who played violin and clarinet. My Uncle Yankl, my grandfather's brother, also played in the band, but he immigrated to America just after World War I. I never saw him, but I heard he was a good violinist. We lost all contact when the war [World War II] came." (I later learned that when Yankl Bughici came to America, he anglicized his name to Jack Boogich and stayed involved with klezmer for a few more years. He composed two tunes, "Bulger No. 19" and "Serba La Booga No. 31," both of which are well known among current klezmer musicians.)

"My grandfather's band played throughout Moldavia and made a good living, unlike most other bands. By age thirteen I was in my father's band, playing the accordion.

"The weddings in Iasi were beautiful and full of traditions. You had to know the exact repertoire for each dance that was performed before and immediately after the chuppah. In the summertime a wedding might start as late as 9 P.M. At a typical wedding my father played only as a soloist, accompanied by the *sekund*. He played all the Yiddish material especially for the bride and groom, then we played Jewish dances like a mitzvah *tants, sirba,* and *khusidl,* but as the evening continued we played more and more modern dance tunes, like tangos, fox-trots, and so on. It was hard work because we usually played until four or five in the morning.

"My father was sought after by Jews and non-Jews, religious and non-religious. Once my father was asked to play for the Stefaneshter *rebe* for the Lag B'Omer holiday festival. They played Hasidic *nigunim* music, which everyone loved. Before my father left to return to Iasi, the Stefaneshter *rebe* gave him a special gold coin. Then the *rebe* made a blessing and drank a *L'chayim* with some *tzuica*. My father carried that gold coin in his pocket his whole life because he believed it kept away the evil eye.

"In Iasi, unlike any other city that I know of, we had a klezmer syndicate. Every Monday evening we got together to talk about business and play cards and chess. During the business part of our meetings we discussed many matters, like who was in need of some financial help. There were klezmers not as successful as we were but deserved our help. Since everyone who belonged to the syndicate paid a small monthly dues according to their earnings, we were able to give money to certain klezmers' families who were poor and had difficulties paying the rent and buying food. We also helped those klezmers who had a contract for a wedding or a restaurant job and were not paid their full amount. If the people still refused to pay, even after the syndicate interceded on behalf of the klezmer or band, then word was given out throughout the city not to play for them or any of their relatives for the next two years.

"Believe me, even though there were a lot of klezmers in Iasi, most belonged to the syndicate or sympathized with us, so it was extremely difficult if not impossible to get any klezmers to play for someone who basically had been banned.

"This beautiful life I cherished as a child all came to a tragic end when the Nazis came. In Iasi there was a huge pogrom in June 28 and 29, 1941. My Uncle Moyshe and his two sons, Julius and Joseph, perished at the hands of the fascists. The day after the massacre another 1,850 men and women died in the grossly overcrowded, sweltering train wagons that left Iasi. Many klezmers were among the twelve thousand Jews murdered."

It was time for Mr. Bughici to go. We shook hands and then we hugged each other tightly. He thanked me for letting him speak so long. And I thanked him for his courage, love, and commitment to Jewish culture even after suffering through the Holocaust.

He opened the door turned around and said, "Remember, Yitskhok, the stories of the klezmers are not well documented. Your work is important. There is a reason why Chagall made the klezmer his leitmotif."

After he left, I waited for Alter-Itsik to lock up. We walked slowly through the dimly lit streets, speaking in hushed Yiddish. It was so lyrical to hear his Yiddish mixed with the clip-clopping of the horses as they pulled their loads down the cobblestone streets.

Mr. Bughici was right. There was something special about Iasi, despite my initial reservations. With one hot kosher meal every day but Shabes and the warmth of the kosher kitchen and shul, I would manage just fine.

Kara the Historian

I hit the mother lode for my klezmer research by coming to Iasi, and his name was Itsik Kara Svart—the leading Jewish historian and folklorist in all of Romania. Dr. Simone Kaufman, who worked at the *kehile* offices, introduced me to Svart at the kosher kitchen when he heard about my research.

Svart—or simply "Kara," as everyone in the *kehile* called him—came to the cantina every day to eat his lunch and get lunch for his wife, Cili, who didn't go out much during the wintertime. He looked like he was in his mid-seventies; he was about five foot six, with graying hair that was a bit topsy-turvy, falling messily over the nape of his neck, and he had a distinctive pointed nose. On the day I met him, he wore a long black wool coat over his rather thin frame. He carried a kind of lunchbox made from four aluminum containers, each one smaller than the other, and designed to fit inside of each other. They were held in place by a metal brace, which formed the handle.

He sat down and began to eat while the waitress took his lunch container to the kitchen to fill it for his wife. Mr. Kaufman came over and said something to Kara in Romanian. Kara nodded his head twice, turned to me while eating his kugel, and in perfect English said, "Please, please sit down. I understand you are a vegetarian klezmer. Do you only sing Yiddish songs about vegetables?"

I laughed and sat down across from this skinny man who ate as if there was no tomorrow. He asked me how long I was staying in Iasi. I told him at least two weeks if not more. He said he would meet me here at the kosher cantina in two days and tell me of the rich history of klezmer music in Iasi and its environs. He was busy revising a book that he'd written in Yiddish, which had been published a year earlier. We talked about what I had found in terms of klezmer in each of the other countries I had been to. He was quite curious about Poland, since many of the folk customs followed by the Jews of Moldavia were based on those brought by the Galicianer Jews.

Just before we said goodbye I asked him why Kara was his pen name. He explained it meant black in Turkish. Since his last name, Svart, meant black in Yiddish, and Moldavia had been a Turkish vassal state, Kara was an appropriate pen name and had become his nickname among many of his friends.

At the front door he turned back to me and said, "*Zingst du vi a zeyg oder a shperel?*" (Do you sing like a saw or a sparrow?)

Then he laughed and went outside. I stood there for a moment as I tried to translate what he'd said, but I didn't know what *zeyg* or *shperel* meant. I ran outside to see if I could catch him and ask him. But with his galloping strides he was already halfway across the field and I didn't want to yell and attract attention.

Two days later, over lunch, Kara told me about the klezmers in Iasi and its environs, speaking in Yiddish, his true mother tongue.

"I was born in Podu Iloaiei, just outside of Iasi. In my shtetl there were no Jewish klezmers, so when there was a wedding we brought them from Iasi by train. When we did not, we hired the Rom. These Rom musicians knew Jewish music very well and played at our local balls and for the Jewish festivals. On Purim they went from house to house accompanying the *Purim-shpilers* [actors who perform little skits from the story of Esther]. The Jews were not ignorant klezmers; they all knew how to read notes. And by the 1920s most klezmers in this region read music because they had gone to the conservatory.

"Several bands, particularly the famous Sigally and Bughici families, made a good living only from music. This was rare for most of the klezmers, but in Iasi with the Yiddish theater, outdoor garden cafés, restaurants, weddings, parties, and the movie theater in the 1930s, there were many opportunities for the klezmers to find work. The Yiddish theater where I worked as a translator and dramaturge had an orchestra made up of only klezmers.

"The reputation of most klezmers prior to the 1920s was not a good one. The klezmer was looked upon like an actor or circus entertainer who lived a Bohemian life, so the public expressed a great deal of uneasiness about him. At the same time his life and adventures seemed to make his music more special. If a klezmer played some Jewish melodies he had learned while in Istanbul, it was more exciting for the guest. At the same time, you didn't want your daughter Rukhl coming home and telling you she was engaged to marry Berl the klezmer.

"Finally the introduction of the gramophone in the late 1920s hurt the small bands. Instead of hiring a band for a dance or to play in a restaurant or café, people played a gramophone. Of course the rich always could afford the best and they kept the Sigally and Bughici bands busy until the war began."

The Gabe *Alter-Itsik*

That night at shul, I asked the whole congregation if they knew anybody who might have an extra room where I could stay for a while. They talked among themselves and then the *gabe,* Alter-Itsik, said he had an extra room and would gladly take me in. They asked me where I was staying and how much I was paying. I told them I was paying ten dollars a night at my hotel and they all agreed I was being ripped off. One man yelled, "Better that you pay half and give it to a Jew rather than those *mumzerim* [bastards]."

So that night I went to my hotel, packed my bags, and went to check out. The hotel clerk asked me if I was already leaving Iasi. I lied, telling him I was catching the 11:33 P.M. train to Bucharest. I thanked him for the "wonderful" accommodations and left.

As I walked down the street toward the train station, I realized that he was watching me, so I decided to duck into a restaurant, order something, and hang there for a while before I went over to Alter-Itsik's place. I figured for the rest of my stay in Iasi I would hang around the *kehile* offices, kosher kitchen, and shul. There was certainly no point in walking past this hotel in broad daylight. Why fuel their already suspicious imaginations?

Alter-Itsik lived near another shul in Iasi that I didn't even know existed. Built in 1875, it was called Podu Ros (Romanian, Red Bridge). The neighborhood where it was located (Tirgu Cuculi) was once very Jewish, but attrition had taken a toll on the Jewish element in the neighborhood. Now only a few old Jews lived here. The shul was still open for *davening* every Shabes, but because Alter-Itsik was the *gabe* of the Mare, he rarely went to the Podu Ros shul.

His apartment was one street away from the shul. He lived in a second-floor walk-up. The place was very clean and had an extra room where he kept all of his Jewish books. There was no bed, but there was a couch, which became my bed for the next two weeks. The hot water only worked a few hours of the day, but Alter-Itsik kept a huge samovar filled with water on the stove. The stove itself looked like it was from the nineteenth century. It was huge, cast iron, and heated with wood or coal. It provided enough heat for his tiny apartment. Finally, I wouldn't have to sleep in my sleeping bag, which in truth was beginning to smell just a bit.

Alter-Itsik gave me a spare key and told me his place was now mine and I could come and go as I pleased. He just reminded me not to turn on the lights on Shabes, nor to light a fire in the stove if by any chance it went out, as he observed the Shabes. That night I ate some fried kreplach filled with brinze and onions, some carrots, and a piece of honey cake, which we both washed down with some plum-flavored *tzuica*. I slept better than I had all week in the hotel. It was equally warm from the stove and from Alter-Itsik's hospitality.

A Visit to a Shtetl

Izu Gott was a musician in his fifties with red hair, small squinty eyes, and glasses. When I met him, he was rehearsing his ensemble for the Iasi's Purim celebration. He was very friendly, and on his suggestion I went to the nearby town of Dorohoi for Purim. Izu was born there and his brother Marcu and father Berko lived there.

I took the train to Dorohoi carrying only my violin and camera and a few toiletries. It was such a pleasure to travel to another town without having to shlep my nearly hundred pounds of gear.

When I arrived at Marcu's apartment, he said, "First comes the stomach, then comes the brain. Without proper sustenance a klezmer couldn't perform well."

The lunch included a great vegetable soup. During lunch Berko told me a funny story about a time in 1934 when he'd played with his father and some other klezmers for a Jewish wedding in the small town of Darabani.

"During the party the bride's brother came up to my father and asked him to stop playing while he sang a song he wrote for his sister. My father asked if he wanted some accompaniment but the man insisted on singing solo. Well, I hadn't noticed at first but this *zhlob* was a bit drunk, but in a friendly way, so we all stopped and went to a back table to listen. This man couldn't sing a note if the messiah himself was whispering in his ears. While he sang he took swigs from a whiskey bottle and became drunker by the minute.

"Finally the groom's family became rather irritated, so my father started to play a *freylekhs* and gently placed the drunk on a chair. While we played and others danced the *zhlob* still sang, completely oblivious to others. Just as I thought that was the end of it, this guy started to dance. Then I noticed he began to turn green and began to heave. Just like that, he threw up all over

the newlyweds' table and then fainted. Apparently he'd had a bit too much to drink and the dancing in circles didn't help matters. Everyone went over to the bride and groom as they quickly got up and ran out to change. Then a couple of guys grabbed the man's feet and arms and carried him outside as well. We continued to play, but this incident took the life out of the party and people began to leave. From then on, whenever we played this *freylekhs* I joked with my father and called it the *brekhekhts tants* [vomit dance]."

Marcu laughed throughout the story and so did his wife. Of course it made it a bit harder for me to keep eating—especially the mashed eggplant salad they had made.

Dorohoi was really like a preserved shtetl. There were few cars, mostly horse and wagon, and the buildings for the most part looked as though they hadn't been touched with a paintbrush or hammer since the turn of the century. There were four shuls still in operation. I found the Dorfishe *shil* (Romanian Yiddish dialect, village synagogue). It had been built by the Jewish farmers that lived outside town and wanted their own shul for Shabes. The shul was locked, so I went up to the windows to take a peek inside. There was the main sanctuary and the *besmedresh*. I could tell the *besmedresh* was still in use because I saw prayer books, *tallisim,* and Shabes candles about the room. Later, Berko would tell me that the shul had been sold to the city. In its place the city was going to build some apartments.

ANOTHER RUN-IN WITH THE LAW

As I photographed this relic from the nineteenth century, I heard a whistle blow, but I ignored it. Then it blew again and I turned around to see what it was. Up on the hill was a policeman, coming my way. I decided to pretend I didn't see him, so I just began walking behind the shul and down this hill toward some homes. As I walked I felt my adrenaline pumping. I kept telling myself I'd done nothing. I put my camera back inside the camera bag so I wouldn't draw any unwarranted attention to myself.

Suddenly a car swerved by me and stopped abruptly. A policeman got out and pushed me into the car. This all happened in just fifteen seconds. I was so startled I didn't even try to resist.

Once inside the car, the policeman (who had blown the whistle at me earlier) asked for my passport. I had no choice, so I gave it to him. As he looked at it he spoke with the two policemen sitting in the front seat. Fortunately, all of my film and cassette recordings and my violin were in Iasi at Alter-Itsik's home.

We drove for five minutes before coming to some gates. Once inside, the gates closed and we all got out. It looked like I was in some kind of police compound. There was one building, a one-story wooden edifice. All three policemen went inside with my camera, film, tape recorder, and passport. I was escorted to what looked like the garage where I was told to sit down, given some tea, and guarded by two young soldiers not more than eighteen or nineteen years old.

My nervousness quickly evaporated. They had nothing on me, and if they kept the one roll of film I'd shot and even the recording of Berko Gott speaking and Duvid playing I could replace the material or just forget about it.

An hour went by and still there was no sign of the police coming out. I tried to make some sort of conversation with my guards, but they were busy looking at a pornographic magazine—which, by the way, I thought was illegal in Romania. I guess it had been confiscated from some poor unsuspecting shmuck and now had become part of the police station's library. Finally I got the guards' attention and indicated I had to go to the toilet, which happened to be inside the station. One guard accompanied me inside, where I found the police sitting around playing cards and eating pastries while my gear was laid out on the table. I stopped to ask if I could go.

In broken English, one policeman, about thirty, with blond hair and a handlebar mustache, said, "No problem, we check passport. You live in Iasi?"

"Yes, I am visiting the Jewish community here for the day."

"Please, you go have good time in Dorohoi."

"*Multse miesc*" (Romanian, thank you), I replied.

"You like music? Go Enescu museum."

I couldn't believe it—how long would I have sat there watching those two *yolds* read porn if I hadn't said something?

After I used the toilet they escorted me to the gate. As I walked down the street to the museum I exhaled and laughed, feeling trouble-free and triumphant.

Purim at the Shtetl

That night's Purim festivities were held in the kosher cantina. Rabbi Dov Wasserman read the *megile* while everyone participated with their various *grogers* (Yiddish, rattles, noisemakers), using them every time Haman's name

The Mare synagogue (right) in the shtetl of Dorohoi

Palave

PILAF

Makes 4 to 6 servings

There is no greater evidence of the influence of the Ottoman Empire on Eastern Europe than this traditional Romanian dish.

2 cups uncooked basmati or long-grain
   rice

4 Tbsp. unsalted butter

½ cup sunflower seeds

1 cup chopped leek, white parts only
   (about 3 leeks)

Two 2-inch cinnamon sticks

½ onion studded with 5 whole cloves

4 cups chicken or vegetable stock

Salt to taste

1 plum tomato, chopped

½ cup golden raisins

½ cup loosely packed fresh mint leaves,
   finely chopped

½ tsp. ground allspice

½ tsp. ground cinnamon

Fresh ground pepper, about 18 twists, or
   to taste

1. Rinse the rice several times, until the water runs clear. Drain in a colander.

2. Melt 2 tablespoons of the butter over medium heat in a heavy skillet (10-inch or similar size). Stir in the sunflower seeds and toast, stirring occasionally, for about 4 minutes. Remove the seeds with a slotted spoon and set aside.

3. Add the remaining 2 tablespoons of butter to the pan and melt over low heat. Stir in the leek, cinnamon sticks, and onion. Cook, stirring occasionally, over low heat until the leek is soft, about 7 minutes. Add the drained rice and cook over medium-low heat until the grains turn slightly opaque, about 5 minutes, stirring frequently.

4. Stir in the stock and add salt to taste (if using canned broth, go easy on the salt). Stir in the tomato, raisins, mint, allspice, cinnamon, and pepper. Cover and cook on low until the liquid is absorbed, about 20 to 25 minutes. Stir with a fork. If the rice is not yet tender at this point, add another ½ cup stock or water; cover, and cook another 5 to 7 minutes, then stir again. Cover the pan after stirring and remove it from the heat. Let stand for 15 minutes.

5. Remove the cinnamon sticks and onion. Gently stir again and mix in the reserved sunflower seeds before serving or reheating.

was read—and sometimes when it hadn't been. I was surprised to see that the *kehile* was as vibrant as it was. A number of teenagers and younger kids participated in the chorus after the reading, singing Hebrew and Yiddish songs. Then the choral leader took his guitar and started playing some Israeli folk songs while people got up and started doing Israeli folk dancing. It was really an intimate atmosphere, one that could have been a replica of times I spent at the Jewish Community Center back home. Then there were refreshments, Romanian style: apricot, cherry, and poppy seed hamantaschen, a parsnip *tsimes,* and some kind of grain dish with raisins in it called *palave.* Some people called it *kish-mish* and told me it was originally from Turkey.

Klezmer Lessons

Back in Iasi after Purim, I visited Izu at his home. He had promised me a klezmer lesson.

We got down to business immediately. I interviewed Izu for only fifteen minutes because he didn't really have much more to add to what his brother and father had already told me, and I really wanted to hear him play.

The tunes were really good. One, "Baveynen Di Kale" (Yiddish, The Bride's Lament), ended up being the only *baveynen* (Yiddish, crying) melody I collected during the entire trek. The *baveynen* would be played while the bride was seated with all of her female attendants before she was married. At that time she generally had her long beautiful hair (often braids) cut, which invariably caused her and her friends to cry. Jewish married women did not go in public with their hair uncovered, as it was immodest, so she wore either a kerchief over the shorn hair or a *shaitel* (Yiddish, wig). While Izu played the tune he sang along with it and rocked back and forth in his chair as if he were *davening.* There was definitely something very prayerlike, almost haunting in the first part of the melody. And when he repeated this melody he never played it the same way twice. It explicitly had an improvisational feel to it. Despite its mournful air it ended with an upbeat *freylekhs.*

Altogether he played for over half an hour, then apologized because he had to run off to another rehearsal with the philharmonic. Besides being the leader of the Jewish choirs in Iasi and in Bucharest, he played the contrabass in the symphony orchestra.

As I walked through town, all of the melodies I had heard over the last two days reverberated in my head, mixed with unbridled happiness. Everyone's

"Baveynen Di Kale" (The Lamenting of the Bride)

Collected by Yale Strom

generosity and trust in me throughout this entire journey had been so genuine and forthright. I knew someday I'd be returning to visit my friends in Eastern Europe.

Hebrew Class

Sunday—the day of Kara's class—came and I walked to the Mare shul with Alter-Itzik. He would always arrive an hour early to warm up the *besmedresh*. I helped him stoke the fire with wood and coal. Slowly but surely the chill in the room evaporated. At 12:45 the students started arriving. Some I had met at the kosher kitchen, others I was meeting for the first time. All were young, between the ages of eight and seventeen.

Kara got there exactly at 1 P.M. and introduced me in Hebrew. Then he asked me to tell the students in Hebrew why I was in Romania. Of course, with every other word (I was breaking my teeth trying to remember my Hebrew), Kara corrected the tense or my choice of words. Then before I started to play some klezmer tunes Kara had the students ask me questions in Hebrew. He finally took pity on me and let me speak in English while he translated my answers into Romanian.

The students were very bright and inquisitive. Many had relatives in Israel and most were eager to join them after they finished college in Romania. One student loudly said in English that paranoia was insidious throughout the country and was destroying the social fabric of the people. He then looked up at the ceiling and said, "I know, Mr. Ceausescu, you can hear me. Please consider this concert of Jewish music a gift from us to you. *Ameyn!*"

Well, with that introduction, I began to play a *freylekhs,* and another and another. Then I played some spirited Hasidic *nigunim.* I purposely stayed away from anything that sounded sad. If Ceausescu was actually listening, I wanted him to know that the Jews were capable of creating joyous uplifting music (even in Romania) and not just lamentations, though daily life was often a Jobian task. After I finished playing I had some tea with Alter-Itzik in the back room while Kara taught the students.

After class I walked back with Kara to his home. His small, cluttered one-bedroom apartment was literally a museum of Romanian Jewish culture. Every nook and cranny held books, pamphlets, magazines, papers, photos, and little objects like Shabes candle sticks, menorahs, and mezuzahs.

Cili, his wife, was in the kitchen cooking dinner. She was a wisp of a woman with short silver hair, and when she spoke she had such an endearing smile. Cili had circulation problems; that was why she didn't go out during the wintertime. Though she moved a bit slowly, there was an intensity to her that was contagious. She was so excited and thrilled to know that a young man like myself had come so far just to find klezmer. She invited me to stay for dinner and while she cooked I perused Kara's amazing archive.

I sat down to listen to more of Kara's lecture of the history of the Jews in Moldavia. During Kara's discourse, every once in a while he interrupted himself to show me a photo, document, or book to emphasize something he was talking about.

As he spoke, a capricious thought began to take hold and flourish in my head. Maybe I could do a master's degree studying the contemporary Jewish life of Iasi. Kara was such a genius that I knew if I followed through on this I would have to have Kara as one of my academic advisors. He spoke mostly in English, but when he wanted to emphasize a particular point he said it in Yiddish.

Soon enough, dinner was served: a garlicky eggplant dish and kreplach.

While we ate, Kara told me that he knew the history of klezmer in Moldavia very well, but Cili was the one who actually remembered some old

Cili Svart cooking in her kitchen in Iasi

Mincare de Vinete cu Usturoi

EGGPLANT WITH GARLIC

Makes 4 to 6 servings

4 Japanese eggplants

4 plum tomatoes

5 cloves garlic, finely chopped

Salt and pepper to taste

3 Tbsp. olive oil

2 large onions, thinly sliced

1. Preheat the oven to 350°. Prick the eggplants with a fork and arrange on a baking sheet. Bake 30 to 40 minutes, until softened. Remove from the oven, keeping the heat on. Peel while hot and let drain. Slice lengthwise into strips.

2. While the eggplant is baking, prepare the tomatoes: bring a small pot of water deep enough to cover the tomatoes to a boil. Make an "X" on the end of each tomato opposite from the stem end and drop into the simmering water. Watch closely; after a few moments the skins will start to fall away from the tomatoes. With a slotted spoon, transfer the tomatoes to a colander and rinse with cold water. The skins should peel off very easily. Slice the tomatoes.

3. In a baking dish, arrange a layer of eggplant, then a layer of sliced tomatoes. Sprinkle with some of the garlic, and salt and pepper. Repeat with another layer of eggplant, tomatoes, garlic, and salt and pepper, until all have been used.

4. Fry the onions in the oil over medium-high heat until browned. Take out the onions and place on paper towels to drain, reserving the oil in the pan.

5. Pour the oil from the pan over the eggplants and tomatoes in the baking dish. Bake for 30 to 40 minutes, or until the garlic is soft. Sprinkle the onions on top. Serve hot, warm, or cold.

Potato-Cheese Kreplach

Makes about 2 dozen

I have an extremely complicated and time-consuming recipe for kreplach dough, which must be rolled paper thin. Save yourself the trouble—use Chinese wonton wrappers. I once took a cooking course with a chef who taught me how to make ravioli dough—it was only after I'd successfully completed the dish that she told me to use wonton wrappers the next time! They are available in most markets and work perfectly in this dish, too.

1½ sticks unsalted butter	2 oz. cheddar, grated
1 medium onion, finely chopped	Salt and pepper to taste
3 large potatoes, peeled, boiled, and mashed	1 package large wonton wrappers (about 24)
¼ lb. farmer cheese	1 egg white, slightly beaten

1. To prepare the filling, melt 6 tablespoons of butter in a small skillet over medium heat. Add the onion and sauté until browned, about 15 minutes. Remove from the heat and allow to cool slightly.

2. In a large bowl, combine the mashed potatoes and cheeses. Add the sautéed onions with their butter and mix well. Season with salt and pepper.

3. To assemble the kreplach, place a teaspoon of the filling in the middle of each wonton wrapper. Brush the edges with egg white and fold the dough over the filling to form a triangle. Press the edges firmly together with the tines of a fork to seal.

4. Place the kreplach on a lightly floured large baking sheet about 1 inch apart and keep covered with a damp tea towel.

5. Meanwhile, in a large pot, bring 6 quarts of salted water to a boil. Reduce the heat to medium so the water simmers and carefully lower half the kreplach into the water. Boil, stirring occasionally with a wooden spoon to prevent sticking, until they rise to the surface and are cooked through, 6 to 7 minutes. With a slotted spoon, carefully remove the kreplach to a colander and drain thoroughly. Transfer to a deep serving bowl and toss with the remaining butter.

"BOSNIAN WALTZ"

Collected by Yale Strom

Yiddish songs that he had never seen in any Yiddish song collection. So out came my tape recorder onto the table with all of the delectable food. Cili began to sing several songs in a tranquil, delicate voice. After each song I asked her to repeat the words slowly so I could write them down; her Romanian Yiddish accent was so thick I wasn't catching every word.

After dinner Cili could see I was beginning to get a cold and a headache, so she made me my first ever Gogl-Mogl. (This Yiddish term for an egg flip comes from Gog, leader of the land of Magog, mentioned in Ezekiel—he led the evil forces that one day would rise up against the Lord in the final climactic battle.) My dad had once told me that when he was a kid his mother would make him a Gogl-Mogl when he wasn't feeling well, particularly if he had a cold or fever. Cili's Gogl-Mogl consisted of raw egg, cider, sugar, and plum schnapps—a lot of schnapps. The taste was a bit disconcerting, but my headache did go away.

I cleared the table and washed all the dishes for Cili. Afterward I played a little concert for the cute couple as they sat side by side like two turtledoves on the couch. Then it was time to go. I gave Cili a big hug and said good-bye, since I would be leaving in two more days and I was sure I wouldn't be back at their home. As I walked down the six flights of stairs (probably another reason why Cili didn't get out much), Cili hummed a beautiful klezmer

Gogl-Mogl

Makes 2 servings

4 egg yolks	3 Tbsp. cider
6 Tbsp. brown sugar	½ cup plum brandy

Beat the egg yolks with the sugar until creamy. Place over a double boiler, add the cider and brandy, and heat, stirring constantly, until the mixture thickens. Pour into a bowl and let cool.

waltz she had learned when she was a little girl in Bosnia. The melody wafted through the stairwell as I carefully walked down in the dark, and it followed me outside as I strolled to my apartment in the crisp night air, under a starlit sky.

How quickly impressions of a place can change! Only two weeks earlier I had lamented the fact that I had to stay in Romania for a month and a half. Now I realized I felt really appreciated and cared for here, and I didn't want to leave.

Good-Bye, Iasi

The next day I got up with Alter-Itsik and had breakfast with him. He told me he was sad to see me go—I had been like a son for him over the last three weeks. He was such a sweet old man I felt bad leaving him. I paid him for all the days I stayed, but he refused to take the money. I insisted it was a small token of my appreciation and his hospitality. Alter-Itsik was stubborn and refused, so I suggested he use the money for the shul. This he would agree to. The shul needed to fix some broken windows and this money would cover that cost. Then Atler-Itsik gave me a bag of cookies and some fruit. We hugged (as he cried) and wished each other *gezint un parnose* (Yiddish, health and livelihood).

As I walked to the train station I was sadder than when I'd left any of the other cities. Iasi and the *kehile* had grown on me. No wonder so many talented klezmers came from this city.

BUCHAREST

The Bucharest train station was abuzz with activity. There were people buying tickets, getting on trains, selling food and drinks, moving baggage from the train to storage. On top of this normal hustle and bustle, there were also homeless people begging for food and money; illegal money changers preying on unsuspecting tourists; prostitutes hawking their services; and ragtag children running around harassing passengers and homeless people, stealing from the food carts, getting high on glue fumes, even running across the tracks to play chicken with the locomotive engines. A large group of kids ran up to me begging for money and candy. It was just mayhem. And who was watching all of this insane activity? The demented police. All I knew was I didn't want to draw their attention to me. I just kept my head down and walked out of the station as quickly as possible.

The combined stench of truck exhaust and seeping vapors from the sewers, the dim streetlights, and the noisy crowds of pedestrians made my head spin. I was not looking forward to spending two weeks here. I was ready to return to the train depot and get on the first train back to Iasi.

But after walking a few blocks and getting my bearings, I thought perhaps things wouldn't be so bad in the capital city. I went to the first hotel I saw, the Oltenia. Sometimes you get what you pay for. It was cold and dirty but I was too tired to look for anything else.

I decided against going to the kosher kitchen. I figured there would be plenty of days to eat the same cuisine I'd eaten up in Iasi, so I bought some bread, cheese, and fruit at a large grocery store. The lines weren't as long as they had been in Iasi. Ceausescu probably wanted to at least keep the local population somewhat satisfied. People in Iasi had told me that there would be more of certain food products in Bucharest's stores than in Iasi's. I suppose the government reasoned that if there were ever going to be a demonstration to protest the shortages, better for it to happen in the provinces, where it wouldn't cause much of a media stir and could be contained quickly and harshly, without attracting the attention of foreign news correspondents.

Theodore Remembers His Klezmer Days

On my first visit to the *kehile* offices I didn't have much luck finding anyone to talk to, so I ended up exploring, eventually finding myself in the Tailors' Shul. One year earlier the shul had been converted into a museum presenting the 2,500-year-old history of the Jewish people in Romania from the Roman times to the German occupation in 1940.

Walking slowly and gazing at the displays, I met Theodore, a *kehile* bookkeeper on his lunch break. Soon we had made an appointment to meet at the *kehile* offices after work.

Coming into the *kehile* for the second time that day, I was stopped and thoroughly searched. My passport was taken and would be held until I left. I was so used to this routine that before the policeman could ask for my passport I had already taken it out of my pocket to hand to him.

Theodore met me at the front desk and took me to his office. He told me not to speak too loudly and only in his room after he'd locked the door. I asked him what he was worried about. Wasn't Yiddish a Jewish language appropriate for a Jewish establishment?

Theodore said, "Yitskhok, these are difficult times in our country. There was no heat in our homes for most of the winter; sometimes there was no bread in the stores for several days and no cheese and milk as well. People are working but are poorly paid and barely have enough to pay for food and rent. Just below the surface, the man on the street is very angry and the government knows this. Any slight provocation and the police will take you to the station and harass and threaten you until you confess to something you never did or even knew about.

"And worst of all, if you are seen with someone from the West, rumors start, and people talk, and before you know it you are getting a visit from the Securitate. Everyone is paranoid of the other. And just like there were Jews who sold their souls to the devil during the war just to save their own skin or to gain certain privileges from the fascists, there are Jews who work in this very *kehile* I don't trust. So be careful while you are here in Bucharest. You want to be able to leave the country with all of your film and recordings. Enough of this now—let's talk about klezmer."

Then Theodore's demeanor, so fraught with angst a moment earlier, became aglow with enthusiasm. He told me he was born in Botosani. His father was a glazier, his mother a homemaker, and he had two brothers and a sister. He became interested in playing the violin when he saw a local klezmer band playing for the Yiddish troupe that was traveling throughout Bukowina (then a Romanian province, today in Ukraine) from Czernowitz. After one performance he asked the violinist if he would give him some lessons. He began to play and eventually, whenever the Yiddish troupe came to Botosani, Theodore got a job playing some incidental music for the audience before the play began.

Theodore asked to borrow my violin and began to play some melodies he had learned from the band. I could tell he hadn't played the violin for some time, but slowly his fingers began to respond to his will power and memory.

When I told Theodore I was staying at the Oltenia, he just laughed and said the klezmer before World War II stayed in better inns than I was staying in. I agreed, but basically I was too tired to look for another place that night.

The Choral Temple

The main shul, the Choral Temple, was where Rabbi Moses Rosen presided. For twenty-five years Rabbi Rosen had been the chief rabbi of all of Romania.

His father had preceded him as rabbi and at the time of my visit he was the only rabbi elected to a government in the Eastern bloc. I had heard from some Jews in Iasi that Rabbi Rosen had a difficult job: on the one hand he was the leader of the Jewish community; on the other hand he had to serve in a government most Jews hated. This catch-22 situation and controversy never lifted throughout Rabbi Rosen's career.

Because Romania had diplomatic relations with Israel, Rabbi Rosen was the liaison between the Romanian government and all Israeli official governmental and nongovernmental persons.

The Choral Temple, built in 1866, was huge. The man who let me inside to look around told me that it could seat some three thousand worshipers. Architecturally it wasn't that stunning, but it did incorporate the Moorish qualities I had seen in some of the Hungarian shuls. The doorway and two main windows were framed by an array of arched bricks. Above each of these windows was a stone design made up of four half circles that combined to make a floral pattern. The shul façade was made of pink and yellow bricks and the top of the building had four tiny towers, each finished like a little minaret. I took a few photos of the interior, but when I walked outside and saw three policemen standing just across the courtyard, talking and smoking, I quickly put away my camera. There was actually a back door, and without telling the gentile caretaker I went back into the shul and went out the back way, which led me to another residential street. Now I was thoroughly infected with Ceausescu disease—paranoia.

Klezmer at the Yiddish Theater

One day I stumbled across a musical library. I went in and asked the librarian if there were any books on Jewish music. Sure enough, they had one book. It had mostly Yiddish songs but there was one chapter with klezmer instrumental tunes for weddings. I asked if there was a photocopier in the library. The librarian just laughed, so I sat down and spent the next four hours copying by hand tune after tune until my hand was too sore to write. Of fourteen tunes, I was able to copy seven. When I came back the next day, the librarian smiled and showed me to the same desk where the book was waiting for me. While I copied the rest of the tunes she asked me if I had been to the Yiddish theater. If I wanted to find some more information and klezmer tunes, she suggested, that would be a good place to research. She was right—I had almost forgotten about the Yiddish theater. When I left

I took one of the overcrowded and barely operational electric buses to check it out.

The theater was located in a neighborhood that used to be predominantly Jewish even up until the 1960s, but now it was nearly all Rom. Walking with my violin case, I attracted a lot of stares, smiles, and whispers. I wanted to stop and talk with some of the Rom, but I also didn't want to get waylaid into going to another wedding—at least not just yet. So I waved hello and marched on to the theater.

There were no lights turned on and it was chilly inside, obviously due to a lack of both funds and city-supplied energy. I saw an older man sitting behind a desk with theater posters in Yiddish and Romanian displayed for people to buy. I asked him in Yiddish where I could find the artistic director or Mr. Bughici (just in case he was in town). Unfortunately the man didn't speak Yiddish, but he showed me a dark corridor and told me to go down and turn left.

I found the office of the artistic director, Israel Bercovici. I heard muffled voices inside, so I sat down on the floor outside and waited. The conversation was in Romanian with a little Yiddish sprinkled in. Sometimes voices were raised, other times they seemed to be whispering. Finally, after nearly an hour, the door opened and out walked a woman with reddish-blond wavy hair—later I would find out this was Elena Waldman, the theater's star actress. She passed me as if I wasn't even there. Her demeanor and gait gave the impression she was not in the best of moods.

I walked in and introduced myself to Mr. Bercovici. He had heard about me from Dumitru Bughici and was happy to meet me. I asked him if he had a little time to talk about the theater and klezmer. He had only fifteen minutes before he had to run to a rehearsal; the theater was preparing to present the play *Mirele Efros* by Jacob Gordin.

He told me that Kara was still working with the Yiddish theater, doing translations and offering dramaturgical advice. The musicians in the pit orchestra were Jewish and non-Jewish, all conservatory-trained. The audience that came to the theater was made up of mostly Jews and some non-Jews. They particularly enjoyed the Jewish music and songs, but it wasn't quite authentic klezmer. His main concern was finding good actors willing to learn Yiddish and finding plays that touched upon matters that they could relate to in their day-to-day life in Romania. Nostalgia was good for the soul but didn't always feed the brain.

Our fifteen minutes were up, so I decided to watch some of the rehearsal, then go over to the kosher kitchen for my first meal there.

Julian and His Hora

The kosher kitchen was abuzz with guests from Israel and the United States for Passover. I had almost forgotten Passover was in two days. I figured I would eat at the seders (ceremonial festive meals for the first two days of Passover) that would be held at the kosher kitchen.

As usual, foreigners had to pay a higher price—and since it was my first time there and hadn't made friends with any of the cooks, I paid the full price. Lunch was good. It consisted of mamaliga, salad, vegetable soup, and vegetable latkes, with strudel for dessert.

Romanian Vegetable Latkes

Makes 6 to 8 servings

3 medium potatoes, peeled

1 medium onion, chopped fine

3 Tbsp. olive oil

1 lb. fresh spinach, stems removed

3 or 4 large eggs, beaten

½ tsp. turmeric

½ tsp. cumin

2 cloves garlic, finely chopped

Salt and pepper to taste

Oil for frying

2 tomatoes, cut into wedges, for garnish

1. Peel and cube the potatoes and boil until tender; drain and mash.

2. Sauté the onion in the olive oil until softened.

3. Wash and dry the spinach thoroughly; chop fine. Add to the onions and cook, stirring, for a minute or two, until wilted.

4. Transfer the sautéed mixture to a large bowl and stir in 3 eggs, the mashed potatoes, the turmeric, cumin, garlic, and salt and pepper. If the mixture is too dry, add another egg.

5. Heat the oil in a large frying pan; add the mixture by spoonfuls and flatten to form 3-inch pancakes. Fry until golden on both sides, about 6 to 10 minutes. Garnish with the tomato wedges and serve.

At the kitchen I met Julian, a young man who was studying physics at the university. He explained that the Jewish choir and orchestra rehearsed and presented musical programs in this building.

Julian had some time before his next class, so he offered to give me a little tour of some of the better-known Jewish landmarks. We walked by Strada Gaster, named after Dr. Moses G. Gaster, a rabbi and bibliophile who was expelled from Romania in 1885 because of his vigorous protests against the treatment of his fellow Jews. Eventually he became chief rabbi of the Sephardic *kehile* in England.

Across the street from the Tailors' Shul was another shul I hadn't noticed before, more of a *besmedresh*. Julian explained it was known by two different names: the Tailors' Wives' Shul and Besmedresh Dov Moshe Zusso (Zusso was an eminent nineteenth-century Hasidic rabbi). In fact, there were sixteen shuls in Bucharest that still operated, a few every day but most just on *erev* Shabes and Shabes.

Julian next showed me a building that now housed offices but had once been a Yiddish school for students through high school. This school, along with others in Iasi and in Timisoara, had been a government-sponsored school in which the language of instruction was Yiddish, but it had closed sometime in the mid-1970s. There were just fewer and fewer students enrolling.

We finally ended up at the Jewish cemetery. Julian wanted to show me the monument to the ill-fated SS *Struma*. The *Struma* was a tiny, decrepit ship filled with 769 Jewish refugees that had set sail from Romania in 1941 and tried to dock in Istanbul, but was turned back because none of the passengers had visas for Palestine. It sank in the Black Sea after hitting a mine. All but one passenger perished. On the monument was a list of all of the names of those who died. Yet another plea for help that fell on the world's deaf ears.

Julian's Surprise

I had learned that tickets to the seders were hard to come by and expensive for a foreigner. But the next day Julian met me at the kosher kitchen with good news: he had asked if I could come to the seders and was told I could—and at the student price.

Then he pulled out a yellowed, frayed piece of sheet music he said he thought was an old klezmer tune. He liked going to antique bookstores looking for old Jewish books, and once he had bought a novel and found this sheet music inside. I swiftly took out my violin and plucked out the melody. Sure enough, it was definitely a klezmer hora.

I asked Julian if I could photocopy or even hand-copy it, but he insisted it was mine. At first I didn't want to accept (it wasn't that long, so I could have copied it in twenty minutes), but he insisted. He said he wasn't a musician, and better that it go to someone who would play the melody so it would live. Plus, he had spoken the night before to Kara (who used to be his Hebrew teacher in Iasi before he came to the university in Bucharest), and Kara had spoken so glowingly of me that Julian said it was *beshert* that we had met. Julian loved Kara like an uncle, so much so that he called him once a week to see how he was doing. I thanked Julian for everything he had done for me so far and asked if there was anything I could do for him.

"Yale, if you could, please play the song I just gave you tomorrow at the seder. Everyone will be so happy."

I told him it would be my pleasure to play the hora the next night. Then we finished lunch quickly as the cooks were closing the kosher kitchen early. They had to kosher the whole kitchen for Passover in just a little less than twenty-four hours. We left together, then Julian went home to help his aunt and uncle prepare for the holiday and I went to see Theodore one more time.

Good-Bye to Theodore

Like most Jews in Bucharest, Theodore was just getting ready to go home to prepare for the holiday. He asked me how I was feeling and if I had collected any more klezmer music. I told him that I had been given this old sheet music, but that he had been the best informant in Bucharest. He smiled proudly. Then he asked if he could play my violin just one more time. As he played, I could see in his eyes and expression that the music was taking him back to another time and place that was full of bliss for him. I really wanted to give him the violin—I knew he didn't have one and couldn't afford to buy one. There were so many things I would have liked to do over the course of my journey if I had had more money. I could have been this magnanimous wandering klezmer, helping those Jews who helped me by buying them medicines, food, some luxury items, gasoline, and so on. But instead I offered what I could and always did give freely—my music.

Theodore finished and we exchanged addresses and said good-bye. I asked if I could walk him home, but he gently refused. He didn't want to be seen walking with me because he was afraid we might pass one of his neighbors on the street and he didn't want to give them any excuse for gossip. I understood and left Theodore standing at the doorway looking through the dirt-streaked windows as I walked down the street. I turned once and waved. He waved back and pantomimed playing the violin. I returned the gesture and disappeared into the sea of pedestrians.

Performance at the Seder

I put on my best clothes and even tried to wash my shoes so I would look presentable for the *seder*. When I got there, there was a long line of guests, all dressed in their holiday best. At least I had my violin—carrying it made me look like I was supposed to be there, someone who had a mission to accomplish. Then as I got to the door where the police were checking bags, I realized I didn't have a ticket and didn't know where Julian was. They wouldn't let me in.

I tried to explain and even asked them to ask Rabbi Rosen to come to the door. He would, I hoped, vouch for me. But they just laughed and said I would have to wait for the person who had my ticket. I tried to speak to some of the guests as they walked in, but they all just ignored me.

I'd stood outside for about an hour when finally Julian realized I was still outside. He had been looking for me inside the main hall, where there were some three hundred people sitting at many beautifully set tables. He thought I had forgotten, but I explained to him what had happened and he apologized for the tight security and ridiculousness of some of the Jewish officials of the *kehile,* who he claimed ran it as if it were their own personal fiefdom.

I missed hearing the Four Questions sung but came in just when Rabbi Rosen was leading everyone in singing "Dayenu" (Hebrew, And It Was Enough). When Rabbi Rosen saw me, he smiled politely and I smiled back, then found my seat between Julian and his uncle. I was very curious to hear the Passover melodies and to see how they would be different from or similar to the ones I'd grown up with.

The reading of the Haggadah—the collection of adages, tales, hymns, psalms, and songs recited at the festive meals on the first two nights of Passover—was done in both Hebrew and Romanian. Some guests followed along intently, while others just listened and still others talked to their neighbors.

I tried to follow in the Haggadah but I was drawn to looking at the people—most, if not all of whom I knew I'd probably never see again. In my thoughts I began to relive certain episodes of my journey over the past year—

Passover Macaroons

Makes 2½ dozen

2 cups blanched almonds

1 cup sugar

3 large egg whites, unbeaten

½ tsp. almond extract

Dash of salt

30 whole blanched almonds, halved, for garnish

1. In a food processor fitted with a steel blade, grind the two cups of almonds with the sugar until the nuts are finely chopped but not pulverized. Transfer to a bowl. Stir in the egg whites, almond extract, and salt.

2. Heat the oven to 350°. Line a baking sheet with parchment paper.

3. Roll a tablespoonful of dough between your palms to make a ball. Place on the cookie sheet and compress it slightly. Press a blanched almond into the top. Repeat with the rest of the dough, leaving 4 inches between cookies.

4. Bake on the middle oven rack for 15 to 18 minutes, until the cookies spread and brown a little. Remove them from the oven, cool on the sheet, and separate with a spatula, taking care not to break them.

even the ones that had been so troublesome, like my border escapades. Now I was able to laugh and even reminisce about them. I was looking forward to telling these stories to my buddies back home, maybe even embellishing a few. They were my badges of derring-do. Now it was hard to believe it was all coming to an end. And to think it had all begun with my standing at the door of the Home for the Aged in Zagreb, sweaty, wet, and exhausted.

When it came time to eat, Julian had already spoken to the waitress about my being a vegetarian, so she knew to bring me extra of whatever I could eat. I wasn't worried; there was plenty of matzah and charoset (a sweet paste usually prepared from nuts, apples, spices, and wine, eaten to signify the mortar the Jews used in Egypt in making the bricks). However, this charoset was different from what I had eaten growing up. It was a Sephardic recipe, made with dates instead of apples. The main course was chicken and *flanken* (flank steak), but I ate eggplant salad, *matzah* kugel, boiled potatoes, kasha, and a green salad. Dessert was stewed fruit and almond macaroons.

Just like at home, many people got up to leave after the meal was served. I was disappointed because I knew I wouldn't be playing my tune until the very end. Finally it came time and Rabbi Rosen called me up. Julian had told him of the music and had made the arrangements for me to play. Rabbi Rosen made a few remarks in Romanian that elicited some applause from the guests. Then he turned to me and said in Yiddish, "Yistkhok, play this song so that the Jews from the time in Egypt will hear these holy notes."

Nothing like putting me on the spot! Luckily, I had practiced the tune Julian had given me several times earlier that afternoon. I began a little tentatively and tried not to look at anyone in the audience. The first time through was OK; by the second and third times I had found my confidence, and I began to sway to the rhythm of the music. Finally, as I played the tune for the fourth and last time, I hummed along with it. When I finished there was a moment of silence. I felt as if I was standing there naked, the silence was so deafening.

Then the applause began gradually and before I knew it they were clapping for more. I hoped that I had touched many with that hora, which probably hadn't been heard in Romania since the war.

I wanted to sit down (really, I did) but Rabbi Rosen insisted I play one more tune. So I explained in Yiddish, while the rabbi translated into Romanian, that I would play a tune specifically played on Passover.

I played a melody that I learned as a child from my dad and uncle that I knew had originated with the Stoliner Hasidim. I tore into the violin and let it sing to the rafters. Afterward the applause was again very appreciative, but I immediately began to walk back to my seat.

I remembered well Leopold whispering to me back in Krakow at the Jewish Club, "Leave them wanting more," and I did just that.

Right after the meal, I said good-bye to Julian and thanked him for his generous hospitality. We exchanged addresses—as I had done at least a hundred times before—and I told him to visit me in America. He laughed and said when and if he got the money for a ticket he was going to visit Israel first, then maybe the United States afterward.

I found a taxi at the taxi stand, loaded my gear into the trunk, and was sped off through the dimly lit streets to the railroad station. As I watched the buildings and people go by, I realized I'd never found out what Kara had said to me in Yiddish that day. Now I had a good excuse for returning.

Books

The Book of Klezmer: The History, the Music, the Folklore from the Fourteenth Century to the Twenty-First by Yale Strom (A Capella Books, 2002)

The Essential Klezmer: A Music Lover's Guide to Jewish Roots and Soul Music from the Old World to the Jazz Age to the Downtown Avant Garde by Seth Rogovoy (Algonquin Books, 2000)

"His Name Is Aaron" and Other Amazing Chassidic Stories and Songs by Mordechai Staiman (Otsar Sifrei Lubavitch, 2002)

A Hole in the Heart of the World: Being Jewish in Eastern Europe by Jonathan Kaufman (Penguin, 1998)

In Memory's Kitchen: Legacy from the Women of Terezin edited by Cara De Silva (Aronson, 1996)

Uncertain Roads: Searching for the Gypsies by Yale Strom (Simon & Schuster, 1993)

A Vanished World by Roman Vishniac (Noonday Press, 1986)

The Wayfarers by Stuart F. Tower (Lighthouse Press, 2003)

World Music: Klezmer by Yale Strom (Universal Edition, 2004)

Films

All are available on videotape.

Carpati: 50 Miles, 50 Years, Yale Strom, director

Green Fields, Jacob Ben Ami, director

Ivan and Abraham, Yolande Zauberman, director

Klezmer on Fish Street, Yale Strom, director

Korczak, Andrej Wajda, director

The Last Klezmer: Leopold Kozlowski, His Life and Music, Yale Strom, director

Partisans of Vilna, Josh Wiletsky, director

Shop on Main Street, Jan Kadar, director

A Tickle in the Heart, Stefan Schwietert, director

Audio Recordings

Between Heaven and Earth: Music of the Jewish Mystics, Andy Statman (Shanachie)

Cafe Jew Zoo, Yale Strom with Hot Pstromi & Klazzj (Naxos World Records)

Carpati: 50 Miles, 50 Years, Yale Strom & Klazzj (Global Village)

Di Naye Kapelye, Di Naye Kapelye (Oriente Rien)

Fidl, Alicia Svigals (Traditional Crossroads)

Garden of Yidn, Yale Strom with Hot Pstromi & Klazzj, featuring Elizabeth Schwartz (Naxos World Records)

Jewish Stories from the Old World to the New (KCRW)

King of Klezmer, Naftule Brandwein (Rounder)

Master of Klezmer Music, Vol. 1, Original Recordings, 1929–1949, Dave Tarras (Global Village)

Voices of the Shoah: Remembrances of the Holocaust (Rhino)

YALE STROM is a world-renowned filmmaker, composer, violinist, photographer, ethnographer, lecturer, author, and playwright. He was a pioneer among klezmer revivalists in conducting extensive field research in Central and Eastern Europe and the Balkans among the Jewish and Rom communities since 1981. Initially his work focused primarily on the symbiotic relationship between these two groups. His focus gradually increased to examining all aspects of their cultures, from post–World War II to the present. He is the author of ten books, including *The Book of Klezmer: The History, the Music, the Folklore from the Fourteenth Century to the Twenty-First* (2002) and *World Music: Klezmer* (2004), the world's first "Music Minus One" instructional guide to klezmer. Strom is also one of the only composers of "new Jewish" music to carry on the tradition of writing original songs, with Yiddish lyrics, about humanitarian and social issues, inspired by the journey recounted in this book.

ELIZABETH SCHWARTZ is an internationally acclaimed Yiddish vocalist specializing in contemporary Yiddish song. A former Hollywood executive, she is an independent film producer and writer.

Yale Strom and Elizabeth Schwartz live in New York City with their daughter.

Printed in the United States
90940LV00004B/65-66/A